Lotus

Illustrated DICTIONARY of LIBRARY & INFORMATION SCIENCE

Complied and Edited by:
Rita James

Lotus PRESS
4735/22, Prakash Deep Building
Ansari Road, Darya Ganj,
New Delhi-110002

Lotus *Illustrated*

DICTIONARY *of*

LIBRARY & INFORMATION SCIENCE

ISBN 81 89093 42 8

Published by:

Lotus Press : Publishers & Distributors
Unit No. 220, 2nd Floor, 4735/22,
Prakash Deep Building, Ansari Road, Darya Ganj,
New Delhi- 110002, Ph.: 41325510, 09811838000
• E-mail : lotuspress1984@gmail.com www.lotuspress.co.in

Printed & Published by : **Lotus Press Publisher & Distributors,** New Delhi-02

Preface

The book contains innumerable terms and cross-references. Broad in scope, this dictionary includes not only the terminology of the various specialisations within library science and information studies but also the vocabulary of publishing, printing, binding, the book trade, graphic arts, book history, literature, bibliography, telecommunications and computer science. It might prove immensely helpful to librarians and information specialists in their work. Entries are descriptive, with examples provided when appropriate. Definitions unrelated to library and information science are generally omitted. Alphabetisation is letter-by-letter.

Library and Information Science is drawing more and more attention world over and becoming a more popular discipline in every passing day. This splendid work is designed to be a hypertext reference resource for library and information science professionals, university students and faculty; and users of all types of libraries. The primary criterion for including a term is whether a librarian or other information professional might reasonably be expected to encounter it at some point in his (or her) professional career, or be required to know its meaning in the course of executing his or her duties and responsibilities as a librarian. A newly coined term is added when it seems likely to become a permanent addition to the lexicon of library and information science. All the users of the book can

contribute constructively to its growth, often suggesting additional terms and commenting on existing definitions. Considering the diverse reader base of the book, it has been written in a very lucid and easy-to-read manner. Expansion of the dictionary is an ongoing process. Suggestions for expansion and improvement are always welcome.

a.k.a.
an abbreviation of 'also known as'.

abbreviation
a shortened form of a word or phrase used for brevity in place of the whole, consisting of the first letter or the first few letters, followed by a period (full stop), for example, assoc. for association or P.O. for post office. Some terms have more than one abbreviation (v. or vol. for volume). Abbreviated abbr.
Also used as an umbrella term for any shortened form of a word or phrase, not an acronym, initialism or contraction, for example, the postal code CT for Connecticut.

abecedarium
a book containing the letters of the alphabet and basic rules of spelling and grammar, used in Europe as a primer before the invention of the printing press. Early printed examples (sometimes in the form of a broadsheet) displayed the alphabet in uppercase and lowercase letters in both roman and gothic type, with separate lists of vowels, dipthongs and consonants.

aberrant copy
a copy of a book containing obvious printing and/or binding errors which are more serious than minor defects.

accession
to record in an accession list that a bibliographic item has been added to a library collection. Also refers to the document added. The process of making additions is known as accessions. The opposite of deaccession. In archives, the formal act of accepting and documenting the receipt of records taken into custody, part of the process of establishing physical and intellectual control over them. In the case of donated items, a deed of gift may be required to transfer legal title.

accession number
a unique number assigned to a bibliographic item in the order in which it is added to a library collection, recorded in an accession record maintained by the technical services department. Most libraries assign accession numbers in continuous numerical sequence, but some use a code system to indicate type of material and/or year of accession, in addition to order of accession.

accession order
the arrangement of books or other documents on shelves in the chronological and numerical order of their addition to a specific category or class, as opposed to an arrangement based entirely on a classification system.

accession record
a list of the bibliographic items added to a library collection in the order of their addition. Normally such a list includes the accession number, brief bibliographic identification, source and price paid for each item. Synonymous with accession catalogue, accession register and accession list.

■ **accompanying material**

related material issued with an item, for example, a floppy disk, CD-ROM, slide set, answer book, teacher's manual, atlas, or portfolio of prints or plates intended by the publisher to be used and stored with it, often in a pocket inside the cover or loose inside the container. When such an item is catalogued by a library, the presence of accompanying material is indicated in the physical description area of the bibliographic record.

■ **accountability**

the extent to which persons in government and the workplace are held answerable for their conduct in office and for the quality of their performance of assigned duties, particularly when incompetence, dereliction, or malfeasance is at issue.

■ **accreditation**

the regular evaluation process by which an educational or service organisation establishes that its program of study or services, or the institution as a whole, meets certain pre-existing standards of quality.

■ **accuracy**

the quality of correctness as to fact and precision as to detail in information resources and in the delivery of information services. In libraries, it is essential that the resources used by librarians to provide reference service be free of error. Accuracy is also an important criterion in judging the reliability of information provided on the Internet. The accuracy of a statement can be verified by checking other sources that provide the same information. The opposite of inaccuracy (the quality of being incorrect or mistaken).

■ **acid migration**

the movement of acid from a material containing acid to one that is less acidic, pH neutral, or alkaline. The process can occur through direct contact or vapour transfer. One of the most common problems in document preservation is the migration of acid from the boards, endpapers, or paper covers of a book to the less acidic paper of the text block (or vice versa). Acid can also migrate from bookplates, inserts, tissues used in interleaving and labels that are not acid-free. The result may be discoloration and eventual embrittlement. The process can be arrested by removing the contaminating material and subjecting the sheet(s) or volume to deacidification. Synonymous with acid transfer.

■ **acid paper**

paper that has a pH value less than 7.0 (neutral). The primary source of acid in paper is lignin, an organic substance contained in untreated wood pulp, but acid can also develop from the addition of certain types of sizing or from residual chlorine used in bleaching. It can also be introduced by acid migration or atmospheric pollution (sulphur dioxide). Because acidity weakens the cellulose in plant fiber, it can cause paper, board and cloth to yellow and become brittle over time, making it an important factor in the preservation of printed materials. To ensure durability, publishers are encouraged to use acid-free permanent paper in printing trade books. Buffering helps neutralise acids that develop after manufacture. Acid can be removed from fiber-based materials by means of an expensive process called deacidification.

■ adobe acrobat

a document exchange program created by Adobe Systems which allows data files created on one software platform (DOS, Windows, Macintosh, etc.) to be displayed and printed on another without loss of text formatting. This capability is particularly important in communication over the Internet which interconnects computers of all types and sizes. Adobe Systems sells the software required to create or convert documents to its Portable Document Format, but does not charge users for the software needed to read PDF documents.

■ adobe acrobat reader

a program for viewing PDF files, used in many full-text electronic journals. The reader program is free and if you do not have it on your machine when it is needed to access an article, instructions for downloading it will usually appear on your screen.

■ adult

a fully grown, mentally competent person of sufficient age to be considered capable of making mature decisions and held legally accountable for the consequences of his (or her) actions. Libraries operate on the assumption that adult patrons are capable of deciding independently what they wish to read and borrow. Although it is the responsibility of the parent to supervise the actions of a child, it is appropriate for librarians to provide guidance to children in the selection of materials suitable to their age level and interests, if asked to do so.

■ adult education

courses designed specifically for adults who have spent their lives outside the system of formal higher education. Because non-traditional students often lack the library skills of students who follow a traditional course of study, they may require more assistance at the reference desk and a more basic level of bibliographic instruction.

adult learner

a person older than traditional college age, who pursues an independent, organised course of study, usually without the benefit of formal instruction at an established educational institution. When enrolled as a nontraditional student at a college or university, such a person may require reference services and bibliographic instruction at a more basic level than traditional students.

adult services

materials, services and programs intended to meet the needs of the adult users of a public library, as opposed to those designed for children and young adults.

advance copy

a copy of a book or other publication bound in advance of the normal press run to enable the publisher to check that all is in order before binding of the edition proceeds. Advance copies are also sent to booksellers, book club selection committees and reviewers before the announced publication date, sometimes unbound or in a binding other than the publisher's binding, often with a review slip laid in. Copies sent unbound are known as advance sheets. Synonymous with early copy.

advance on royalty

an amount paid to the author(s) of a new book prior to its publication against the royalties it is expected to earn, usually offered as an inducement to sign a book contract with the publisher. Synonymous with author's advance.

advance order

an order placed for a new book prior to its date of publication, usually in response to prepublication promotion. The number of copies ordered in advance may assist the publisher in determining the size of the first printing, the price and how much to spend on advertising.

advertorial

advertising text written in editorial style and format. To avoid confusion, most magazine publishers add the word 'Advertisement' to the running head.

■ **adverts**

advertisements bound into a book, usually at the end of the back matter. Abbreviated ads or advrts.

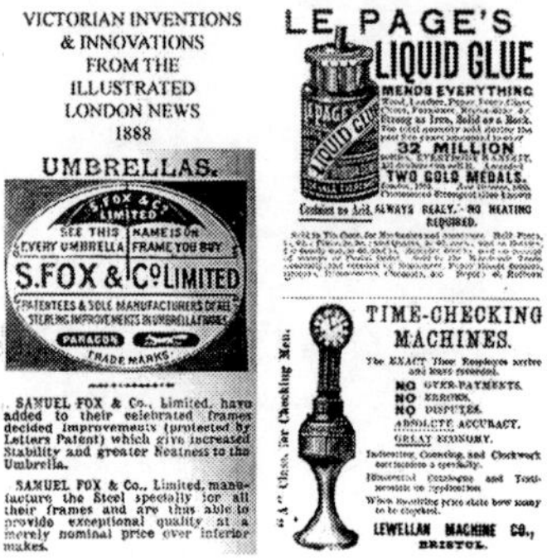

■ **aerial map**

a map of the earth, or of another planetary body, composed of one or more photographs taken from a position above its surface, usually from a passing aircraft, satellite, or space vehicle.

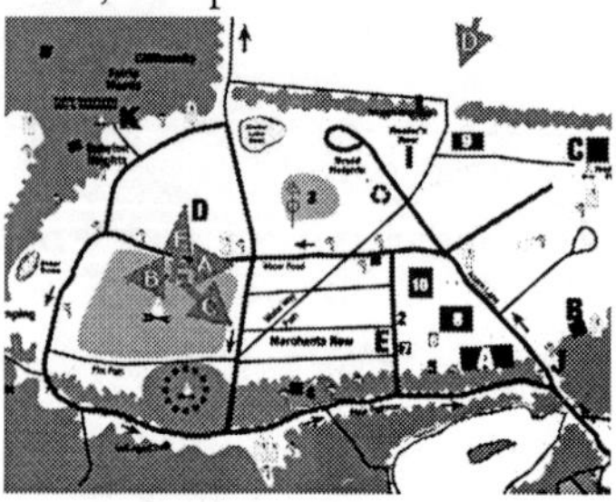

■ **affiliate**

a separately administered organisation closely connected with another by formal agreement.

■ **affiliated library**

a library which is, by formal agreement, part of a larger library system but administered independently by its own board or management structure. Medical and law libraries at large universities often fall into this category.

■ **against the grain**

a popular expression meaning 'contrary to natural inclination' originally used in the printing trade to refer to machine-made paper folded across the grain of its fibres. In book production, sheets are printed with the grain running from top to bottom of the leaves, allowing them to flex easily lengthwise after they are bound. When folded with the grain, paper tears easily and cleanly along the fold. When folded across the grain, it cracks and leaves a ragged edge when torn.

■ **agency**

for archival purposes, any commercial enterprise, organisation, institution, or other corporate body that creates and manages records of its business, activities, or affairs. In very large organisations, subordinate units (sections, departments, offices) may function as separate agencies.

■ **agenda**

a list of topics or issues to be discussed at a meeting, sometimes solicited from prospective attendees in advance by the person who calls or chairs the meeting. It is customary to distribute the agenda before the meeting begins, to allow attendees time to prepare. A hidden agenda is a goal or intention consciously or unconsciously concealed, usually to gain the advantage of surprise, a tactic that often backfires when unsuspecting persons discover that they have been manipulated.

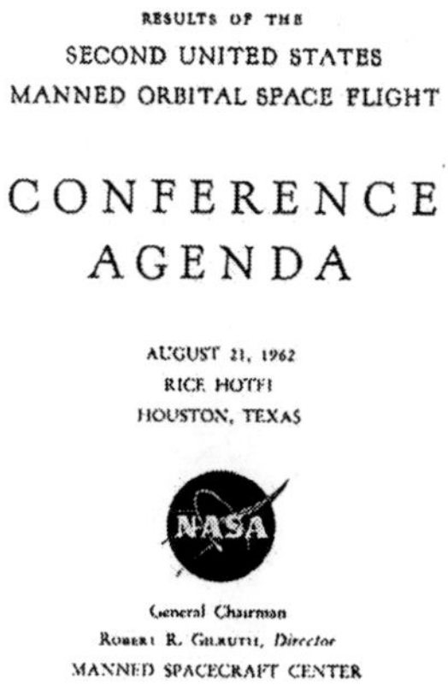
RESULTS OF THE
SECOND UNITED STATES
MANNED ORBITAL SPACE FLIGHT

CONFERENCE
AGENDA

AUGUST 21, 1962
RICE HOTEL
HOUSTON, TEXAS

General Chairman
ROBERT R. GILRUTH, Director
MANNED SPACECRAFT CENTER

■ -ana, -iana

a suffix added to the name of a person, place, or institution to signify the body of related literature, information, memorabilia, etc., that has accumulated over time. In libraries such materials are usually housed in special collections.

■ analects

from the Greek analekta meaning 'things gathered up.' A collection or 'gleaning' of miscellaneous literary excerpts or fragments (example: the teachings of Confucius).

■ analogue

a representation of an object, physical condition, or process, that closely replicates the original, reflecting any variations in its state. In technology, analogue devices are designed to monitor conditions such as sound, movement, or temperature and convert the resulting measurements into electrical signals or mechanical patterns representing the fluctuations of the actual phenomenon (example: sounds recorded on a phonograph record). Analogue data is encoded in signals that are continuous over a range or interval of values, for example, data transmitted over a telephone line which must be converted by a device called a modem into the discrete values of digital code in order to be processed by a digital computer.

■ analytical bibliography

the comparative and historical study of books as physical objects, including the methods and techniques of book production and their influence on texts. Synonymous with critical bibliography. Analytical bibliography has three main branches:

Historical bibliography: the history of books and their methods of production.

Textual bibliography: the relationship between the text as conceived by the author and the text as published.

Descriptive bibliography: the close description of the physical characteristics of books.

■ analytical entry

an entry in a library catalogue for a part of a work (chapter in a book) or for an entire work (story, play, essay, or poem) contained in an item, such as an anthology or collection, for which a comprehensive entry is made. Analytical entries are made under the author, title and subject of the part and include a reference to the title of the work containing the part. Because preparation of analytical entries is time-consuming, the level of bibliographic description provided in a catalogue depends on the administrative policy of the library and its assessment of local needs. Synonymous with analytics.

■ **analytical note**

the statement in an analytical entry indicating the relationship of the work, or part of a work, to the more comprehensive work of which it is a part, for example, the title of an anthology containing a short story, play, essay, or poem.

■ **animated graphics**

a graphic design technique in which a sequence of related still images, such as cartoon drawings or diagrams, is displayed in such rapid succession that the illusion of continuous motion is created on a computer screen. Animated graphics require less bandwidth than full-motion video when transmitted over the Internet (and also less memory), so they can be downloaded more quickly when a Web site containing them is selected by the viewer.

■ **animation**

the illusion of continuous motion created on film by photographing a sequence of drawings, still pictures, or cartoon cells, each representing a slight change from the preceding one and viewing them in rapid succession. Developed into an art form by animators in the studios of Walt Disney, the technique continues

to provide pleasure to audiences worldwide.

■ **annals**

a periodical in which the transactions of a society or organisation, or events and developments in a specific discipline or field of study are recorded. In a more general sense, a list of events recorded in chronological order.

■ **annex**

an addition to an existing library or archive, or a nearby facility used as an addition to the main building, usually of smaller size. A library annex is sometimes used to store low-use materials in closed stacks.

■ **annotate**

to add notes to a written document to explain, comment on, or evaluate its content, as in an annotated edition. Also, to add brief notes, called annotations, to the entries in a bibliography or catalogue to describe, explain, or evaluate the sources listed.

antonym

a word or phrase which is the opposite in meaning of another term. Dictionaries of antonyms are available in the reference section of larger libraries. In some indexing languages, one of the terms in a pair of opposites may be selected to represent both, with a cross-reference made from the other. The opposite is synonym.

aperture card

a card containing one or more small windows in which individual frames cut from a strip of microfilm are mounted. This format allows microfilm images to be used independently and provides a convenient surface for recording pertinent information about each frame. Synonymous with image card.

aphorism

a very concise sentence or statement that expresses, in a pointedly memorable way, a universally recognised truth or principle. A maxim (example: 'Well begun is half done.'). Aphorisms published in collections are usually shelved in the reference section of a library.

apocryphal

writings which scholars consider to be of dubious authorship or authenticity (not genuine), for example, the 14-15 books of the Greek translations of the Old Testament (Septuagint), known as the Apocrypha, accepted as authoritative by the Roman Catholic and Greek Orthodox churches, but rejected in Judaism and not considered canonical in Protestantism.

apostil

a marginal note or annotation in a book or manuscript.

appendix

a part of a written work, not essential to the completeness of the text, containing complementary information such as statistical tables or explanatory material too long to be included in the text, or in footnotes or endnotes. An appendix differs from an addendum in having been planned in advance as an integral part of the publication, rather than conceived after typesetting occurs. Appendices usually appear in the back matter, following the text and preceding the notes, glossary, bibliography and index.

applicant

a person who has made a formal request to be considered for employment, usually by filling out an application form or by sending a resume or curriculum vitae with cover letter to a prospective employer in response to a job posting.

■ appraisal

the monetary valuation of gifts, usually done at the request of an archives, library, or museum, by a professional appraiser familiar with the market for the type of item(s) donated. Also refers to the process of evaluating records to determine whether they are to be archived indefinitely, retained for a shorter period, or disposed of in some other way (sold, donated, destroyed, etc.).

■ approval book

books received by the library through an arrangement with a publisher or dealer, in which all titles matching certain criteria are automatically sent and billed; the library may return any titles rejected after examination.

■ approval plan

a formal arrangement in which a publisher or wholesaler agrees to select and supply, subject to return privileges specified in advance, publications exactly as issued which fit a library's pre-established collection development profile. Approval profiles usually specify subject areas, levels of specialisation or reading difficulty, series, formats, price ranges, languages, etc. Some plans provide advance notification slips instead of sending the actual physical item.

■ approval shelf

a shelf or shelves, usually located in or near the acquisitions department of a library, where new books ordered on approval are stored pending examination by the selectors responsible for deciding whether they are to be added to the collection or returned to the publisher or wholesaler.

■ approvals

new books sent automatically by a publisher or wholesaler in accordance with a pre-established profile of the library's needs, rather than ordered title-by-title by the selectors responsible for collection development. Approvals not returned within an agreed upon time are understood to have been accepted by the library.

■ arabesque

an elaborate Islamic-style design consisting of intricately interlaced lines which may include flowers and foliage, or geometric patterns, stamped as a decoration on the cover of a book or used by a printer to ornament a text.

■ Arabic numeral

one of the ten digits (0 1 2 3 4 5 6 7 8 9) developed in India in the 6th century to indicate number in a system of place value based on ten. Arabic numerals were adopted by the Arabs around 900 AD, who introduced them in Europe via Spain about 100 years later, where they replaced roman numerals. Colonisation introduced them to the rest of the world. The notation used in Dewey Decimal Classification is composed entirely of arabic numerals.

■ archetypal novel

early fictional tales and romances considered to be precursors of the novel in its modern form.

■ Association Of Vision Science Librarians (AVSL)

an international association of information professionals employed at educational institutions, eye clinics and hospitals and private companies whose library collections and services include the literature of vision, AVSL is a special interest group of both the Association of Schools and Colleges of Optometry and the Medical Library Association. The organisation publishes standards and guidelines for vision science libraries, a union list of vision-related serials and a core list audiovisual collection.

■ associative relation

a semantic relation in which two words or phrases are conceptually connected, sometimes within a specific context, but are not related hierarchically.

■ asterisk

a special character in the shape of a star (*) produced on a standard keyboard by pressing the Shift+8 keys. The asterisk is used as a reference mark in printing to indicate a footnote or other reference on the same page. A series of asterisks is sometimes used in text to indicate ellipsis, for example, to suggest an unprintable word (D***). In most bibliographic databases, the asterisk is used as the end truncation symbol in keywords searches.

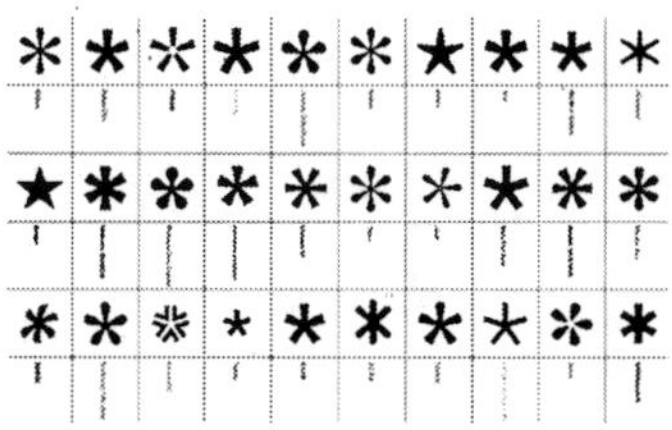

■ astronomical map

a map of the planets, stars, galaxies, or other heavenly bodies, usually printed against a dark ground. Synonymous with star map.

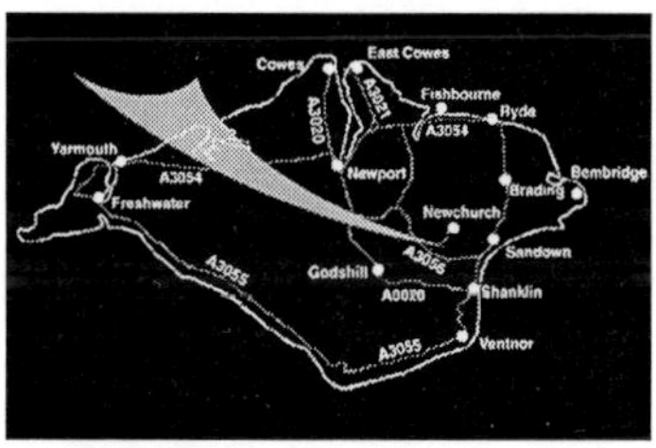

■ asynchronous

occurring at different times. In communications, a response that is delayed due to the nature of the transmission medium. The opposite of synchronous.

■ asyndetic

lacking cross-references.

■ athenaeum

the temple of Athena, goddess of knowledge and learning, where scholars and writers met in the city of Athens in ancient Greece to exchange ideas. In early 19th century New England, the name was applied to certain proprietary libraries, reading rooms and buildings containing libraries.

■ atlas

a bound or boxed collection of maps, usually related in subject or theme, with an index of place names (gazetteer) usually printed at the end. The first bound collection of maps is known to have been issued in Europe in the mid-16th century. In most atlases, the maps are printed in uniform style and format, on a fairly consistent scale. An atlas may be issued as an independent publication or as accompanying material, with or without descriptive text, plates, charts, etc. Some have a special focus, others are intended for a specific use (road atlases). In a library, large atlases may be stored in a specially designed atlas case.

■ atlas case

a free-standing piece of display furniture used mainly in libraries, usually about waist-high with a sloping top and a book stop along the front edge for displaying an open atlas. Most atlas cases are made of wood, with several deep, wide, closely-spaced shelves for storing oversize reference works. Some designs have sliding shelves to facilitate use.

■ atlas folio

the largest widely used folio, usually about 16 x 25 inches in size, used mainly for large atlases.

■ atlas

usually, a volume of maps; also used for a volume of plates illustrating any subject, particularly in anatomy.

■ attachment

a computer file of any type linked to an e-mail message in such a way that the two are transmitted together to the designated address. Nontext attachments, such as graphics and database files, may require special encoding and decoding software. Particular care should be taken when opening attachments as they are sometimes used to transmit computer viruses.

■ authority control

the procedures by which consistency of form is maintained in the headings (names, uniform titles, series titles and subjects) used in a library catalogue or file of bibliographic records, through the application of an authoritative list called an authority file to new items as they are added to the collection. Authority control is available from commercial service providers.

■ authority file

a list of the authoritative forms of the headings used in a library catalogue or file of bibliographic records, maintained to ensure that the headings are applied consistently as new items are added to the collection. Separate authority files are usually maintained for names, uniform titles, series titles and subjects. All the references made to and from a given heading are also included in the authority file.

■ authority record

a printed or machine-readable record of the decision made concerning the authoritative form of a name (personal or corporate), uniform title, series title, or subject used as a heading in a library catalogue or file of bibliographic records, listed in an authority file governing the application of headings to new items as they are added to the library collection.

■ authority work

the process of deciding which form of a name, title, series title, or subject will be used as the authorised heading in a library catalogue or file of bibliographic records, including the establishment of appropriate references to the heading and its relationship to other headings in the authority file.
Example: Shaw Bernard, with references from Shaw G. B. and Shaw George Bernard.

■ authorisation

in computing, a username, password, PIN, or other access code issued to a person who is allowed access to a specific electronic resource, application program, network, or other computer system, which the user must enter correctly in order to log on. Authorisation codes are usually subject to periodic renewal. A single authentication may have multiple authorisations.

■ authorised biography

a biography written with the explicit consent and sometimes the cooperation of its subject, or the subject's family if the biography is deceased. Authorised biographies are more likely to be scrutinised by reviewers for bias because the biographer may have been expected to overlook or downplay embarrassing events or unflattering qualities in exchange for access to first-hand information and confidential sources.

■ authorised edition

an edition issued with the explicit sanction of the author or holder of rights in the work or, in the case of a biography, by the person who is its subject or the subject's family if the biography is deceased. The opposite is unauthorised edition.

■ author's advance

an amount paid by the publisher to the author of a work before the completed manuscript is submitted for publication, established by contractual agreement between the two parties, usually refundable if the work is not completed. Synonymous with advance on royalty.

■ author's copy

one of six or more complimentary copies of a published work normally provided to the author free-of-charge by the publisher at the time of first publication. Faculty members sometimes donate complimentary copies of their works to the academic library at the college or university with which they are affiliated.

■ author's edition

an edition of all the unpublished and previously published works of an author, issued in one or more uniform volumes, usually bearing a collective title or some other indication on the title page that all known works are included. Synonymous with complete works and uniform edition. Also refers to an edition published with the author's consent (authorised edition).

■ author's editor

an editor familiar with the publishing industry, employed by a university or research institution to assist faculty and researchers in preparing their work for publication and to help them negotiate the intricacies of the publishing process, as distinct from an editor employed by a publishing company to help prepare a manuscript for printing once it has been accepted for publication.

■ authorship

the origin of a manuscript, book, or other written work, with reference to its author(s). In a more general sense, the source of an idea or creative work in any form, with reference to its creator or originator, for example, the composer of a musical work. When authorship of an anonymous work cannot be determined with reasonable certainty, it is said to be of unknown authorship.

■ autobiography

an account of a person's life written by its subject, usually in the form of a continuous narrative of events considered by the author to be the most important or interesting, selected from those he or she is willing to reveal. The first fully-developed autobiography, the Confessions of St. Augustine, was written in the 4th century A.D. Some autobiographies are largely fictional (example: Confessions of Jean-Jacques Rousseau). Contemporary autobiographies of famous people are often written with the assistance of a ghost writer. An autobiography differs from a diary or journal in being written for others, rather than for purely private reasons.

■ **autograph**

a manuscript written entirely in the author's own handwriting. Also refers to a person's own signature.

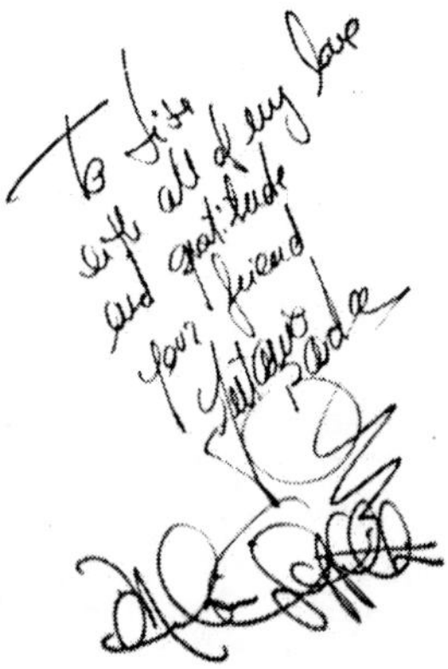

■ **autographed copy**

a copy of a book or other published work signed by the author. Autographed copies may be of considerable value to collectors if the author is very well-known and signed copies rare.

■ **autographed edition**

an edition of a work in which all the copies are personally signed by the author, possible only in relatively small editions.

■ **average price**

the sum of the prices of individual items within a specific category (or a representative sample), divided by the number of items selected for the purpose of calculation. In library acquisitions, average price per title is used to compute the annual rate of inflation in the cost of various types of materials, an important consideration in budgeting and the allocation of funds.

■ **axonometric map**

a very detailed, large-scale map of a city, in which the buildings and other structures are shown in perspective, usually on an incline.

■ **back**

the sewn or binding edge of the gathered sections of a book, to which the lining is applied. The back may be flat, but more often it is given a convex curve in a binding procedure called rounding. A flexible or hollow back is preferable because it allows a volume to open flat. All the issues of a periodical which precede the current issue, usually bound in annual volumes or converted to microfilm or microfiche to conserve space. In the catalogue record, the extent of the back file is indicated in the holdings note.

■ **back fold**

the fold along which a signature is gathered to form the binding edge of a book, left uncut in sewn bindings but trimmed in perfect binding to allow the adhesive to bond more securely.

■ **back issue**

any issue of a periodical that precedes the current issue. Back issues are usually retained in a back file which may be stored in a different location in the periodicals section of a library, sometimes converted to a more compact format, such as microfilm or microfiche. In the catalogue record, the extent of the back file is indicated in the holdings note. Synonymous with back number.

■ bathymetric map

a topographic map showing the depth and features of the sea floor, including coastal zones (bays and estuaries), usually by means of contour lines called isobaths.

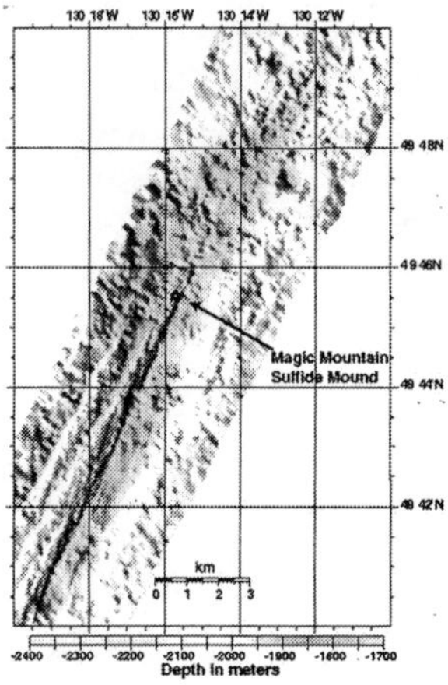

■ battledore

a type of school primer used in the late 18th century, made of folded paper varnished on the inside, resembling a horn book when opened, but sometimes lacking a handle.

■ baud

unit measuring the speed of transmission of data over telecommunications lines.

■ beast epic

a series of stories popular during the Middle Ages in which the characters are animals with human qualities, usually written in the form of an allegory satirising the Catholic Church, the royal court, or some other powerful person, group, or institution (example: Pierre de Saint-Cloud's 12th century Roman de Renart). A more recent example is George Orwell's Animal Farm (1945), written in the same tradition.

■ bevelled boards

a technique used in hand-binding in which the upper surface of the edges of heavy boards are cut at a sloping angle, instead of the usual 90-degrees, to give the cover a more elegant appearance or in conscious imitation of an earlier style. Also spelled bevelled boards.

■ bevelled edge

any edge tapered at less than a 90-degree angle to make the transition from upper to lower surface more gradual than in a right-angle cut. Bevelled boards are sometimes used in hand bookbinding. The edges of mats used in framing are normally bevelled at a 60-degree angle.

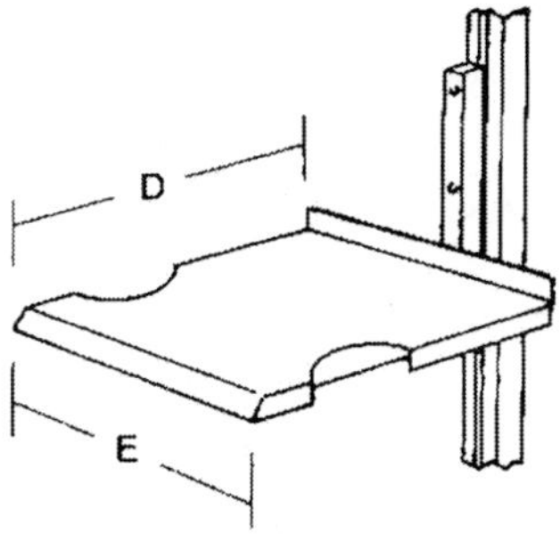

■ **bi-annual**

a publication (e.g. a magasine) which is issued twice a year. Because of confusion with the term biennial (a publication issued every two years), the terms 'half-yearly,' 'twice yearly' or 'semi-annual' are more commonly used.

■ **bias**

judgment unfairly influenced by subjective opinion when the situation calls for reliance on objective fact. Bias exists even in reference books.

■ **bibelot**

a French term for a small decorative object of exceptional beauty, rarity, or curiosity. In literature, a book of unusually small size, elegantly designed and crafted from the finest materials. Also known as a thumb book.

■ **bible paper**

a strong, thin, opaque printing paper made from new cotton or linen rags, or from flax fiber, used to reduce the bulk of large volumes such as dictionaries, encyclopaedias, bibles and prayer books that would otherwise be too thick to be easily handled. Sometimes used synonymously with India paper.

■ **bible style**

a general term for any flexible leather binding that has rounded corners, especially one of dark colour.

■ **biblia pauperum**

latin for 'Bible of the Poor,' a block book issued in large numbers beginning in about 1450, consisting mainly of pictures with explanatory text in Latin or German providing lessons from the Scriptures.

■ **biblio**

from the Greek word biblion meaning 'book,' used in combination to form a host of terms pertaining to books and libraries (bibliography, bibliomania, bibliophile, bibliophobia, bibliotherapy, etc.). In interactions with patrons, most public services librarians avoid the 'B-words' because the general public is not familiar with the technical terminology of librarianship.

■ **bibliocaper**

a term coined by George Eberhart to refer to an odd or wacky event, harebrained prank, or bizarre petty crime involving libraries, librarians, library patrons, or books.

■ biblioclast

a person who destroys or mutilates books, for one reason or another. Fortunately for bibliophiles, this form of aberrant behaviour occurs infrequently.

■ bibliogony

of or relating to the production of books in all their forms. Synonymous with bibliogenesis.

■ bibliographee

a person concerning whom a bibliography is compiled, as in a list of references at the end of a biographical essay or book-length biography.

■ bibliographer

a person who describes and lists books and other publications, with particular attention to such characteristics as authorship, publication date, edition, typography, etc. The result of this endeavour is a bibliography. A person who limits such efforts to a specific field or discipline is a subject bibliographer.

■ bibliographic citation

(synonym for bibliographic reference) identifying information about a publication, used in catalos and indexes as well as in lists of 'literature cited' or 'references' in scholarly publications. Formats vary, but a book citation generally includes at least information on the author, title, publisher and date of publication; an article citation includes author, title, date and information on the periodical in which it was published.

■ bibliographic control

a broad term encompassing all the activities involved in creating, organising, managing and maintaining the file of bibliographic records representing the items held in a library or archival collection, or the sources listed in an index or database, to facilitate access to the information contained in them. Bibliographic control includes the standardisation of bibliographic description and subject access by means of uniform catalogue code, classification systems and preferred headings; the creation and maintenance of catalos, union lists and finding aids; and the provision of physical access to the items in the collection.

■ bibliographic database

1. a computer file consisting of electronic entries called records, each containing a uniform description of a specific document or bibliographic item, usually retrievable by author, title, subject heading (descriptor), or keyword(s). Some bibliographic databases are general in scope and coverage, others provide access to the literature of a specific discipline or group of disciplines. An increasing number provide the full-text of at least a portion of the sources indexed. Most bibliographic databases are proprietary, available by licensing agreement from vendors, or directly

from the indexing and abstracting services that create them.

2. an electronic version of a catalog or index. A bibliographic database allows the user to identify publications by author, subject, title, or other search terms. It generally provides at least a full citation to the item and often other information such as abstracts and assigned subject headings.

■ bibliographic description

in a general sense, all the elements of data necessary to conclusively identify a specific document, presented in some form of record. In library cataloguing, the detailed description of a copy of a specific edition of a work, intended to identify and distinguish it from other works by the same author, of the same title, or on the same subject. The bibliographic record representing an item in the catalogue includes the following standard areas of description: title and statement of responsibility (author, editor, composer, etc.), edition, material specific details, details of publication and distribution, physical description, series, notes and standard number and terms of availability (ISBN, ISSN, price).

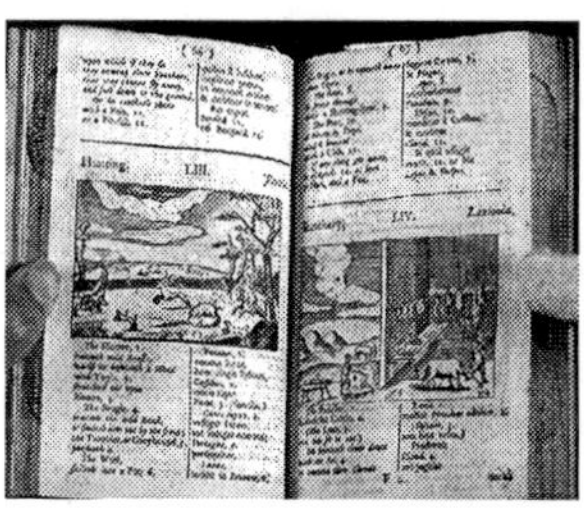

■ bibliographic essay

a critical essay in which the bibliographer identifies and evaluates the core literature of a subdiscipline or field of study, providing guidance to students, researchers and collection development librarians.

■ bibliographic format

the standardised sequence and manner of presentation of the data elements constituting the full description of an item in a specific cataloguing or indexing system. The machine-readable MARC record format has become the standard for library catalos in many countries of the world.

■ bibliographic Instruction (BI)

instructional programs designed to teach library users how to locate the information they need quickly and effectively. BI usually covers the library's system of organising materials, the structure of the literature of the field, research methodologies appropriate to the discipline and specific resources and finding tools (catalos, indexing and abstracting services, bibliographic databases, etc.). In academic libraries, bibliographic instruction is usually course-related or course-integrated. Libraries which have a computer-equipped instruction lab are in a position to include hands-on practice in the use of online catalos, electronic databases and Internet resources. Instruction sessions are usually taught by an instructional services librarian with specialised training and experience in pedagogical methods. Synonymous with library instruction and library orientation.

■ bibliographic item

a document or set of documents in any physical format (print or nonprint), given a single bibliographic description in library cataloguing based on the fact of having been published, issued, released, or otherwise treated as a single entity. As defined in FRBR (Functional Requirements for Bibliographic Records), a single concrete exemplar of a manifestation of an expression of an intellectual or artistic work, in most cases a single physical object, such as a copy of an edition of a single-volume monograph. All the items constituting a manifestation normally contain the same intellectual/ artistic content and are identical in physical form, but variations can occur subsequent to production, as in the case of a monograph rebound by a library. In some cases an item consists of more than one physical object, for example, a video recording released on more than one cassette or a multivolume set of reference books.

■ bibliographic record

an entry representing a specific item in a library catalogue or bibliographic database, containing all the data elements necessary for a full description, presented in a specific bibliographic format. In modern cataloguing, the standard format is machine-readable, but prior to the use of computers, the traditional format was the catalogue card.

■ bibliographic retrieval

the process in which a user queries a library catalogue or bibliographic database, usually by author, title, subject heading (descriptor), or keyword(s) and receives a list of records representing items that satisfy the parameters of the search. Most commercial databases allow the searcher to use techniques such as Boolean logic, truncation and proximity to refine search statements.

■ bibliographic utility

an organisation that provides access to and support for machine-readable bibliographic databases directly to member libraries or through a network of regional bibliographic service centres, usually via a proprietary interface.

■ bibliotherapy

the use of books selected on the basis of content in a planned reading program designed to facilitate the recovery of patients suffering from mental illness or emotional disturbance.

■ biennial

1. issued every two years. Also refers to a serial publication issued every two years.
2. a serial publication issued every two years.

■ bifolium

in bookbinding, a pair of conjoint leaves (as opposed to a single leaf), forming four pages when folded. Plural: bifolia.

■ **bildungsroman**

from the German word 'Bildung' (meaning: education, culture) and the French word 'roman' (novel). A novel in which the author traces the maturation of the hero or heroine, from the subjectivity of childhood and early adolescence through the development of objective self-awareness (examples: The Magic Mountain by Thomas Mann and The Tin Drum by Gunter Grass).

■ **bilingual edition**

a book or periodical published in two languages, usually because both languages are spoken in the country in which the work was published or because the work was co-published in countries with different national languages.

■ **blind page**

a page in a book, usually the half-title, title page, dedication, or a blank page, included in the pagination but not given a page number.

■ **blind reference**

a cross-reference in an index or catalogue, directing the reader to a heading that does not exist in the same index or catalogue.

■ **block book**

a form of book containing text alone, or text with pictures, printed entirely from woodcuts on only one side of each leaf. Block books originated in Europe during the 15th century at the same time as printing from movable type and may have been an inexpensive alternative to books produced on a printing press. The best known example is the Biblia Pauperum (Bible of the Poor) printed in large quantities during the second half of the 15th century. Fewer than two dozen copies are known to have survived.

■ **block letter**

a letter printed in a typeface that has strokes of equal width and boldness, straight and without serifs, a style used for legibility in headlines, but considered less legible for printing text matter. Synonymous with sans-serif.

■ **blockbuster**

a slang term for a new book for which the sale of a very large number of copies is virtually guaranteed, usually due to the reputation or popularity of the author. Public libraries often order such titles in multiple copies to satisfy initial demand. Also refers to the willingness of publishers to repeatedly sign such authors and promote their works, sometimes to the neglect of writers of lesser fame whose works deserve to be read. Synonymous with megabook.

blocked

the status of the borrower account of a patron who is barred from checking out materials from the library, usually because fines for overdue items remain unpaid. Most electronic circulation systems are designed to automatically block a patron record under conditions prescribed by the library.

blocking

the process of impressing letters or a decorative design on the cover of a book in ink, metal foil/leaf, or blind, using an engraved plate called a brass (binder's die) mounted on a blocking press. Also refers to the tendency of the leaves of a book or other bound publication to stick together, forming a solid block after they have been exposed to water, a problem that can be mitigated by standing the wet item on end with the leaves fanned open to allow them to air dry. Leaves of coated paper can be difficult to separate without damaging the printed surface, especially after drying has commenced.

blue pencil

to mark corrections in a manuscript or typescript during the editing process, derived from the colour of pencil traditionally used by editors. The term has also been applied to the editing of text by a censor.

blueprint

a photographic copy of the detailed plans for constructing a building or other structure, originally printed in white against a blue ground. Blueprints are usually produced in sets, one for each floor for each phase of construction. They are collected by architecture libraries and by archives and special collections for construction projects of historical significance. Blueprints are used by libraries in planning and overseeing the renovation, expansion and new construction of facilities.

blurb

1. the publisher's description and recommendation of a new book, usually printed on the front flap of the dust jacket, portions of which may be used in advertisements published in book trade journals and review publications and in the publisher's catalog. Brief excerpts from favourable reviews are usually printed on the back of the dust jacket.

2. a brief summary or description of a work printed on the book jacket, publisher's catalog or advertisement to entice potential purchasers.

■ board

a general term for the sheet of rigid material forming one side of the cover of a book bound in hardcover. In early bookbinding, wood was used for this purpose (usually seasoned oak), but by the 15th century pasteboard had been introduced. In modern bindings, the cover is usually made of binder's board or of strawboard, chip board, or pasteboard in less expensive editions, all made from various fibrous materials, pulped or laminated and then pressed into large flat sheets cut to size in binding. The lay term is cardboard. In computers, the flat piece of plastic or fibreglass designed to hold microchips and other computer hardware. The main circuit board in most systems is called the motherboard and all the component chips that plug into the main board are called cards or boards. Also refers to a group of prominent persons, elected or appointed to serve as trustees responsible for overseeing the policies and major management decisions of an organisation or institution, such as a library or library system.

■ board book

a durable book of small size designed for very young children, consisting of a few unnumbered pages made of pasteboard covered in glossy paper printed with colourful illustrations and little if any text. Board books are often alphabet books or counting books.

■ body

in printing, the main portion of a book, beginning with the first page of the text and including any footnotes and illustrations, but excluding the front matter and back matter. In bookbinding, the block of sections sewn or glued together in preparation for attachment to the case or cover. In an e-mail message, the text of the message, as opposed to the header (e-mail address of sender, address(es) of recipient(s), subject of message) and any footer.

In typesetting, the small rectangular unit of cast metal bearing a single raised character on one end (the face) from which an impression is taken in letterpress printing. Synonymous in this sense with shank. Also refers to a group of people with an official function.

■ body matter

the text of a work to be printed, as distinct from any display matter (headings, ornaments, illustrations, etc.).

■ boldface

a typeface conspicuous for being thicker and darker but not larger than the medium weight type of the same font, used mainly for contrast or emphasis and for headings. The words thicker and darker in the preceding sentence are in boldface. Variations include semi-bold, extra-bold and ultra-bold. Also spelled bold face. Synonymous with bold and black face.

■ bolt

the folded edge of a single sheet of paper at the head, tail, or fore-edge of the block in an uncut or unopened book, known respectively as the head-bolt, tail-bolt, or fore-edge bolt. In binding, the fourth edge, called the back fold, is sewn and glued to the other folded and gathered sections to form the back of a book.

■ book

a collection of leaves of paper, parchment, vellum, cloth, or other material (written, printed, or blank) fastened together along one edge, with or without a protective case or cover. Also refers to a literary work or one of its volumes.

■ book announcement

a brief statement by the publisher announcing the availability of a new book or backlisted title, published as an advertisement in book trade journal or review publication, or in an advertising section included in another book published under the same imprint. A book announcement usually includes the title of the work, the name of the author(s) or editor(s), ISBN, projected date of publication, list price and prepublication price if offered. It may also include a blurb or brief excerpts from favourable reviews and a picture of the front cover.

■ book art

the form of art expressed through the medium of the book. The artist's input extends beyond authorship and illustration, making the physical appearance of the book as an object a manifestation of creativity in and of itself. In some art books, the traditional format of the book is not altered (example: an illustrated collection of poems in which the words and images are embossed rather than printed on paper pages). In other works, the artist experiments with format, even to the extent of challenging the concept of reading (example: a book with the covers and leaves consisting entirely of double-sided mirrors).

■ book auction

a public or private sale at which rare books and used books are sold to the highest bidder, usually on commission. A firm specialising in such sales is known as a book auction house. Extremely rare and valuable books and manuscripts are usually sold by international auction houses.

■ book band

a strip of printed paper (usually colored) placed around the jacketed cover of a book to call attention to a special characteristic, such as availability at a reduced price, receipt of an award, or special loan status (reserve or interlibrary loan).

■ book block

all the sections of a book sewn or glued together, plus the endpapers and any other materials added by the binder, before the cover is applied.

book burning

the intentional destruction by fire of books considered objectionable or dangerous, usually by a religious or secular authority, as in the mass burning of book considered politically incorrect by the Nazi Party in pre-World War II Germany, or by a mob, usually in the frenzy of political revolt.

book card

a piece of stiff card stock of standard size (three inches wide and five inches high), with space at the top for the call number, name of author and title of item and blank lines below for recording the due date and the library card number or name of the borrower, used in manual circulation systems to maintain a card file of items currently checked out. The book card is reinserted in the book pocket inside each item at check-in. Some libraries use coded-coded book cards to indicate type of material or applicable loan rule.

book catalogue

a library catalogue in the form of a bound or loose-leaf book, whether handwritten, printed, or computer-generated, practical only for small collections.

book club

a commercial company that sells new books and backlisted titles by mail to subscribers who agree to purchase a minimum number of titles per year at discount prices, usually from main, alternate, or special selections offered on a monthly basis which may be rejected or returned by the subscriber. To attract new subscribers, an introductory offer of free or heavily discounted titles may be offered in exchange for a minimum purchase commitment. Some book clubs offer books of general interest, others specialise by genre (example: mystery), subject (gardening), or academic field or discipline (history). Directory information for book clubs is available in Literary Market Place, a reference serial available in most libraries.

book club edition

an edition of a book offered for sale mail-order by a book club. Copies may be purchased by the club from the publisher's stock (usually at a discount) or specially reprinted for club distribution. An edition produced solely for distribution to book club subscribers can usually be distinguished from the trade edition of the same title by the inferior quality of the paper and binding and by the absence of a price on the dust jacket.

book collecting

the process of acquiring a collection of books based on their content, history, antiquity, rarity, beauty, monetary value, or other characteristics. A person who systematically acquires books for the pleasure of owning them, as an investment, or with the intention of bequeathing them to a library or other institution is known as a book collector.

■ book contract

a legally binding written agreement between a writer and publisher in which the author grants the publisher the rights to a specific work in exchange for compensation (usually royalties as a percentage of net sales on copies sold) and a commitment to publish the work in specified form within a designated period of time. Synonymous with publisher's agreement.

■ book cradle

a low stand or rack, made of wood, metal, or plastic, designed to display an open book, usually as part of an exhibit.

■ book culture

the habits, skills, institutions, etc., of a given people concerning books in all forms, including their manufacture (publishing, printing and binding), marketing and promotion, bookselling and collecting, book clubs and reading groups, bibliography and conservation, activities of libraries and archives and the writing, illustrating, reviewing and reading of books. In the United States, the persistence of book culture is evident in the presence of small cafes intended for readers on the premises of large bookstores and in the success of companies that manufacture and sell giftware, decorative items and accessories for readers.

■ book drop

a slot, chute, bin, or box to which books and other items borrowed from a library may be returned, especially during hours when the facility is closed. Book drops may be free-standing (usually outside the walls of the library) or built into the circulation desk or an exterior wall. Security is an important consideration in the design of an after-hours book drop. Libraries have suffered damage from hazardous materials deposited in book drops by malicious persons.

■ book fair

a trade exhibition, usually held annually, at which book publishers and distributors display their products in spaces called booths leased for that purpose. The first international book fair was held in France at Lyon during the late medieval period. Also refers to a non-trade exhibition of books and the book arts, which may include presentations by authors, illustrators, publishers, binders, etc.

■ book hand

a formal style of handwriting used by scribes to prepare books before the invention of the printing press, distinct from the cursive hand used for writing letters and other informal documents.

■ book history

the study of the origins and development of written works, from the cuneiform clay tablets and papyrus scrolls of antiquity, through the manuscripts and incunabula of the Middle Ages, to modern printing and publishing. Synonymous with history of the book.

■ book jobber

a book supplier.

■ book label

a card, strip, etc., smaller than a bookplate, usually made of paper, affixed to the inside of a book, in most cases to indicate ownership.

■ book lease plan

an acquisitions plan offered by some book jobbers which allows a library or library system to lease an agreed upon number of popular fiction and nonfiction titles, usually for a fixed monthly fee. After a prescribed period of time, or a decline in demand, titles are returned for credit toward new books usually selected from a monthly list provided by the jobber. Because leased books arrive fully catalogued and processed for circulation, some public libraries rely on leasing plans for high-demand items. Leasing is also used in academic libraries with limited space for a permanent collection of popular fiction and nonfictions. Synonymous with rental plan.

■ book lice

a species of minute (1/16-inch) soft-bodied, wingless insect (Liposcelis divinatorius) of worldwide distribution, which damages old books by feeding on the glue and paste in their bindings. Book lice also consume mold, cereal products and the bodies dead insects, which makes them a menace to botanical and soological museum specimens. Keeping relative humidity low helps to control them in libraries and exhibit spaces. Book lice also fall prey to book scorpions.

■ book lift

a fixed mechanical device similar to a dumb waiter, designed for transporting books from one floor or stack level to another in a library, without having to use a stairway or full-size elevator.

■ book light

a very small electric light designed to attach, usually by means of a clip, to the cover of a book for reading in a dark place (airplane seat, bed, tent, etc.) without disturbing others.

■ book list

a selected list of books, usually on a specific topic or in a particular genre, arranged in some kind of order (by author, title, subject, theme, etc.), which may include brief descriptive annotations, used mainly in readers' advisory.

■ book number

the portion of the call number following the class notation, added to identify a specific item within its class. A book number is composed of an author mark appended by the cataloguer to sub arrange works of the same class by name of author, followed by a work mark added to sub arrange works of the same author by title or edition.

■ book of hours

a book of common prayers for the Catholic laity, to be said at seven appointed hours in each day, introduced during the 11th century in England and France and used in Europe until the 16th century. Some medieval examples are magnificently illuminated.

■ book paper

a grade of paper suitable for printing books, pamphlets, periodicals, catalos, etc., as opposed to various other grades (newsprint, tissue paper, wallpaper, wrapping paper, etc.). Book papers vary in content, coded, finish, opacity, weight and permanence. For books which are to be retained indefinitely in the collection, librarians prefer permanent papers, acid-free and of high rag content.

■ book pocket

a three-inch wide strip of stiff paper with a small pocket folded and glued across the bottom third of its height to hold a book card, affixed to items held by a library that does not have an automated circulation system. Available ungummed or with a self-adhesive back, plain or with a date due slip printed at the top, pockets are affixed to the inside cover or endpaper in books, or to some other part in nonbook items. To enable circulation staff to match card to item at check-in, the front of the pocket and the top of the corresponding card are marked with the call number, name of author and title of item.

■ book press

a mechanical device consisting of two thick composite boards with a long screw at each of the four corners, used like a sandwich to apply pressure to a book, to ensure that glued or pasted surfaces adhere properly in binding, rebinding and repairing. In heavy-duty models, the boards are positioned on a base between two sturdy metal uprights to which a horizontal bar is attached, with a single large screw for increasing the downward pressure of the bar.

■ book size

the height and width of a book, usually measured in inches or centimetres from head to tail and from spine to fore-edge of the cover. Historically, the size of a printed book was determined by the number of times a full sheet of printing paper measuring approximately 19 x 25 inches was folded, once to form signatures of two leaves (four pages) known as folio, twice to form four leaves (eight pages) known as quarto, three times to form eight leaves (sixteen pages) known as octavo, to form twelve leaves (twenty-four pages) known as duodecimo, four times to form sixteen leaves (thirty-two pages) known as sextodecimo, etc. In modern book production, the size of an edition depends on the size of the unfolded sheet used in printing. In the bibliographic description of rare books, the historical dimensions are is still used, but in modern book production, size is based on the height and width of the binding.

■ book stamp

a wood, metal, or rubber stamp used to make an inked impression on the cover, edge, endpaper, or title page of a book as a mark of ownership.

■ book stock

the total number of books in a library's collections, subject to growth through acquisition and to diminution through loss, damage, theft, weeding, etc. Synonymous with book collection.

■ book stop

a narrow ridge or ledge along the lower edge of the sloping top of a dictionary stand, atlas case, or lectern, allowing an open book or sheaf of papers to rest at an angle convenient for reading without sliding off.

■ book talk

an event, usually scheduled in a library, bookstore, or educational institution, at which the author, a librarian, or other interested person discusses a book and reads excerpts from it to encourage readership and promote reading in general. Also spelled booktalk.

■ book trade

the operations and arrangements that exist in a specific country for the manufacture, distribution and sale of books to the public, including publishers and their associations, printers and binders, retail booksellers and their trade associations, jobbers and dealers and the generally accepted practices, standards and codes governing their activities.

■ book trade journal

a periodical issued by publishers, booksellers and others engaged in the book trade for the purpose of announcing and promoting newly published titles. Book trade journals also include trade news, bestseller lists, author interviews, book reviews, feature articles, regular columns, analysis of current trends and issues and information about book production/ distribution, book fairs and book signings.

■ book truck

a wheeled metal or wooden cart with two or three shelves, used by a page or other library staff member for transporting books and other materials from one area of the library to another. Book trucks are available from library suppliers.

■ book

handy, portable printed information storage device commonly forming a large portion of a library collection and not requiring mediating technology for use.

■ bookbin

a wheeled box for transporting books, sometimes with a bottom equipped with a spring mechanism to allow the space inside to fill gradually as books and other materials are returned to a book drop built into the circulation desk or wall of a library.

■ **bookbinding**

the process of fastening the leaves of a book together and enclosing them in a protective cover, formerly done by hand but now largely mechanised.

■ **bookcase**

a set of two or more single- or double-sided shelves in a rigid frame, used to store books, periodicals, videocassettes and other materials. In libraries, bookcases are usually made of wood or metal with fixed or adjustable shelves.

■ **bookend**

an L- or inverted T-shaped movable piece of wood, metal, tough plastic, or other rigid material, placed at the end of a row of books, periodicals, videocassettes, etc., to keep them upright on a shelf. Bookends manufactured as gift items may be covered in leather, carved in wood or fine stone, or cast in metal and given a decorative finish.

■ **bookish**

pertaining to a book, or to books and reading in general, usually in the literary sense. Also refers to a person who is fond of reading books or excessively studious. As a term of disparagement, any person whose knowledge of life is acquired largely by reading books, rather than from actual experience.

■ **bookman**

a man in the business of publishing, making, or selling books. Also, a man of literary or scholarly inclination who is familiar with books.

■ **bookmark**

a narrow strip of paper, leather, ribbon, or other thin, flexible material placed between the pages of a book to mark a place. Hand-crafted decorative bookmarks are sometimes given as gifts. In older and more expensive editions, a piece of narrow ribbon longer than the length of the pages is sometimes glued to the top of the spine to serve as a bookmark. A ribbon used in this way is called a register. In computing, to mark a document or a specific location in a document for subsequent retrieval. Most Web browser software includes a 'bookmark' option that allows an Internet address (URL) to be archived, enabling the user to revisit the site without having to retype the address or repeat the original search from scratch.

■ **bookmobile**

a large motorised van equipped with shelves to accommodate a small library collection and a desk for a librarian or paraprofessional member of the library staff, serving as a travelling branch library in neighbourhoods and communities too remote to be easily served by the nearest public library.

■ bookseller

a person in the business of selling books and related materials to the retail trade at the full net published price, especially one who owns a bookstore. Also refers to anyone in the business of selling used books.

■ bookstall

a small open-air retail book outlet, usually found in airports and railway stations and at fairs and markets. In France, quay-side bookstalls have been an important part of Parisian culture for centuries.

■ bookstore

an enclosed store devoted to the retail sale of books, usually in both hardcover and soft cover. Some bookstores specialise in used books, rare books, children's books, or materials on a specific subject or in a particular genre (science fiction, comics, etc.). Large trade bookstores may also sell magazines and newspapers, maps, calendars, greeting cards, nonprint media (videocassettes, DVDs, audiocassettes, CDs, CD-ROMs) and reading paraphernalia. Bookstore chains have outlets in most large cities in the United States, offering nearly identical stock (Barnes & Noble and Borders Books & Music). College bookstores sell mainly textbooks and trade editions for the use of students.

■ bookworm

the larval form of a moth or beetle that damages books and other printed materials by boring small holes through leaves and bindings, creating a highly undesirable condition called worming. Also spelled book-worm. Also, a slang expression used as a term of disparagement for someone who prefers reading over most other activities and can usually be found with his or her nose in a book.

■ boolean

a system of logic developed by the English mathematician George Boole (1815-1864) which allows the user to combine words or phrases representing significant concepts in a keywords search of an online catalogue or bibliographic database. Three logical commands (sometimes called 'operators') are available in most search software:

1. The OR command is used to expand retrieval by including synonyms and related terms in

the query. Search statement: violence or conflict or aggression.
2. The AND command is used to narrow search results. Each time another concept is added using 'and' the search becomes more specific. In some online catalos and databases, the 'and' command is implicit (no need to type it in a keywords search). In other interfaces, terms will be searched as a phrase if not separated by 'and.' Search statement: violence and television and children.
3. The NOT command is used to exclude unwanted records from search results. Search statement: television not cartoon.
When two different Boolean commands are used in the same search statement, parentheses must be included to indicate the sequence in which they are to be executed (syntax). This technique is called nesting.

■ breach of contract

failure to keep the terms of an agreement or contract. Some employment contracts include penalties for breach of certain provisions, such as length of notice required at time of resignation, but enforcement is usually at the discretion of the employer.

■ broken up

a book disassembled to enable its parts (usually plates or other illustrations) to be sold separately. Copies of the Gutenberg Bible have been broken up and the leaves can be sold separately.

■ browsability

the ease with which a library catalogue, index, bibliographic database, or other list of resources can be searched in a casual, unsystematic manner. A printed index is often more browsable than its online counterpart because the page format makes it easy for the user to scan a list of headings to find related information.

■ browse

to look through a library collection, catalogue, bibliography, index, bibliographic database, or other finding tool in a casual search for items of interest, without clearly defined intentions. To facilitate browsing, libraries assign similar call numbers to items on the same subject, which groups them together on the shelf. In information retrieval, a search directed by the user in a dynamic but casual way. A clearly formulated query may determine the initial point of entry into an index or database, but searches that begin systematically often give way to an exploratory approach as new terminology is revealed in the results retrieved. Some researchers consider printed indexes to be more browsable than electronic databases because page format allows the user to scan with ease the headings and entries that precede and follow the initial point of access. Also, to search for information available on the World Wide Web in a casual, serendipitous manner. Hypertext is designed to facilitate online browsing by providing embedded links to related documents and electronic resources (this online dictionary is an example).

browser

1. software used to access Web documents (e.g. Netscape, Internet Explorer).
2. a person who searches a library collection, catalog, index, bibliography, bibliographic database, or other list of resources in a casual, unsystematic manner. Also refers to a type of application software called a Web browser, designed to facilitate searching for information available on the Internet.

browser cache

the portion of microcomputer memory reserved by Web browser software for storing the contents of Web pages previously visited by the user, reducing the amount of time required to revisit a page using the same machine. Clicking on 'Reload' or 'Refresh' in the toolbar of a browser will cause the Web page displayed on the screen to be retrieved from its original remote address, rather than from the cache. Most browsers allow the user to specify the length of time search history will be retained before it is automatically deleted.

buckram

a strong, durable book cloth consisting of a heavy woven base in cotton, linen, or jute filled with starch or impregnated with pyroxylin, used to cover volumes for which heavy use is anticipated (bound periodicals, periodical indexes, children's picture books, etc.).

budget

the total amount of funds available to meet a library's expenditures over a fixed period of time (usually one or two years). In most budgets, funds are allocated by category of expenditure, called lines. In chronically under-funded libraries and library systems, budgeting can be a major source of frustration for librarians and library administration.

buffer

in computing, temporary storage (usually RAM) used for data while it is being processed, or for special purposes such as the transfer of data between two system components which have different operating speeds, for example, a printer and a CPU capable of processing data more quickly than output can be printed. A buffer may be a section of memory reserved for a specific processing function, or a portion of general memory allocated and deallocated as needed. In papermaking, a substance or mixture of substances added to paper stock during manufacture to control the acidity or alkalinity of the product. In document preservation, a substance or mixture used to maintain the acidity or alkalinity of paper (or of a solution) at an optimum level.

buffered paper

printing paper to which an alkaline substance, such as calcium carbonate or magnesium carbonate, is added in manufacture to neutralise any acid produced internally as a result of aging, or introduced by acid migration or exposure to atmospheric pollution. Non-buffered paper is required for certain types of photographic prints.

buffering

in papermaking, the addition of an alkaline substance such as calcium carbonate or magnesium carbonate to the pulped fiber to neutralise any acid that may develop as paper ages, or be introduced through acid migration or exposure to atmospheric pollution. Extent of buffering is indicated as a percentage of the paper weight, usually no more than 2-3%.

bug

in computing, a slang term for a persistent error in software or hardware. Once it has been located, a software bug can be corrected by altering the program, a process known as debugging. To correct a hardware bug, it is usually necessary to reconfigure circuitry. Also refers to an electronic eavesdropping device installed in a telephone receiver, or in some other hidden location, usually for the purpose of espionage.

bulk

the thickness of a book without its cover, normally less after binding than in its unbound state. Also, the thickness of a sheet of paper in relation to its weight, as measured in thousandths of an inch. The thickness of printing papers is also measured in pages-per-inch. Publishers sometimes 'bulk' a short text by printing it on thick, low-density paper. India paper and bible paper are used to reduce the bulk of a large volume.

bulk lending

the lending of a large volume of materials by one library to another, usually for a period of time longer than the normal borrowing period. Books published in large print and books-on-tape are sometimes loaned in bulk to the branch libraries within a public library system, or even outside the system.

bull

narrowly speaking, a document, letter, edict, or decree issued by the Pope, to which his official seal (Bulla) is affixed. Also refers to any statement of belief or doctrine, whether ecclesiastical or not.

bulletin

a periodical, usually in the form of a pamphlet, issued by a government agency, society, or other institution, containing announcements, news and information of current interest, usually more substantial than a newsletter. In a more general sense, any brief report on the latest developments in an ongoing process or situation, issued in print or nonprint format. Abbreviated bull.

LA LETTRE DE LA BIBLIOTHÈQUE

■ bulletin board

a flat notice board, usually attached to a wall near the entrance to a library, used to display announcements of forthcoming events, dust jackets removed from new books recently added to the collection, reading lists, comments and suggestions from library users (sometimes with responses from the library administration) and other information pertinent to library operations. Some libraries use a kiosk for this purpose.

■ Bulletin Board System (BBS)

1. the electronic equivalent of a notice board, generally subject-specific. A BBS is a form of electronic mail in which users post messages to a common receiver (the bulletin board) and have access to all messages posted.
2. an online messaging system and discussion forum that allows users to post notices and comments to members of an interest group connected to the same network. A BBS is similar in function to a Web site, but lacks graphics and has its own telephone number which the user must dial with the aid of a communications program.

■ bumped

the condition of a binding that has at least one corner bent, compressed, or rounded by forceful contact with a hard surface, such as the floor in a fall from a bookshelf.

■ bureau

an office or department within an organisation or government agency, responsible for collecting and disseminating information, usually on a specific topic, in a particular field, or of a certain type.

■ burlesque

from the Italian word burla meaning 'mockery.' A crude form of satire in which the style of a work, or of an entire genre, is ridiculed by trivialising a serious subject or dignifying a trivial one, usually in the form of a stage performance. The purpose is to amuse and entertain, rather than to inform.

■ burnish

in bookbinding, to polish the colored or gilt edges of a volume with a smooth hard tool, such as an agate, until the surface gleams elegantly in the light. Left unburnished, a gilt edge is antique.

burnout

a serious and sometimes irreversible decline in staff morale due to chronic overwork, which may result in increased absenteeism, backlogs, high turnover and deterioration in quality of service. Also spelled burn-out.

business library

a branch of a metropolitan public library system which serves the specialised information needs of persons engaged in business, usually located in or near the commercial or financial district. Also, a separately administered library associated with the business department of a college or university, administered to serve the curriculum needs of the business faculty and the information needs of students enrolled in courses in business, management, accounting and related fields. The collection usually includes books, periodicals and reference materials on business, as well as company reports, economic and business statistics, business-related periodical indexes and databases, etc., managed by a business librarian.

buying guide

a publication intended for professional librarians, providing authoritative guidance on the purchase of a specific type of resource. Buying guides usually begin with a discussion of evaluation techniques, then provide detailed analysis of possible selections, usually broken down by type of work. The relative strengths/weaknesses of available alternatives may be presented in tabular format to facilitate comparison. Also used synonymously with consumer guide.

byline

a line of type, usually printed at the beginning or end of a newspaper or magazine article to indicate its authorship.

byte

the common unit of computer storage used in digital computers of all types and sizes, composed of eight binary digits called bits. Hardware specifications for computers (microcomputers to mainframes) are indicated in bytes. Each unique sequence of eight bits can encode a single character, for a total of 256 possible characters. In ASCII text, the characters are alphanumeric. Disagreement exists about the origin of the term. It may be an abbreviation of binary table or binary term, or derived from the expression 'by eights.' The clarification is as follows:

1 byte = 8 bits
1 kilobyte (K) = 1,024 bytes
1 megabyte (MB) = 1,024 kilobytes or approximately one million bytes
1 gigabyte (GB) = 1,024 megabytes or approximately one billion bytes

Text and image files are usually measured in kilobytes, portable storage and program files in megabytes and hard disk capacity in gigabytes.

cache

a small section of dedicated high-speed memory built into a microcomputer to improve system performance by providing temporary storage for blocks of data and instructions which would otherwise be retrieved from slower memory. As a general rule, the larger the cache, the greater the enhancement of performance and speed. Pronounced 'cash.'

cadastral map

from the Latin word capitastrum meaning 'register of the poll tax.' A map showing boundaries and subdivisions, made to record ownership and rights in land and to describe and establish the value of property, usually for the purpose of tax assessment.

caldecott medal

a literary award given annually since 1938 under the auspices of the American Library Association to the illustrator of the most distinguished children's picture book published in the United States during the preceding year. The medal is donated by the family of Frederic G. Melcher.

calendar

a list of the days in a year, usually arranged by month and within each month by week, sometimes indicating the dates of important events such as national and religious holidays. Also, an almanac listing days of the year which are of special significance to a particular culture or political entity. Also refers to a list of the documents included in an archival collection (rolls, charters, state papers, etc.), usually annotated to indicate the date, contents and other characteristics of each item.

calendar year

the one-year period beginning on January 1 and ending on December 31. Most journal subscriptions run for a single calendar year, although an incentive may be offered to subscribe or renew for two or more years.

calf

a leather binding made from the skin of a calf usually no more than a few weeks old. The smooth, unblemished surface of calf made it the preferred material in England for hand-binding trade editions, but not on the Continent where printed books were usually sold in paper covers to be bound at the discretion of the purchaser. Calf bindings can be dyed any coded and decorated in various ways (marbled, mottled, speckled, stained, tooled, etc.).

call number

a unique code printed on a label affixed to the outside of an item in a library collection, usually the lower spine of a book or videocassette, also handwritten or printed on a label inside the item. Assigned by the cataloguer, the call number is also displayed in the bibliographic record representing the item in the library catalogue, to identify the work, indicate its subject classification and give its location on the shelf relative to other items of similar classification. A call number is composed of the notation identifying the class assigned to the item, followed by an author mark to distinguish the work from others of the same class, followed by a work mark distinguishing the title from other works of the same class by the same author and sometimes other information such as publication date, volume number, copy number and location symbol.

■ call slip

a brief form that must be filled out by a registered borrower to request an item from the closed stacks of a library, usually retrieved by hand by a staff member called a page, although automated and semi-automated systems are used in some large libraries.

■ calligraphy

the art of elegant handwriting. A highly skilled penman is a calligrapher. The term also refers to handwritten characters, words, pages and even entire documents which meet the aesthetic requirements of highly skilled penmanship. In Far Eastern cultures, calligraphy is done with a pointed brush held in a vertical position. In Western and Islamic cultures, it is done with a reed, quill, or nib pen held at an angle to the writing surface.

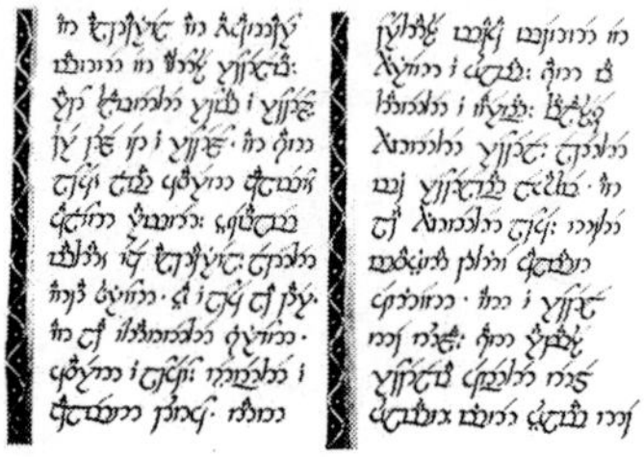

■ cameo

a typeface used for special effect in which the normal method of printing is reversed, the characters appearing in white against a solid or shaded background, instead of in black against a light background.

■ cameo binding

a style of bookbinding popular in Italy from about 1500-1560 in which the centres of the boards forming the cover are stamped in relief in imitation of a coin or medallion. The decoration may be left blind, or embellished with ink, silver, or gold leaf. Synonymous with plaquette binding.

■ cameo stamp

in binding, a metal tool of oval shape, engraved with a design, usually in the form of a picture, used from the 11th to 16th century in blind tooling to make an impression resembling cameo jewellery on the side of a leather-bound book.

■ camera microfilm

in reprography, an image of an original source document, made with a camera on high-quality film, usually retained by the

producer for the purpose of making archival or distribution copies. Synonymous with first generation and master negative.

■ Camera-Ready Copy (CRC)

in printing, copy typed using word processing software, or produced by some other means, which has been fully edited and is ready to be photographed for platemaking without having to be typeset. Synonymous with camera copy.

■ cancel

a new leaf or leaves printed to replace part of a book or other publication when changes are required in the text or illustrations, usually before binding but after the work has gone to press, more common in the 17th and 18th centuries than today because as printing developed, the frequency of printing errors declined.

■ cancelled

said of a regular order, continuation order, or periodical subscription terminated for some reason by the library or the seller. A nonserial item may be reordered if it is still available. Library holdings of a cancelled serial title are noted in the catalogue record in a closed entry. Serial cancellations have increased in recent years, particularly in academic libraries, due to the rising cost of print subscriptions and the availability of full-text in periodical databases.

■ cancellation period

the period of time a library allows a publisher, jobber, or other vendor for shipment of a book or item before the order is automatically cancelled, usually 90-180 days. The item may subsequently be reordered from the same vendor, or a different source.

■ candidate

a person whose application for employment has been accepted and who is being seriously considered for a position. Also refers to a person taking an examination, running for an elected office, considered for an award or degree, or destined for a particular purpose or fate.

■ canon

in literature, the accepted list of works by a given author, considered by scholars to be authentic, for example, the thirty-seven plays of William Shakespeare. Also refers to the approved list of works included in the Christian Bible. In the most general sense, a criterion or standard of judgment applied for the purpose of evaluation.

■ canonical order

the arrangement of headings, parts, divisions, or items in an order established by law or tradition, the classic example being the sequence of the books of the Christian Bible.

■ canto

a major subdivision of a long narrative or epic poem, serving the same function as a chapter in a novel. Cantos are traditionally numbered in roman numerals. Examples of works divided in this way are Dante's Divina Commedia, Spenser's Faerie Queene and Byron's Don Juan.

■ case study

in the social and medical sciences, analysis of the behavior of one individual in a population, or a single event in a series, based on close observation over a period of time. A case study may be published as an article in a journal, as an essay in a collection, or in book form. In bibliographic databases that permit the user to limit retrieval by type of publication, case studies may be one of the options.

■ casebook

a book containing records or descriptions of actual cases that have occurred in a professional discipline (law, medicine, psychology, sociology, social work, counselling, etc.), selected to illustrate important principles and concepts, for the use of students as a textbook and practitioners for reference.

■ case-sensitive

a computer system or software program in which uppercase letters (A, B, C...) and lowercase letters (a, b, c...) are not interchangeable as input (JAVA versus java). On the Internet, Web addresses (URLs) are case-sensitive, but e-mail addresses and filenames usually are not.

■ catalogue

a comprehensive list of the books, periodicals, maps and other materials in a given collection, arranged in systematic order to facilitate retrieval (usually alphabetically by author, title and/or subject). In most modern libraries, the card catalogue has been converted to machine-readable bibliographic records and is available online. The purpose of a library catalogue is to offer the user a variety of approaches or access points to the information contained in the collection.

■ **catalogue card**

in manual cataloguing systems, a paper card used to make a handwritten, typed, or printed entry in a card catalogue, usually of standard size (7.5 cm high and 12.5 cm wide), plain or ruled. With the conversion of paper records to machine readable format and the use of online catalos, catalogue cards have fallen into disuse. British spelling is catalogue card.

■ **catalogue code**

a detailed set of rules for preparing bibliographic records to represent items added to a library collection, established to maintain consistency within the catalogue and between the catalos of libraries using the same code.

■ **catalogue record**

in the manual card catalogue, all the information given on a library catalogue card, including a description of the item, the main entry, any added entries and subject headings, notes and the call number. In the online catalogue, the screen display that represents most fully a specific edition of a work, including elements of description and access points taken from the complete machine-readable bibliographic record, as well as information about the holdings of the local library or library system (copies, location, call number, status, etc.) taken from the item records attached to the bibliographic record. British spelling is catalogue record.

■ **cataloguer**

a librarian primarily responsible for preparing bibliographic records to represent the items acquired by a library, including bibliographic description, subject analysis and classification. Also refers to the librarian responsible for supervising a cataloguing department. British spelling is cataloguer. Synonymous with catalogue librarian.

■ **cataloguing**

the process of creating entries for a catalogue. In libraries, this usually includes bibliographic description, subject analysis, assignment of classification notation and all the activities involved in physically preparing the item for the shelf, tasks usually performed under the supervision of a librarian trained as a cataloguer. British spelling is cataloguing.

■ **cataloguing agency**

a library or other institution that provides authoritative cataloguing data in the form of new bibliographic records and modifications of existing records, for the use of other libraries.

■ **catalogue**

list of materials available in a particular collection, arranged in a systematic order.

■ **catch letters**

a sequence of letters (usually three) printed at the top of a page in a dictionary, gazetteer, or similar work, which duplicate the first few letters of the first or last word on the page. Those printed on the verso indicate the first letters of the first word on the page; those on the recto, the first letter of the last word on the page. In some works, the letters appear in two groups separated by a hyphen, representing the first and last words on the page.

■ catchword

a word or part of a word printed in boldface or uppercase at the top of a column or page in a dictionary or encyclopaedia, which repeats the first and/or last heading appearing in the column or on the page. Synonymous with guideword. In medieval manuscripts and early printed books, a word or part of a word given below the last line on a page, which repeats the first word on the following page to enable the binder to assemble the leaves in correct sequence. Also refers to a word or phrase repeated so frequently that it has become a motto or slogan.

■ catchword title

a partial title composed of an easily remembered word or phrase likely to be used as a heading or keyword in a search of the library catalogue, sometimes the same as a subtitle or the alternative title. Synonymous with catch title.

■ cathedral binding

a cloth or leather binding decorated with architectural motifs of the Gothic period, sometimes even including a rose window, popular in France and England from about 1815 to 1840 when interest in Gothic art underwent a revival.

■ caucus

an interest group within a political faction or party, legislative body, or organisation, formed (sometimes spontaneously) to address an immediate need for action on a given issue or series of related issues, usually by formulating policy, supporting candidates for political office, drafting campaign strategy, lobbying, etc.

■ Caxton, William

England's first printer, Caxton learned the trade relatively late in life while living in Cologne and Bruges. He brought the first printing press to England and installed it in the Chapter House at Westminster Abbey, issuing the first dated book known to have been printed in England (probably his The Dictes and Sayings of the Philosophers) in 1477. By the time he died in 1491, his press had issued approximately one hundred works, including folio editions of Chaucer's Canterbury Tales (1478) and Mallory's Morte D'Arthur (1485) which he sold to English readers in bound copies. He was an expert editor and translated into English many of the works he printed.

■ **cellulose**

the fibrous vegetable material used in papermaking, derived primarily from wood pulp, but formerly from cotton or linen rags. The cellulose in paper and board made from wood pulp is weakened over time by the presence of acid unless lignin is removed in manufacture and an alkaline buffer added.

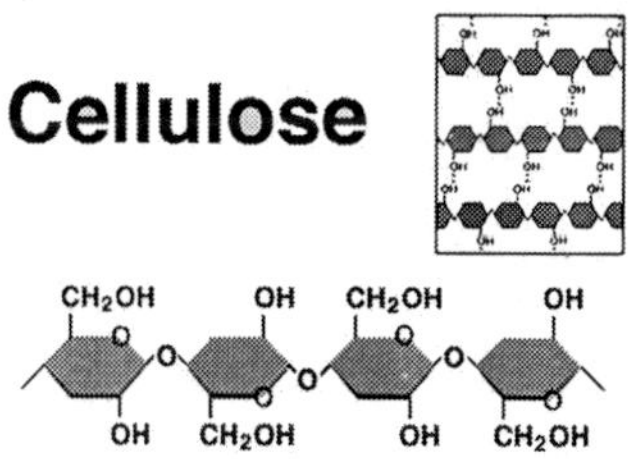

■ **censorship**

prohibition of the production, distribution, circulation, or display of a work by a governing authority on grounds that it contains objectionable or dangerous material. The person who decides what is to be prohibited is called a censor. Commonly used methods include decree and confiscation, legislation, repressive taxation and licensing to grant or restrict the right to publish.

■ **census**

an official count and statistical analysis of the population of a given geographic entity (city, county, state, province, country, etc.) taken at a particular point in time. The earliest known census of taxpaying households was recorded in China in the 3rd century B.C. More complete enumerations were conducted for military and tax purposes in ancient Rome by special magistrates called censors. The development of the modern census began in Europe in the 17th century and today includes questions concerning age, gender, ethnicity, income, housing, etc., formulated to generate data used in social planning, political redistricting, business marketing, etc. In most countries, participation in the census is compulsory and the information collected on individual households and businesses is confidential.

■ **census tract**

one of many small geographic areas into which a state or country is divided for the purpose of gathering and reporting census data.

■ **centrepiece**

in bookbinding of the late 16th and early 17th centuries, an ornamental design such as an arabesque, stamped on the center of the front and/or back cover, usually accompanied by matching corner pieces. Also refers to a piece of embossed or engraved metal attached to the center of the front cover of a book. Also spelled centrepiece.

■ central library

the administrative center of a library system, where system-wide management decisions are made, centralised technical processing is conducted and principal collections are located. Synonymous with main library.

■ Central Processing Unit (CPU)

the hardware component of a computer that houses the circuitry for storing and processing data according to instructions contained in the programs installed on it, including the operating system, utilities to run peripheral devices and application software. Generally speaking, the more memory and disk storage a CPU has, the more processing it can handle within a given amount of time and the faster it can accomplish a task.

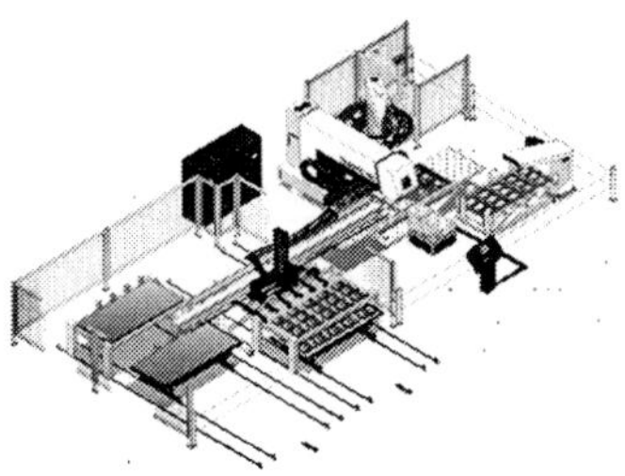

■ centralised cataloguing

the preparation of bibliographic records for books and other library materials by a central cataloguing agency which distributes them in printed and/or machine-readable form to participating libraries, usually for a modest fee. Also refers to the cataloguing of materials for an entire library system at one of its facilities, usually the central library, to achieve uniformity and economies of scale. Also spelled centralised cataloguing.

■ centralised processing

the practice of concentrating in a single location all the functions involved in preparing materials for library use, as opposed to technical processing carried out at multiple locations within a library or library system. Centralisation allows processing methods to be standardised, but increased efficiency may be offset by the cost of distributing materials to the units where they will be used.

■ certificate of issue

in a limited edition, the statement in each copy giving the total number of copies printed and the copy number. In an autographed edition, the certificate may also bear the signature of the author, editor, or illustrator.

■ certification

in archives, the formal act of attesting to the official identity and nature of an original document or its reproduction. Also, the process by which a state agency, or a nongovernmental agency or organisation authorised by a state government, evaluates the qualifications of an individual, organisation, or institution to perform a specific service or function, for the purpose of granting a credential.

■ cessation

a serial or annual that has ceased publication.

■ cf.

an abbreviation of the Latin confer meaning 'compare.'

■ CGI

Common Gateway Interface; a programming mechanism for servers.

■ challenge

a complaint lodged by a library user acting as an individual or representing a group, concerning the inclusion of a specific item (or items) in a library collection, usually followed by a demand that the material be removed. Library programs may also be targeted. Public libraries are challenged far more frequently than other types of libraries because they are supported by public funds and must provide resources and services for a highly diverse clientele ('this library has something to offend everyone'). An unambiguously worded collection development policy is a library's best defence against such objections.

■ changed title

the title proper of a publication that has undergone a change of title from the one under which it was previously published. Title changes occur most frequently in periodicals, compounding the work of serials librarians and complicating access for users. In library cataloguing, a note is included in the bibliographic record representing the new title and a similar note is added to the record for the previously published title. Synonymous with title change.

■ channel

a pathway along which data is transmitted electronically from one computer, terminal, or device to another. The term also refers to the physical medium carrying the signal (optical fiber, coaxial cable, etc.) and to the properties that distinguish a specific channel from others. In data storage, a track on a specific storage medium (magnetic tape, magnetic disk, CD-ROM, DVD, etc.) on which electrical signals are recorded. In communications, a band of frequencies assigned by the Federal Communications Commission (FCC) to a radio or television transmitting station for its exclusive use. Also refers to the blank space dividing columns of text written or printed on a page.

■ chapbook

from the Anglo-Saxon root ceap. A small inexpensive paperbound book or pamphlet containing a popular legend, tale, poem, or ballad, or a collection of prose or verse, hawked in the streets of London from the 16th to the 18th century by travelling peddlers called chapmen. The content was usually sensational (abduction, murder, witchcraft etc.), educational (travel), or moral. Chapbooks were typically of small size (6 x 4 inches), containing up to 24 pages illustrated with woodcuts, usually with a decorated cover title. Also refers to a modern pamphlet of the same type. Also spelled chap-book.

■ chapter

one of two ore more major divisions of a book or other work, each complete in itself, but related in theme or plot to the division preceding and/or following it. In works of nonfictions, chapters are usually given a chapter title, but in works of fiction they may simply be numbered, usually in roman numerals. Chapters are listed in order of appearance by title and/or number in the table of contents in the front matter of a book.

■ chapter drop

the position below the chapter heading at which the text of a chapter begins—lower than on succeeding pages of the text and, in most books, the same for all chapters.

■ chapter heading

a display heading in a book or manuscript, usually consisting of a roman numeral indicating the chapter number, followed by the chapter title, written or printed on the first page of the chapter in uniform style and position above the first paragraph of the text. Set in a type size larger than the text and running heads, chapter headings are sometimes embellished with an illustration or head-piece in older editions.

■ chapter title

the title that appears at the beginning of a chapter in a book, usually bearing some relation to the content of the division of the work. Chapters may simply be numbered (usually in roman numerals), or given a number and a title. They are listed in order of appearance by number and/or title in the table of contents in the front matter.

■ character

any mark, sign, or symbol conventionally used in writing or printing, including letters of the alphabet, numerals, punctuation marks and reference marks. In indexing, the smallest unit used in the arrangement of headings. In data processing, a sequence of eight binary digits (one byte) representing a letter of the alphabet, numeral, punctuation mark, or other symbol.

Also, a fictional person in a novel, play, short story, or other literary work. A character study is a work in which the primary theme is the inner development of a person or group of persons (example: Hamlet). In Library of Congress subject headings, 'Characters' is a standard subdivision used in personal name headings for writers of fiction, particularly playwrights (example: Shakespeare, William, 1546-1616 - Characters - Falstaff).

Well-known characters may be given a separate heading, followed by a parenthetical qualifier, as in Jeeves (Fictitious character).

■ character set

a group of symbols in a specific font, used for printing and/or electronic display. Character sets for languages written in the roman alphabet usually contain 256 symbols of which the first 128 are the same.

■ charge

to record the loan of a book or other item from the circulating collection of a library to a borrower. In modern libraries, this task involves the use of a computer. Also refers to the library's record of such a transaction, including the identity of the borrower, the title and call number of the item and its due date. Also refers to a fee or payment required of a library patron, usually for the use of non-traditional services, such as rental collections and certain methods of document delivery.

■ chart

a map designed to meet the requirements of navigation, or one showing meteorological phenomena or heavenly bodies. A nautical chart indicates soundings, currents, coastlines and other important maritime features. An aeronautical chart shows features of interest to aircraft pilots. Also refers to an opaque sheet on which data are displayed in the form of graphs or tables, or by other graphic techniques.

■ charter

a legal document recording the franchise or granting of specific rights to an individual or corporate body by a governmental authority such as a legislature or sovereign (example: the Charter of the United Nations). The texts of important charters are usually available in the government documents or reference section of large libraries. The originals are preserved by the institutions that own them, usually in archives or special collections.

■ chase

in letterpress, the portable rectangular metal frame in which assembled type and display matter, composed into pages, is firmly locked into position. The resulting form is then ready to be transferred to the bed of the press for printing. The expression in chase means 'ready for printing.'

■ chased edges

a small wavy or crimped repeating pattern impressed as decoration on the gilt edges of a book, using heated finishing tools called gauffering irons, popular in 16th and 17th century ornamental bindings. Synonymous with gauffering and goffered edges.

■ chat

a real time computer conferencing capability between two or more users of a network (LAN, WAN, Internet) by means of a keyboard rather than voice transmission. Most Internet service providers offer a chat room to their subscribers.

■ check digit

a digit added to a sequence of digits, related arithmetically to the sequence in such a way that input errors can be automatically detected whenever the sequence is entered as data into a computer (example: last digit of the ISBN).

■ checked out

the circulation status of an item that has been charged to a borrower account and is not due back in the library until the end of the loan period. In the online catalogue, the due date is usually displayed as a status code in the catalogue record to indicate that the item is currently not available for circulation. Synonymous with on loan.

■ check-in record

a separate record attached to the full bibliographic record for a serial publication, in which the receipt by the library of individual issues or parts is entered, usually by an assistant working in the serials department. Most online catalogues allow users to view the check-in record to determine if a specific issue has arrived. The check-in record may also indicate whether an issue is missing, claimed, or at the bindery.

■ checklist

a comprehensive list of books, periodicals, or other documents, which provides the minimum amount of description or annotation necessary to identify each work—briefer than a bibliography. Also, the log kept by a library to record the receipt of each number of a serial publication, or part of a work in progress. Also refers to a list of items required, or procedures to be followed, such as the steps in a library's opening or closing routine. Also spelled check-list.

■ chemise

a loose leather or cloth cover designed with pockets to fit over the wooden boards of a hand-bound book, sometimes secured to the boards with bosses, used in Europe from the 12th to 15th century as a substitute for full binding.

■ Chief Information Officer (CIO)

the title of the person in a commercial company or nonprofits organisation who is responsible for managing the flow of official information, including computing and any library services—a relatively new position in companies and organisations that recognise the need for such a management function.

■ chief source of information

the source of bibliographic data preferred by cataloguers in preparing the bibliographic description of an item, usually the title page or a substitute, for example, the title frame at the beginning of a filmstrip or motion picture, or the title screen of a Web page.

■ chiffon silk

extra-thin but strong silk tissue used to mend or strengthen a leaf in a book or other document printed on paper.

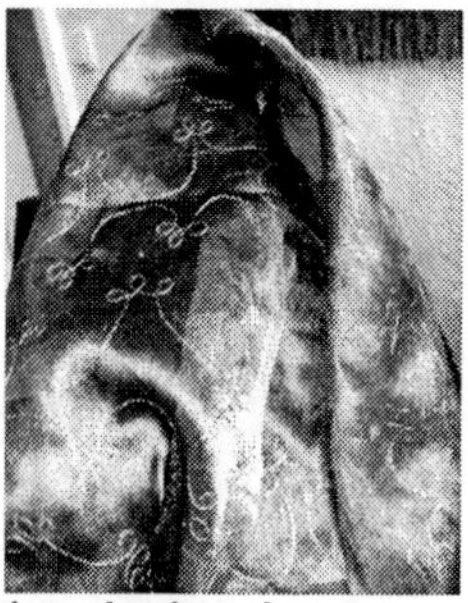

■ children's book

a book written and illustrated specifically for children up to the age of 12-13. Included in this category are juvenile fiction and nonfictions, board books, nursery rhymes, alphabet books, counting books, picture books, easy books, beginning readers, picture storybooks and storybooks. Children's books are shelved in the juvenile collection of most public libraries and in the curriculum room in most academic libraries.

■ children's librarian

a librarian who specialises in services and collections for children up to the age of 12-13. Most children's librarians have extensive knowledge of children's literature and are trained in the art of storytelling.

■ children's literature

literary works created specifically for children, as distinct from works written for adults and young adults, including poetry and prose, fiction and nonfictions. Children's literature began with the oral transmission of nursery rhymes, songs, poems, fairy tales and stories. During the early 17th century, the horn book came into widespread use in Britain and the American colonies, but it was not until the late 17th century with the publication of the popular Tales of Mother Goose by Charles Perrault (1628-1703) that written literature for children emerged as a separate genre. By the mid-18th century, the British writer, printer and publisher John Newbery (1713-1767) perceived that a market existed for children's books and began publishing illustrated works intended to be morally instructional (Little Goody Two-Shoes). Not until the 19th century did children's literature break away from didacticism, first with the publication of the fairy tales of Hans Christian Anderson (1805-1875) and the brothers Grimm and later with Edward Lear's Book of Nonsense (1846), Alice's Adventures in Wonderland (1865) and the sequel Through the Looking Glass (1871).

■ children's room

the area in a public library or one of its branches, reserved for collections and services intended specifically for children up to the age of 12-13, usually staffed by at least one children's librarian and furnished to accommodate persons of small stature. Some children's rooms include a comfortable corner or alcove designed for group storytelling, puppetry, etc.

■ children's services

library services intended for children up to the age of 12-13, including juvenile collection development, lapsit services, storytelling, assistance with homework assignments and summer reading programs, usually provided by a children's librarian in the children's room of a public library.

■ Chinese style

in China and Japan, the evolution of the book proceeded as in the West, from scroll to leaves enclosed in a cover, but by a different route. Instead of binding separately cut leaves in codex form, a continuous roll of writing material was accordion-pleated, creating a series of folded leaves left uncut at the fore-edge with writing (and later printing) on one side only. Also known as Japanese style.

■ chip

a shortened form of microchip, a high-speed miniaturised integrated circuit, etched in a semi conducting material (usually silicon) on the surface of a tiny, wafer-thin piece of metal, for use as microprocessor and memory in computers and other electronic equipment. The design of increasingly powerful microchips has been the driving force behind the information

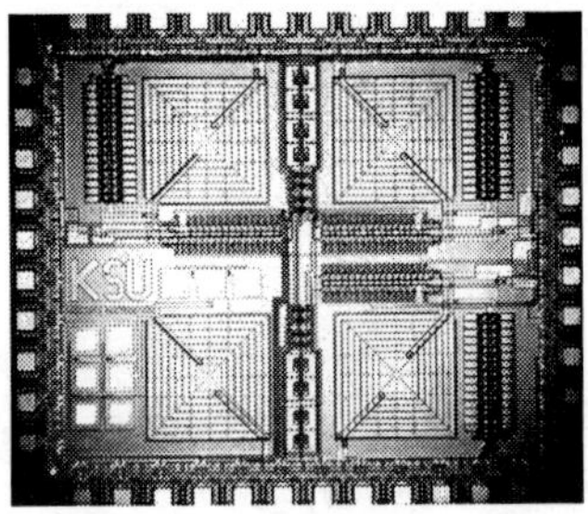

technology revolution that began in the second half of the 20th century.

■ chip board

a thin, cheap, low-density board manufactured from recycled paper and other cellulose fibres. Although chip board is sometimes used in case binding, binder's board is preferred in hardcover trade editions. Also spelled chipboard.

chipped

the condition of a book that has small pieces missing from the edges of its cover, dust jacket, or pages, not as priced in the market for antiquarian books as a copy in mint condition.

choropleth map

a map on which colour, shading, or some other graphic technique is used to show the density or frequency of a variable (e.g., mortality, population, precipitation) in each of several areas, based on the average number of occurrences per unit of area.

chorus score

the score of a musical work originally written for solo voice and chorus, which shows only the choral parts and any accompaniment arranged for keyboard instrument.

chrestomathy

a collection of choice passages from the literary works of an author (or authors), especially one compiled as a sample of literary specimens as an aid in the study of a language.

Christian fiction

novels and stories in which Christian religious belief is a major (sometimes predominant) element in the development of plot, theme and character. The market for Christian fiction has expanded considerably in the United States in recent years. New titles are regularly reviewed in Booklist and Library Journal.

chronicle

originally, a detailed chronological record of contemporary events, usually written over an extended period of time, with no pretense of literary style and little or no interpretation or analysis. The first extant example is the Anglo-Saxon Chronicle which begun in the 9th century during the reign of King Alfred, which covered the history of England from 60 BC to the 12th century. In modern usage, a list of events described and recorded in the order in which they occurred. The treatment is fuller and more connected than in annals.

chronicle play

a drama based on material from the chronicle histories of England, for example, those written by Hall and Holinshead. Popular during the Elisabethan period, chronicle plays were at first loosely structured, but evolved into sophisticated character studies, exemplified by the history plays of William Shakespeare. A more recent example of a history play is A Man for All Seasons by Robert Bolt (1960).

chronological

the arrangement of data, records, items, headings, entries, etc., according to their relation in time, from earliest to latest. In library classification systems, the period subdivisions added to subject headings are listed in chronological order (example: Antiquity—Medieval—Renaissance—then by century from the 15th to 20th). The opposite of reverse chronological.

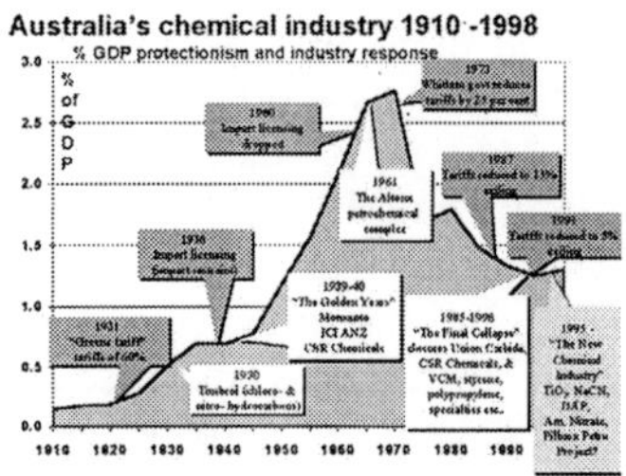

■ chronology

a book or section of a book that lists events and their dates in the order of their occurrence. Most chronologies are limited to a specific period (example: Roman Empire), event (World War II), or theme (women's history). Book-length chronologies are usually shelved in the reference section of a library.

■ chrysography

from the Greek words chrys ('gold') and graphia ('writing'). The art and craft of writing letters in gold, as practiced by the skilled copyists who produced medieval illuminated manuscripts. Also refers to writing done in gold letters.

■ cinema

a broad term encompassing the motion picture industry and distribution system, the films produced and the art form they represent. It is also used in Europe and the UK to refer to the theatre in which motion pictures are publicly shown.

■ cipher

the initials of a personal name, written or arranged in ornamental form of such complexity and/ or artistry as to form a private mark or symbol. In a more general sense, secret writing or code intended to be understood (deciphered) only by those who know the key to it. In data processing, an encrypted character that can only be decrypted with a key.

■ circa

a Latin word meaning 'about,' used to indicate lack of certainty but reasonable probability concerning a date, for example, the approximate birth and/or death date(s) of a person for whom official records are lacking. Abbreviated c. or ca. Example: c. 1922 (about 1922)

■ circular

an advertisement, announcement, or directive, usually in the form of a printed letter or leaflet, distributed to a large circle of people at the same time and intended to be passed on to others to whom its content might be of interest.

■ circulating book

a book that can be charged to a borrower account for use inside or outside the library facility, as opposed to one restricted to library use only.

■ circulating collection

books and other materials which may be checked out by registered borrowers for use inside or outside the library. In most academic and public libraries in the United States, circulating materials are shelved in open stacks to facilitate browsing.

■ circulating library

a library containing materials that can be borrowed by persons authorised to do so, usually for a fixed period of time, after which prompt return is expected. The idea of a subscription library to circulate fiction and other books of general interest was first conceived and implemented by London booksellers in the 17th century. By the Victorian period, this type of library was sufficiently widespread to provide a market for the publication of quality fiction in Britain.

■ circulating

library material that may be checked out by patrons.

■ circulation

the process of checking books and other materials in and out of a library. Also refers to the total number of items checked out by library borrowers during a designated period of time and to the number of times a given item is checked out during a fixed period of time, usually one year. In public libraries, low circulation is an important criterion for weeding items from the collection. Books for which circulation is anticipated to be high may be ordered in multiple copies to satisfy demand, or given a more durable binding to withstand heavy use. Some online circulation systems provide circulation statistics by classification and material type, for use in collection development. Circulation is a fundamental to access services. Abbreviated circ. In publishing, the number of copies distributed of each issue of a serial publication, including complimentary copies, single-copy retail sales and copies sent to paid subscribers.

■ classic

1. a widely read work recognised as outstanding in its field. Such a work remains in print long after initial publication; is translated, adapted and issued in multiple editions; and continues to be the subject of criticism, commentary, study and analysis (example: The Adventures of Huckleberry Finn by Mark Twain). Also refers to a feature film or documentary that has withstood the test of time.
2. all the non-Christian works written in the Greek and Latin languages prior to 600 AD (example: The Republic of Plato). In a broader sense, outstanding books

on any subject, fiction or nonfictions, written for adults or children.

■ classification

the process of dividing objects or concepts into logically hierarchical classes, subclasses and subsubclasses based on the characteristics they have in common and those that distinguish them. Also used as a shortened form of the term classification system or classification scheme.

■ classification schedule

the names assigned to the classes in a classification system, listed in the order of their symbolic notation. In a hierarchical classification system, the arrangement of the schedule(s) indicates levels of specificity.

■ classification system

a list of classes arranged according to a set of pre-established principles, for the purpose of organising items in a collection, or entries in an index, bibliography, or catalogue, into groups based on their similarities and differences, to facilitate access and retrieval. In the United States, most library collections are classified by subject.

■ classified

the status of a document to which access is restricted to a few authorised individuals within a military or government agency, research institution, private corporation, or other organisation, usually because it contains highly sensitive information which might be misused by unauthorised persons. When secrecy is no longer required, the document may be declassified. Also refers to a reference tool (catalogue, index, dictionary, encyclopaedia, etc.) organised according to a classification system, usually by subject or some other arrangement based on content, as opposed to a strictly alphabetical or numerical listing of entries.

■ classified catalogue

a type of subject catalogue in which the entries are filed according to a pre-established classification system, with bibliographic records entered under as many subject headings as apply to the content of each item. An alphabetical subject index facilitates the use of a classified catalogue, which is usually maintained alongside an author and/or title catalogue.

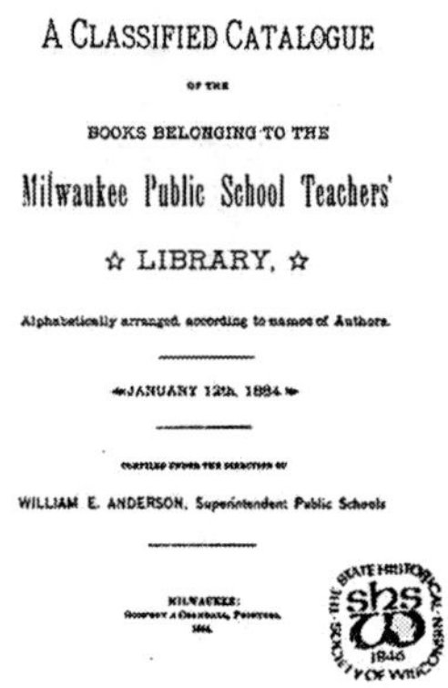

A CLASSIFIED CATALOGUE

OF THE

BOOKS BELONGING TO THE

Milwaukee Public School Teachers'

☆ LIBRARY. ☆

Alphabetically arranged according to names of Authors.

JANUARY 12th, 1884

WILLIAM E. ANDERSON, Superintendent Public Schools

MILWAUKEE:

■ classified index

an index in which entries are arranged under headings and subheadings indicating hierarchical divisions and subdivisions within classes based on the subject matter indexed, rather than in alphabetical or numerical sequence. To use such an index effectively, a subject index is required.

classroom collection

a small semi-permanent collection of library materials selected by a school library or academic library for the general classroom use of an instructor and the students enrolled in a course (or courses).

classroom library

a small collection of library materials located permanently in a school classroom for the use of instructor and students in support of the general curriculum. Such a collection may include reference materials such as a dictionary, thesaurus, atlas, general encyclopaedia, etc.

classroom loan

a small collection of library materials on temporary loan from a school library or academic library to a classroom, for the use of instructor and students, usually in support of a specific project or curriculum unit.

clay tablet

the earliest known books were inscribed on small, thin, wet slabs of clay, using a thin, sharp instrument called a stylus to incise the wedge-shaped cuneiform characters of the written languages of ancient Mesopotamia. The finished tablets were sun-dried or kiln-fired, then enclosed in a protective outer shell of dried or fired clay inscribed with a title or abstract of the contents. Although clay tablets were too heavy to be portable in large numbers and too small to record long texts effectively, they were much more durable than the papyrus scrolls that superseded them.

clearing house

an organisation or unit within an organisation that functions as a central agency for collecting, organising, storing and disseminating documents, usually within a specific academic discipline or field. A clearinghouse may also assist the research process by maintaining records of information resources for referral.

cliche

from the French word clicher meaning 'to stereotype.' A word, phrase, or expression so overused that it has lost its impact and, to some degree, its original meaning. Considered unimaginative, cliches are avoided by serious writers and speakers, except in dialogue when the author wishes to make a point about the mentality of the speaker. Dictionaries of cliches are available in the reference section of larger libraries. In literature, an overused plot element or character type whose lack of originality detracts from the quality of the work.

click-and-drag

to change the position of an icon, filename, window, or other movable element on a computer screen by clicking on it with a pointing device, such as a mouse and then holding down on the button to shift the element to another location on the screen. The technique can be used to reposition windows on a microcomputer desktop, move computer files from one directory or subdirectory to another in storage and organise bookmarked Web sites in folders in most Web browsers.

■ client

1. software program that is used to contact and obtain data from a server software program on another computer, often across a great distance.
2. a person who uses the services of a professionally trained expert, or of a professional organisation or institution, usually in exchange for payment of a fee. Librarians employed in academic and public libraries usually refer to the people they serve as users or patrons because libraries have traditionally provided most services without charge. Information brokers who operate on a fee-for-service basis can be more appropriately said to serve 'clients.'
3. Also refers to a computer connected to a network such as the Internet, equipped with software enabling the user to access resources available on another computer, called a server, connected to the same network.
4. a computer (or more specifically, a software application such as a browser) that uses resources provided by another computer (the server).

■ clientele

all the persons who use a library's services and collections on a regular or irregular basis, usually those who live in the district that funds it operations or are members of the institution it serves. Successful collection development depends on the librarian's knowledge of the information needs and preferences of the library's clientele.

■ client-server

wide-area (WAN) or local-area network (LAN) architecture that makes it possible for a client computer (usually a PC workstation) to download information or processing from a server machine, as opposed to a system that uses dedicated terminals connected to a minicomputer or mainframe. The size and speed of computer required as a server (microcomputer, minicomputer, or mainframe) depends on the nature of the applications to be installed and the amount of anticipated use. Also refers to the software used to establish the connection between a client and server.

■ clipboard

a small amount of computer memory reserved as a temporary storage place in the exchange of data between software applications. In word processing, this is normally accomplished by selecting the option to 'cut' or 'copy' from one document and 'paste' into another. Data transferred to the clipboard is lost when another cut/copy operation commences, unless saved as a separate file.

■ **clipping**

a page, piece of a page, or pages cut or torn from a printed publication, usually from a newspaper or magazine, by a person who wishes to save an article, editorial, letter to the editor, photograph, cartoon, etc. Large collections of clippings are usually stored in a clipping file, arranged by subject or some other method of classification. Synonymous with cutting.

■ **clipping service**

a service, usually performed in a special library, in which news announcements, articles, photographs and other items of interest to the host organisation are clipped from current periodicals and news services on a daily or weekly basis, to be forwarded to appropriate personnel within the organisation, based on pre-established interest profiles. Directory information for clipping services is available in the reference serial Literary Market Place. Synonymous with clipping bureau.

■ **cloisonne**

an elegant style of book cover produced by Italian and Greek craftsmen of the 11th century in which an ornamental design in narrow metal strips was soldered onto a metal plate and the open spaces between the strips filled with enamel in various colours, to form the outer surface of the cover. Books bound in this style are usually very valuable, especially if they are in good condition.

■ **close classification**

a classification system in which the main classes and divisions are minutely subdivided, allowing very specific characteristics of each subject to be differentiated. The opposite of broad classification.

■ **close out**

a book title offered for retail sale at a significantly reduced price because the publisher is allowing it to go out of print. A rebate may be offered by the publisher to the bookseller for copies that do not sell.

■ **close score**

a vocal music score in which all the parts are given on a minimum number of staves, usually two, as in a hymn.

■ **Closed Caption (CC)**

a continuous moving line of text (called a crawl) along the bottom of the screen in a television broadcast, giving the narration or dialogue and noting any non-speech vocalisations (laughter, screams, dogs barking, etc.) or sound effects (music, applause, doorbells, etc.). Used mainly for the hearing-impaired and in bilingual programming, closed captioning is visible only with the aid of a special decoder. In library cataloguing, the phrase closed captioned is entered in the note area of the bibliographic description to identify an item that includes the feature.

■ closed catalogue

a library catalogue to which new bibliographic records are no longer added, or in which additions are restricted to certain categories, although existing records continue to be removed as they are revised, corrected and/or converted to machine-readable format. After retrospective conversion is completed, a closed catalogue is usually removed from public access and eventually discarded.

■ Closed Circuit Television (CCTV)

a video system used internally in some large libraries, for conferencing and to monitor traffic for security purposes.

■ closed entry

a note in the bibliographic record for a serial or continuation, giving the complete information for all the parts or volumes published, or in the holdings note in the catalogue record for such a title, indicating all the parts or volumes held by a the library (example: v. 1-10, 1936-46), as distinct from the open entry for an ongoing serial subscription or continuation order (example: v.1- ,1936-). For periodicals, a closed entry usually indicates that the subscription was cancelled or the publication ceased.

■ closed file

in archives, a collection of documents in which additions or changes are unlikely to occur, or a file of records to which access is restricted or denied, except under special circumstances.

■ closed reserve

an item on reserve which may be checked out by a registered borrower, but may not be removed from library premises. Also, a reserve collection shelved in a closed stack from which requested items must be retrieved by a member of the library staff.

■ closed stacks

a shelving area in a library to which only members of the library staff have access, established to protect the collection or conserve space by using aisles narrower than the standard width in open stacks. Materials are retrieved from closed stacks by staff members upon request.

■ closed-end index

an index covering one or more documents or publications, compiled all at one time.

■ closet drama

a play written to be read rather than performed on the stage, for example, the dramatic works of the French poet Alfred de Musset. Also refers to a drama originally intended for performance, which survives as a work of literature but is rarely if ever performed (Byron's Manfred).

■ closing

all the procedures followed by the staff of a library when the facility closes at the end of a day, such as informing patrons that it is time to leave, checking the premises to be certain all users have vacated, logging off computer systems, turning off lights and equipment, locking doors, switching on pre-recorded phone messages, activating security alarms, etc. Size and design of facility determine the length of time and number of staff required to close. In very large facilities, a checklist may be followed for each floor and one or more security guards may assist in clearing the building.

■ cloth

a generic term for any woven material used since the early 19th century to cover the boards of a book, as opposed to the leather, parchment, or vellum used in earlier bookbinding, or the paper covers used today. Dyed book cloth used in edition binding is woven from cotton or linen, filled with starch sizing, or coated or impregnated with some other compound, then pressed under heat. Because the covers of cloth-bound trade editions are not designed to withstand heavy use, publishers add an attractively designed paper dust jacket for protection (and marketing purposes). Volumes that must withstand heavy use are often given a library binding in a heavier, more durable material such as buckram. The term is also used in publishers' catalos to distinguish the hardcover from the soft cover edition of a work. Synonymous with clothbound.

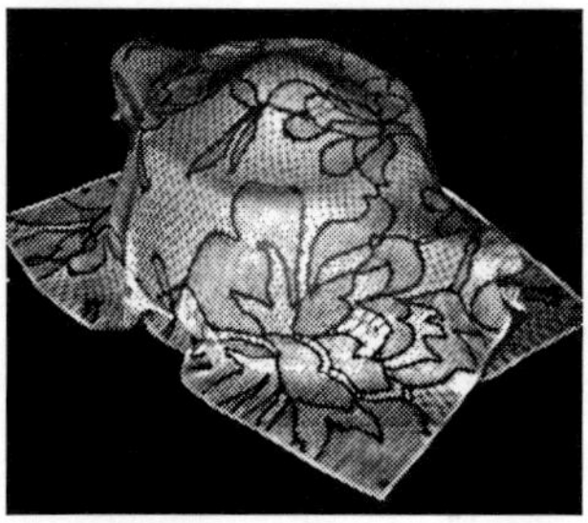

■ cloth book

a small, illustrated children's book printed entirely on sturdy woven fabric and given a flexible binding for toddlers who have not yet developed sufficient manual dexterity to turn paper pages without tearing them. To withstand drooling, the cloth pages may be treated with a moisture-resistant substance. In the 19th century, this type of toy book was called a rag book.

■ cloth joint

a strip of cloth used to reinforce the inside of the front and back joints in some library bindings and in very large, thick, or heavy books. In volumes of normal size and thickness, the unreinforced joints are usually formed on the inside by the fold in each endpaper.

■ club line

a single indented line at the beginning of a paragraph when it appears at the foot of a printed column or page of text, considered awkward by skilled typesetters and avoided whenever possible.

■ co-edition

an edition for which two or more publishers share responsibility, for example. The title page of a co-edition may bear the imprint of the originator, of one of the companies granted distribution rights, or of all the co-publishers.

■ coextensive entry

the principle in indexing that the subject heading or descriptor assigned to a work should encompass all the significant concepts covered in the item (and no more). Thus a book about painters and poets would require the heading 'Painters and poets,' rather than separate headings for 'Painters' and 'Poets.'

■ coextensive heading

a subject heading that indicates all or most of the subjects of a bibliographic item.

■ coffee table book

an expensive book on a popular subject, usually oversize and lavishly illustrated, with the text clearly subordinate to the illustrations. Designed primarily for display and casual browsing rather than cover-to-cover reading, coffee table books are often marketed on the decorative appeal of their colourful dust jackets. In trade bookstores, they may be sold at a deep discount, especially at Christmas to attract gift buyers. Public libraries may add them to the collection when received as gifts, provided demand exists for the subject and their condition is good. Academic library approval plans generally exclude them.

■ cognitive style

the manner in which an individual habitually organises a problem-solving or learning experience, especially whether the person prefers content that is already structured (lecture-style) or is more likely to impose his/her own structure on the material (hands-on approach). Differences in learning style have important implications for the delivery of reference services and bibliographic instruction and for the design of online tutorials and library Web pages.

■ cold boot

to restart a computer by turning the power off and turning it back on again, causing the files in its operating system to be re-executed. This procedure is sometimes helpful in getting a computer 'unstuck' when it locks up unexpectedly during processing and rebooting fails to get it going again, but the user should be aware that powering down will result in loss of unsaved data.

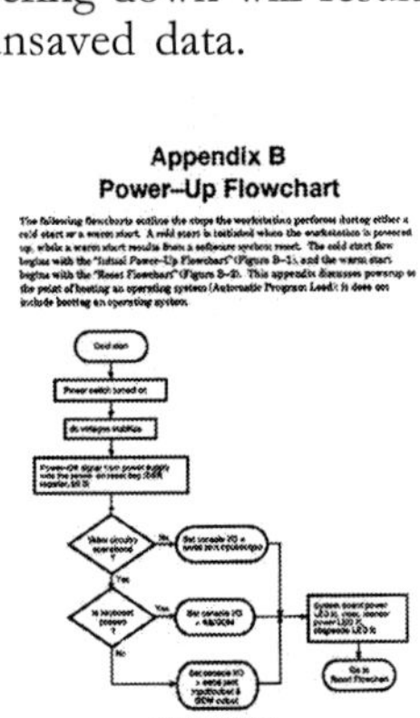

cold-crack

the tendency of the adhesive on the spine of a perfect-bound book to split at very low temperatures, reducing the text block to a pile of loose leaves. The inability of hot-melt adhesives to withstand cold temperatures makes them unsuitable for use in bindings markets in countries like Finland and Russia where winter temperatures can be severe. The problem is eliminated in adhesive binding which uses slower drying, cold-resistant polyvinyl acetate (PVA) adhesive.

collaborator

a person who works closely with one or more associates in producing a work to which all who participate make the same kind of contribution (shared responsibility) or different contributions (mixed responsibility), for example, essays written by different authors for publication in a collection, or illustrations for a children's book in which the text is written by a person other than the illustrator.

collate

to determine, usually by close examination of signatures, leaves, illustrations and other characteristics, if a copy of a book is complete and perfect, or to compare it with descriptions of ideal copies found in bibliographies for the same purpose. Also, to compare two printed works page-by-page and line-by-line, to establish whether they are identical copies or variants of the same text. Also, to check a book before binding to be sure that it is complete and that the sections are gathered in correct sequence, a task is made easier by collating marks printed along the back fold to make misplaced sections easier to spot. The marks are concealed after the lining has been applied to the binding edge. Also, to merge two or more ordered sets of documents, records, pages, or data into a single desired sequence. High-end photocopiers usually have collating capability.

collation

in library cataloguing, a synonym for the physical description area of a bibliographic record, which has fallen into disuse. In binding, a list of the signatures of a book, indicating the number of leaves in each. Also, the process of checking the physical make-up of a book for completeness before binding, particularly the presence of all illustrations, plates and maps not printed with the text. In analytical bibliography, the comparison of two texts of the same work to determine which is the first edition or the definitive text.
Also refers to the merger of two ordered sets of documents, records, pages, or data into a single desired sequence.

collected edition

an edition of the previously published works of an author, issued in a single volume or uniform set of volumes, usually under a collective title.

collectible

any class of things, usually old or rare but lacking intrinsic value, which people accumulate as a hobby or in the expectation that the value will rise (autographs, comic books, phonograph records, etc.). Also used as an adjective to describe something sought by collectors, for example, first editions and incunabula.

collecting archives

an independent organisation, or unit within a larger organisation or institution, responsible for building a collection of records and documents from a variety of sources, in keeping with the mission of the parent institution, for example, a manuscript repository in the library of a major university. Archives of this type may provide online access to a portion of their resources or be completely.

collection

in library cataloguing, three or more independent works or long excerpts from works by the same author, or two or more independent works or excerpts from works by different authors, not written for the same publication or occasion, published in a single volume or uniform set of volumes, for example, a book of essays written by one or more essayists. Selected for publication by an editor, the works are listed in order of appearance in the table of contents in the front matter. Synonymous with collected work. Compare with anthology and compilation. Also refers to a number of documents (books, reports, records, etc.), assembled in a single location by one or more persons, or by a corporate entity and arranged in some kind of systematic order to facilitate retrieval.

collection agency

a commercial enterprise that specialises in collecting past-due bills from people who owe them, usually by informing the person that their credit record will suffer unless prompt payment is received. Most public libraries enter into a contractual agreement with such an agency to handle the collection of unpaid bills for items lost, damaged, or long overdue. Academic institutions have the option of withholding grades or diploma from a student until library fines are paid.

collection assessment

the systematic evaluation of the quality of a library collection to determine the extent to which it meets the library's service goals and objectives and the information needs of its clientele. Deficiencies are addressed through collection development. Synonymous with collection evaluation.

collection development

the process of planning and building a useful and balanced collection of library materials over a period of years, based on an ongoing assessment of the information needs of the library's clientele, analysis of usage statistics and demographic projections, normally constrained by budgetary limitations. Collection development includes the formulation of selection criteria, planning for resource sharing and replacement of lost and damaged items, as well as routine selection and deselection decisions. Large libraries and library systems may use an approval plan or blanket order plan to develop their collections. In small and medium-sized libraries, collection development responsibilities are normally shared by all the librarians, based on their interests and subject specialisations, usually under the overall guidance of a written collection development policy.

■ **collection development policy**

a formal written statement of the principles guiding a library's selection of materials, including the criteria used in making selection and deselect ion decisions (fields covered, degrees of specialisation, levels of difficulty, languages, formats, balance, etc.) and policies concerning gifts and exchanges. An unambiguously worded collection development policy can be very helpful in responding to challenges from pressure groups.

■ **collection level cataloguing**

the encoding level used to control separately published documents (maps, pamphlets, ephemera, etc.) which are unrelated bibliographically and do not warrant the expense of full level or even minimal level cataloguing, but have research value and can be catalogued as a single item under a collective title because they share at least one unifying characteristic (author, issuing body, language, subject, genre, etc.). Synonymous with collective cataloguing.

■ **columnist**

a journalist who writes regular commentary on current issues for publication in a magazine or newspaper, or in more than one newspaper, usually from a political position left or right of center, or expressing an original point of view on a matter of interest to readers. National political columnists are often syndicated. Also refers to a specialist in a particular field or on a given subject who writes regular commentary for a magazine or trade journal.

■ **comb binding**

a form of mechanical binding in which a row of interconnected curved plastic teeth is inserted into slots punched along the binding edge of the leaves of a publication to hold them together, used for binding calendars, lab manuals, instruction manuals and workbooks which must open flat to be used conveniently. If the plastic spine is wide enough, the title may be printed on it.

■ **comedy**

a dramatic work in which an amusing event, or series of events with a happy ending, is presented for the enjoyment of the audience or reader. Comic effect is usually achieved by emphasising incongruity of character in dialogue and/or action. When such an effect is achieved with subtle insight, the result is 'high' comedy, as distinct from 'low' comedy which appeals to cruder perceptions. The earliest surviving examples of classical comedy are the eleven plays of Aristophanes, thought to have been written and performed in Athens in the 5th century B.C.

■ comic book

a booklet, usually printed in colour on paper made from wood pulp, containing one or more stories told pictorially in a continuous strip of cartoon panels, with any dialogue or monologue enclosed in balloons or given in captions. An extended form of the comic strip seen in daily newspapers, comic books are often published in series classified by genre (adventure, fantasy, romance, science fiction, etc.). They are acquired by libraries for special collections on popular culture and are of considerable interest to private collectors.

■ command-driven

a computer interface in which the user must type a command statement or query to achieve the desired result, usually faster than a menu-driven interface, but not as user-friendly for novices who must invest time and effort in learning the system's command language.

■ commentary

a critical or explanatory note or collection of notes on a sacred or literary work, accompanying the text or issued separately, usually written by a person (or persons) other than the author. Commentaries are usually devoted to major works that have been the subject of considerable interpretation (Bhagavad-Gita, Bible, Koran, etc.). Also refers to an historical narrative written largely from personal experience (Seven Commentaries on the Gallic War by Julius Caesar). Synonymous in this sense with memoirs. In a more general sense, a series of remarks or observations, made by someone with authority to speak and be heard on the subject, for example, a journalist writing a column on a political or social issue.

■ commercial journal

a scholarly journal or trade journal published by a for-profit company, as opposed to a journal published by a university press or nonprofit organisation, such as a scholarly society or professional association. Relentless price increases have become an important issue for libraries that subscribe to commercially published journals.

■ commercial publisher

a publisher in the business of producing and selling books and/or other publications for profit, as opposed to a university press or the publishing arm of a scholarly society, professional association, or other nonprofit organisation that operates on a cost-recovery basis. The term includes trade publishers and popular presses. In commercial publishing, the decision to publish is influenced by sales potential, sometimes at the expense of originality and quality.

■ commercial television

television broadcast stations for which profit is the prime concern. In the selection of programming, commercial stations rely heavily on ratings because their advertisers are motivated by the desire to reach the widest possible viewing audience.

■ Common Carrier (CC)

a telecommunication service, such as a telephone or cable company, that provides wire and/or microwave services to businesses and the general public, usually at rates regulated by federal, state, or local government.

■ Common Gateway Interface (CGI)

a program interface installed on a Web server, that allows Web pages to be linked to databases and other programs in such a way that input can be entered via the Web page and sent to a database management system for searching. Results are sent back by the DBMS and presented to the user in HTML format.

■ commonplace book

a book with blank pages in which passages in prose or verse are recorded irregularly by its owner as ideas for future exploration or contemplation, sometimes arranged by subject. The writer may note only his own thoughts and ideas, or excerpt those of other writers or speakers. Commonplace books kept by persons of stature, such as Ralph Waldo Emerson and Thomas Jefferson, have been deemed worthy of publication. Although interest in this form of literary expression has waned, it is still used by poets (example: A Certain World by W. H. Auden).

■ communications

the transfer of information from one physical location to another by electronic means. The term telecommunication refers to both analogue and digital communications, including the transmission of voice and video. Data communications refers to digital communications only, occurring via modem over a telephone line, by direct cable to another PC equipped with file transfer software, from a remote terminal connected to a minicomputer or mainframe, from one node to another on a local area network (LAN), or between client and server in a network environment. A communications device is a piece of hardware, such as a modem, cable, or port, designed to facilitate data transmission.

Compact Disc (CD)

a digital audio recording medium introduced in 1982, capable of storing up to 74 minutes of high-fidelity stereophonic sound in a single spiral track on one side of a 4.75-inch disc, similar to the track on a phonograph record. Designed to be read by a laser beam and decoded inside a device called a CD player, compact discs not only provide clearer sound than phonograph records and audiotape, but are capable of recording a much wider range of volume. In libraries, CDs are usually shelved separately, often in specially designed display cases. Some libraries provide listening equipment on the premises.

compact edition

an edition in which the physical size of a long work is reduced, usually by altering the format without changing the content, for example, The Compact Oxford English Dictionary (second edition) reproduced micro graphically and issued in a slipcase with a microprint reader.

comprehensive

all-inclusive or all-encompassing. An index, bibliographic database, or other work of reference, compiled with the stated goal of covering all possible aspects of a subject, or all the published literature on a subject or in a field or discipline. In bibliography, an attempt to list of all the works that meet the criteria for inclusion established by the bibliographer as to author, subject, publication type, currency, etc. The opposite of selective.

compression

a method (e.g. sipping) for reducing the size of files to save space or transmission time; compressed files must be uncompressed before use.

compulsory arbitration

the process in which representatives organised labour and management, having reached an impasse in contract negotiations, submit their differences to a legally designated arbitrator or arbitration board authorised to hear arguments from both sides on unresolved issues and reach a final binding decision. Both sides are required to accept the outcome.

compulsory retirement

mandatory retirement at a fixed age, usually established by the employer and stipulated in its personnel policy. Compulsory retirement is a controversial legal issue in the United States. Organisations that have no mandatory retirement age may offer periodic retirement incentives to long-time employees, aimed at reducing payroll costs.

computer file

data or programs encoded in machine-readable format for processing by a computer. Data files stored on a computer are usually organised by topic or other characteristic in directories and subdirectories. Synonymous with machine-readable data file.

■ **computer literacy**

the skills required to retrieve information efficiently and communicate effectively using computer hardware and software, based on a conceptual understanding of computer technology and how it can be used to accomplish specific tasks, including an awareness of its inherent limitations, as well as its advantages. Because most hardware and software are progressively upgraded, an ongoing effort is required of the user to remain computer literate.

■ **Computer Output Microform (COM)**

computer output produced directly on microfiche or microfilm without ever having been printed on paper. A device called a COM recorder converts digital data into a form that can be read by the human eye before recording it on film.

■ **computer output microform catalogue**

a library catalogue produced directly on microfiche or microfilm from a file of machine-readable bibliographic records, using a special recording device called a COM recorder. Comcatalogues are more compact than card catalogues, but a microform reader-printer machine is required to display and print individual catalogue records. Prior to the development of online catalogues, this format was preferred for state, regional and consortial union catalogues.

■ **computer program**

a set of instructions written in a programming language to enable a computer to process data, perform operations and solve logical problems. Synonymous with software.

■ **Comstock, Anthony (1844-1915)**

an American reformer with a high school education who in 1873, after serving in the Union army during the Civil War, founded the New York Society for the Suppression of Vice and devoted the rest of his life to waging an aggressive crusade against pornography, abortion, gambling, swindling, medical quackery and other activities he considered morally offensive. Comstock used his influence to persuade Congress to pass what became known as the 'Comstock laws' empowering the U.S. Postal Service to exclude from the mail books and other publications which he considered indecent or obscene, including information about contraception. After Comstock publicly attacked the first American production of George Bernard Shaw's play Mrs. Warren's Profession, the British playwright dubbed his rigid views and repressive methods 'comstockery,' turning his name into a public symbol of censorship based on prudery.

■ **concatenate**

from the Latin con ('together') and catenare ('to chain'). To join two or more data fields within a record to create a single field. In a more general sense, to link items together in a series, for example, several related essays or long excerpts for publication in a collection.

■ concertina

a form of bookbinding in which the spine is continuous with the front and back covers, but folded in narrow accordion-style pleats to which the leaves or folios are attached along the peaks or valleys of the folds. Compare with zig-zag book. Also refers to a method of folding paper in which each successive fold is parallel with, but in the opposite direction to, the preceding one. Synonymous with accordion fold, fan fold and s-fold.

■ concise edition

an edition in which the content of a longer work is stated in the fewest possible words, sometimes aimed at beginners in the field. In the concise edition of a dictionary, infrequently used words and phrases in the full edition are omitted and long definitions may be shortened. In a concise encyclopaedia, the text is shortened and less important entries may be dropped entirely. The adjective 'concise' is sometimes used in the titles of works not based on a longer work, to indicate that the content is expressed succinctly.

■ concordance

an alphabetically arranged index of the principal words or selected words in a text, or in the works of an author, giving the precise location of each word in the text, with a brief indication of its context. A glossarial concordance includes a brief definition of each term. Concordances are usually devoted to very well-known works, such as the Bible, or to the works of a major writer (Chaucer, Shakespeare, etc.).

■ condensed

a typeface narrower in proportion to its height than the normal version of the same style, used in printing to fit more text than normal in a column or on a page. The opposite of expanded.

■ condensed book

a single volume, usually published in inexpensive hardcover edition, containing abridgments or long extracts from several separately published works, usually of fiction.

■ condensed score

the score of a musical work composed for orchestra or band in which the principal parts, usually given by type of instrument (woodwind, brass, strings, percussion), are reduced to a minimum number of staves.

■ condition

the physical state of existence of a book or other document at a particular point in time, designated in the antiquarian and used book trade by a two-part code in which the first part indicates the condition of the book itself and the second part, the condition of its dust jacket. A hyphen or dash following the slash indicates that the dust jacket is missing.

conference

a formal meeting of a group of individuals, or representatives of several bodies, to provide the opportunity for discussion or consultation on topics of mutual interest. When published collectively, the papers presented at such a meeting are called proceedings. Abbreviated conf. Compare with workshop.
Also refers to a formal meeting

of the representatives constituting the legislative or governing authority of a corporate body, usually for the purpose of discussing and acting on issues of importance to the organisation.

conference name

the official name of a meeting, conference, workshop, symposium, exhibition, exposition, festival, athletic contest, scientific expedition, etc., used as the corporate name heading in cataloguing any publications issued in its name. Form of heading is subject to authority control.

conference

in library terms, a gathering in which scholars report their recent research findings to peers in the same field. Papers presented at a conference are often published in volumes known as 'conference proceedings,' which are therefore important sources for current information. The work presented may or may not later be revised and published in a refereed journal.

confidentiality

in the delivery of library services, the right of patrons to have the nature of their research and library transactions remain private. Librarians and library staff members are encouraged to 'protect each library user's right to privacy and confidentiality with respect to information sought or received and resources consulted, borrowed, acquired or transmitted.' For this reason, automated circulation systems are designed to delete from the patron record all indication that a specific item has been borrowed once it has been returned to the library and to limit access to borrower accounts to authorised personnel.

configuration

the physical arrangement and functional relationships of the various components of a computer system, usually established to meet the needs and preferences of its users. The term configurability has been coined to refer to the ease with which a computer system can be modified or customised to meet changing needs and requirements.

■ conjoint leaves

two leaves formed by one piece of parchment, vellum, or paper, usually folded lengthwise down the center. In a book, they may be bound into a section in such a way that they are not adjacent in the resulting sequence of leaves, but when traced through the back of the volume are found to be of a single piece, for example, in a 16-page signature, pages 3-4 (leaf 2) would be the conjugate of pages 13-14 (leaf 7) and vice versa.

■ connect time

the length of time a user is logged on to a remote computer network or system. Some Internet service providers began by charging subscribers on the basis of connect time, but most ISPs now provide unlimited access for a fixed monthly fee. Connect time is still used by some database vendors as the basis for billing.

■ conservation

the use of physical or chemical methods to ensure the survival of manuscripts, books and other documents, for example, the storage of materials under controlled environmental conditions or the treatment of mildew-infected paper with a chemical inhibitor. Non-invasive techniques are preferred as a means of preserving items in their original condition. In a more general sense, any measures taken to protect archival or library collections from damage or deterioration, including initial examination, documentation, treatment and preventive care supported by research. A person educated, trained and experienced in such procedures is a conservator.

■ conservation binding

1. binding or rebinding intended to ensure the long-term survival of a manuscript or book while maintaining the integrity of its original form, as opposed to binding or rebinding for appearance or durability regardless of the implications for conservation.
2. an organisation that specialises in the protection and rehabilitation of printed and photographic materials, especially damaged or deteriorating items. Conservation centres support the enhancement of preservation programs in libraries, archives, museums and other historical and cultural organisations. Some conservation centres also provide disaster assistance.

■ consistency

in indexing, the degree of similarity between the subject headings or descriptors assigned to the same item or document by different indexers, or at different times by the same indexer.

■ consolidated shipment

in the book trade, a batch of materials sent by a publisher, jobber, or other vendor to a library or bookseller which includes both recently ordered titles and items on back order, combined to reduce shipping costs.

■ **consolidation**

the merger of two or more separately administered libraries, or organisational units within a library, into one unit under a single administration, usually for reasons of efficiency and/or economy, or to improve quality of service.

■ **consortium**

an association of independent libraries and/or library systems established by formal agreement, usually for the purpose of resource sharing. Membership may be restricted to a specific geographic region, type of library (public, academic, special), or subject specialisation. Plural: consortia.

■ **conspectus**

a survey of a topic or body of literature that takes a general or comprehensive view of the subject. Also, a summary or digest that retains the basic pattern or structure of a larger work, but condenses the content considerably.

■ **constituency**

the persons represented by a library or library system when it seeks funding for daily operations, new programs and capital improvements and when it lobbies for legislation favourable to its interests. Successful library administration depends on winning the approval of the library's external constituency (voters, users, supporters, etc.) through quality of service, public relations and community outreach programs. A library also has an internal constituency consisting of its employees and management.

■ **consultant**

a person with knowledge and experience in a specialised field, hired by a library or other institution to analyse a problem and provide professional or technical advice concerning possible solutions, especially when the required level of expertise is not available within the organisation or the opinion of an outsider is desirable. A consultant may also participate in the planning and implementation phase of a recommended change.

■ **consultation service**

in-depth reference assistance from a librarian, available by appointment.

■ **consumer guide**

a publication containing practical information and advice for prospective purchasers concerning the quality of products and services available in the market place. Some consumer guides are published serially. High-demand consumer guides may be shelved in the reference section of a library, sometimes in ready reference.

Used synonymously with buying guide.

■ container

a box or holder used for storing a bibliographic item, group of items, or part of an item. Physically separable from its contents, a container can be open or lidded.

■ contemporary

in the antiquarian and used book trade, a work published within the most recent decade. Also refers to a book in which all the parts (particularly the binding) were created at the time the edition was printed.

■ content

the essential matter or substance of a written work or discourse, as opposed to its form or style. In a more general sense, all the ideas, topics, facts, or statements contained in a book or other written work. Synonymous in this sense with subject matter. Also refers to the matter which is the subject of a course of study.

■ content analysis

close analysis of the explicit and implicit message of a work or body of communicated information through classification and evaluation of the important concepts, symbols and themes it addresses, to determine its meaning and account for the effect it has on its audience.

■ content designator

characters used as tags, indicators and subfield codes in a machine readable bibliographic record to identify or provide additional information about the data elements of which it is composed.

■ contents

all the divisions, chapters, articles, or individual works contained in a book, periodical, or other publication, usually listed with locators (page numbers) in order of appearance in the table of contents in the front matter of a book, or on a page near the front of an issue of a periodical. Also refers to all the items physically contained in a box, binder, case, or holder designed for loose materials, for example, a pamphlet file or portfolio.

■ contents note

a note in the bibliographic record for a book, listing its major divisions (books, chapters, etc.) or the works contained in it (essays, interviews, short stories, poems, plays, etc.), usually by title.

■ context

in the most general sense, the entire situation, background, or environment relevant to an event, action, statement, work, etc. In a literary sense, the parts of a sentence, paragraph, or text that occur just before and after a specific word, phrase, or passage and determine its precise meaning. Quoting out of context may give a misleading impression of the intentions of the original speaker or author. Context is included in certain types of keyword indexing.

■ context-sensitive

in computing, an interface designed to provide assistance to the user at the point when help is needed, as opposed to a program that provides a general help screen which the user must first locate and then navigate to find instructions or advice concerning a specific problem.

■ contingency fund

a special fund set aside in a library budget to cover unanticipated expenditures and emergencies. Contingency funds are commonly included in budgets for major capital improvements to allow for possible cost overruns.

■ contingency plan

an alternative plan of action prepared in advance to be put into effect should it become impossible to implement normal arrangements, or when certain predetermined conditions arise. An example might be the decision of a library to cut spending on monographs rather than cancel serials subscriptions in the event of an unexpected budget cut.

■ continuation

a book or other uncompleted work continued by another writer, usually after the death of the original author. Also, a work issued as a supplement to one previously published, or a part issued in continuance of a monographic set or series. Libraries normally place such materials on continuation order. In the catalogue record for such a publication, a library's holdings are indicated in an open entry for a publication that is ongoing, or in a closed entry for one that has ceased.

■ continuation order

an order placed by a library with an agent or publisher to automatically supply until further notice each succeeding issue, volume, or part of a serial or series as published. If a continuation order does not specify a maximum price, it is assumed that the item may be shipped regardless of price. Some publishers offer a discount on continuation orders (usually 5-10%).

■ continuing education

formal instruction for persons who have completed an academic degree, moved into the workplace and wish to keep up with changes and innovations in their field. For librarians, continuing education opportunities include courses offered online or traditionally through a library school, training provided by commercial vendors and workshops sponsored by bibliographic service centres and library associations, as well as independent study.

■ continuous pagination

numbering the pages of two or more volumes or parts of a set, or the issues of a periodical comprising a volume, in a single unbroken sequence, beginning with number one.

continuous revision

the process of updating a textbook or reference work by revising a portion of the text and/or illustrations with each printing, as opposed to updating the entire content of the work all at once and publishing the result as a revised edition.

contour map

a topographic map that indicates relief by continuous lines, traditionally shown in brown ink, connecting points of equal elevation, with or without shading. The number of feet represented by the intervals between contour lines varies with the scale of the map. A topographic map of the sea floor is called a bathymetric map.

contract

a legally binding written agreement between an employer and 1) an individual librarian or other member of the library staff, or 2) librarians and/or staff organised in a collective bargaining unit for the purpose of negotiating terms of employment (salaries and wages, duties and responsibilities, promotion and tenure, vacation and sick leave, benefits, etc.) usually for a specified period of time.

contraction

a shortened form of a word or phrase used for brevity in place of the whole, formed by the omission of one or more letters or sounds, usually replaced by a hyphen (e-mail for electronic mail) or an apostrophe (isn't for is not).

contraries

impurities in the rag, waste paper, or other fibrous material from which paper is made, usually bits of wool, feathers, or twine, or hard materials such as metal staples, bone, or plastic which must be removed in the papermaking process to maintain quality of product. Contraries occasionally show as blemishes in a sheet of finished paper.

contrast

the degree of difference between the high and low tonal values in a print, photograph, or image on motion picture film, video, or television, maximum contrast being black and white with no intermediate grey tones.

contributor

one of several persons, each of whom writes one or more signed or unsigned portions of a book, periodical, or other edited work. A contribution may consist of an article or column in a magazine or journal, an essay in a collection, a poem or story in an anthology, an entry in an encyclopaedia, or one or more terms and definitions in a dictionary or glossary. Contributors are usually listed by name in the front matter or back matter of a book, on one page of a periodical, or in the last volume of a reference set, alphabetically by name or in the order in which their work appears.

control key

a key located in the lower left-hand corner of a standard computer keyboard, usually labelled Ctrl or Ctl, which can be used simultaneously with one or more other keys to give a specific command, for example, Ctrl+Alt+Del to reboot the operating system.

controlled access

entry into a library, or use of a library collection, which is limited to registered members of the library's user group or some other category of user specifically granted access. The libraries of large private universities may extend access to all or part of their collections only to registered students, faculty and staff. Use of special collections may be limited to authorised library staff, except by appointment.

controlled vocabulary

an established list of preferred terms from which a cataloguer or indexer must select when assigning subject headings or descriptors in the bibliographic record, to indicate the content of a work in the library catalogue or in an index or bibliographic database. Synonyms are included as lead-in vocabulary, with instructions to see or USE the authorised heading. For example, if the authorised subject heading for works about dogs is 'Dogs' then all items about dogs will be assigned the heading 'Dogs,' including a work titled All About Canines. A cross-reference to the heading 'Dogs' will be made from the term 'Canines' to ensure that anyone looking for information about dogs under 'Canines' will be directed to the correct heading. Controlled vocabulary is usually listed alphabetically in a subject headings list or thesaurus of indexing terms. The process of creating and maintaining a list of preferred indexing terms is called vocabulary control. Synonymous with controlled terms.

convention discount

a discount given on orders placed at a publisher's exhibit booth during a conference or convention, usually 10-20%, with 15% the norm. Librarians sometimes compile lists of selected new books prior to attending a major library conference, to be prepared to take advantage of the anticipated discount. At the end of the conference, display copies may be sold at an even deeper discount, especially if the dust jackets are no longer in perfect condition. Synonymous with show discount.

convention issue

an issue of a trade journal devoted to a forthcoming conference or convention, providing a brief description of the program, information about exhibits, registration procedures, advice about travel and accommodations and whom to contact for more details. Follow-up articles usually appear in the issue immediately following the event.

■ conventional name

a name, distinct from the real or official name by which a thing, place, or corporate body has become known, for example, 'Wall Street' for the New York Stock Exchange.

■ cookbook

a type of how-to book that gives instructions for preparing food, including recipes for specific dishes, notes about tools and ingredients, weights and measures and sometimes directory information for culinary suppliers. Most cookbooks are specialised, focusing on a particular cuisine, type of dish, or category of food. Cookbooks for beginners often include colour illustrations, but those intended by the author to be comprehensive are usually sparsely illustrated. Most public libraries include a diverse selection of cookbooks in the non-fiction section. Synonymous with recipe book.

■ cookie

1. piece of information sent by a web server to a web browser that the browser software is expected to save and send back to the server whenever the browser makes additional requests from the server
2. a small string of data created by a Web server, transmitted to a computer connected to the Internet and stored in the cookie file of its Web browser. Originally intended to reduce the amount of time required for Web site registration by retrieving from the user's hard drive input provided in a previous visit, cookies can also be used to determine what a user viewed on previous visits and on visits to other Web sites. Potential invasiveness has made cookies the subject of debate over privacy. Web browser software can be set to allow the user to accept or reject a cookie at the time it is offered, or to reject all cookies automatically. 'Cookie manager' software provides a wider range of options.
3. a set of information (such as login, registration, shopping cart, or user preference information) sent by a Web Browser program to a Web Server. The Browser software saves the cookie information and sends it back to the Server along with any additional requests to the Server. The cookie enables the Server to customise information sent back to the user, keep a log of the user's requests, or gather other information about the user.

■ cooperative cataloguing

an arrangement in which a library or library system agrees to follow established cataloguing practices and work in automated systems or utilities that facilitate the creation of bibliographic and authority records in a form that can be shared with other libraries.

■ coordinate

one of a number of quantities used to indicate the position of a point, line, or plane with reference to a fixed system, such as a grid. On maps and charts of the surface of the earth and other heavenly bodies, the quantities are usually degrees, minutes and seconds of longitude and latitude, or angles of declination and ascension.

■ co-publishing

the simultaneous publication of an edition by two or more publishers, usually in different countries, to achieve economies of scale when the home market is not sufficient to guarantee a reasonable profit. Typically, a work is printed in the country of the originating publisher and then supplied to a publisher in another country with a title page bearing the imprint of the second publisher (or both). Subsequent printings may occur independently or cooperatively. In journal publishing, the result may be separate editions for each country or a bilingual edition marketed in both countries.

■ copy

to make a duplicate of a document or other work, by hand or any other process. Many early books were produced in only one copy. In medieval Europe, devotional works and the classics were laboriously hand-copied by monks and copyists known as scribes. Modern methods rely on printing and reprography. In data processing, to reproduce data from one file, location, or storage medium to another without alteration. Also refers to a single specimen of a manuscript or printed document. Libraries sometimes purchase heavily-used items in multiple copies. Copy number is indicated in the catalogue record and at the end of the call number, beginning with the second copy. In limited editions, the total number of copies printed and the number of each copy are recorded in the certificate of issue, usually on the verso of the leaf preceding the title page. In publishing, matter that is to be typeset in preparation for printing, or incorporated as text into a hypertext document.

■ copy card

a small plastic debit card available for purchase from a vending machine or at the circulation desk of a library, which can be used in photocopiers and microform reader-printer machines instead of cash to pay for paper copies of documents.

■ copy editor

a person employed by a publisher to meticulously edit and mark up an author's typescript in preparation for printing, usually in accordance with house style as to spelling, abbreviation, punctuation, grammar, syntax, usage, citation style, etc. A good copy editor also checks the accuracy of facts, quotations, citations and is alert to possibilities of libel, plagiarism, etc.

■ copy number

when multiple copies of the same edition are added to a library collection, the cataloguer numbers each copy sequentially, beginning with the second. In the catalogue record for the edition, each copy is listed separately in the holdings, with the copy number given at the end of the call number following the abbreviation cop. It is also printed at the end of the call number on the spine label attached to the outside of the physical item.

■ copyright

the exclusive legal rights granted by a government to an author, editor, compiler, composer, playwright, publisher, or distributor to publish, produce, sell, or distribute copies of a literary, musical, dramatic, artistic, or other work, within certain limitations (fair use). Copyright law also governs the right to prepare derivative works, reproduce a work or portions of it and display or perform a work in public. Such rights may be transferred or sold to others and do not necessarily pass with ownership of the work itself. Copyright protects a work in the specific form in which it is created, not the idea, theme, or concept expressed in the work, which other writers are free to interpret in a different way. A work never copyrighted or no longer protected by copyright is said to be in the public domain.

■ copyright date

the year in which a specific work was granted copyright protection, usually printed on the verso of the title page, sometimes following the letter 'c' with a circle around it. If more than one copyright date is given, the earliest is the date of the first edition, which is the same as the date of first publication. Subsequent dates indicate revisions in the text of an extent requiring renewal of copyright.

■ copyright fee

the payment required by a national copyright depository to register copyright of a creative work, which must be submitted with the completed application form and a deposit copy of the work.

■ copyright piracy

the systematic unauthorised reproduction or use without permission of a work protected under copyright law, usually for the purpose of profiting from such activity. This type of egregious infringement is subject to legal action by the copyright owner(s) in countries that have accepted international copyright agreements, but in countries which have not, the holder of intellectual property rights may have little recourse.

■ core collection

a collection representative of the basic information needs of a library's primary user group. In public libraries, core collections are selected in anticipation of popular demand and maintained on the basis of usage. In academic libraries, selection is based on curriculum need and collections are maintained to meet the research interests of students and faculty. Also refers to an initial collection developed for a new library, usually with the aid of standard lists and other selection aids.

■ core journal

a scholarly journal that reports original research of such significance to the academic community that the publication is considered indispensable to students, teachers and researchers in the discipline or subdiscipline. For this reason, it is included in the serials collections of academic libraries supporting curriculum and research in the field. In public libraries, a periodical so essential to meeting the information needs of a wide range of users that it is included in most general serials collections.

■ core level cataloguing

an encoding level developed for use in the Program for Cooperative Cataloguing (PCC), which allows the cataloguer to create bibliographic records containing fewer data elements than in full level cataloguing, but more than in minimal level cataloguing. Fields of fixed length are fully coded, but a list of exceptions applies to certain fields of variable length.

■ core list

a list of the best books, periodicals, etc., on a subject or in a discipline, usually compiled as a selection aid for librarians whose responsibilities include collection development. Although useful when first published, such lists become outdated within a few years.

■ corner

the juncture of two edges of the cover of a book. Corners can be rounded or square and are sometimes covered in contrasting material, such as leather or heavier cloth, for protection and decorative effect. To make library corners, the turn-in is folded; on Dutch corners, it is cut.

■ corner piece

in bookbinding of the late 16th and early 17th centuries, an ornamental design such as an arabesque, stamped on the corners of a book cover, usually with a matching centrepiece. Also refers to decorative metal corners attached to the binding of a book. In modern usage, a temporary guard made of metal or some other hard material, attached to the corners of a book to protect against damage in shipping. Also refers to an ornament or flourish printed or drawn by hand at the corner of a border around a portion of printed or handwritten text.

■ corpora

initial capital letters inserted by a lubricator in blank spaces left for that purpose by the copyist in a manuscript or by the printer in an early printed book.

■ corporate author

1. a corporate body such as an association, company, government agency, institution, or nonprofit organisation in whose name a publication is issued. In libraries, the official name or title of such a body is used as the corporate name in cataloguing publications issued in its name.
2. an organisation (e.g., a business, government agency, institution, etc.) considered to be the author of a work.

■ corporate body

a commercial enterprise, government agency, association, nonprofit organisation, institution, or group of individuals identified by a collective name, which has the capacity to act as a single entity, including territorial authorities and groups constituted as meetings, conferences, congresses, expeditions, exhibitions, etc., whether operating or defunct. In libraries, the official name or title of such a body is used as the corporate name in cataloguing publications issued in its name.

■ countermark

a smaller, secondary watermark on antique papers, usually located in the center or lower center of the half-sheet opposite the watermark, indicating the name of the papermaker and sometimes the date and place of hand manufacture.

■ countersunk

said of a depression stamped or impressed on the surface of a book cover to display a label, inlay, or decoration.

■ counting book

a picture book designed to teach preschool children to count (usually from one to ten or twelve) by providing illustrations in which the number of objects displayed on each page or double spread corresponds to the numeral printed with them.

■ country code

the last portion of an e-mail or Internet address outside the United States, consisting of two alphabetic characters indicating the country in which the host computer is located. Some Web search engines allow the user to specify country code in a query.

■ country study

a publication that provides factual information about a specific nation, including its history, geography, demography, society and culture(s), economy, government and politics, etc., with statistical information sometimes given in an appendix. Country studies often include at least one map and may be published in series.

■ courier

a person or service hired by a library to retrieve materials on request from an off-site storage facility, or to transport materials from one library to another within a library system or consortium, as opposed to relying on the postal service or a commercial delivery service.

They had a great sale on monitors today

■ course catalogue

a comprehensive list, usually published annually, of all the courses taught at a school, college, or university during a given academic year, usually arranged by department and course number, with brief descriptions of course content and a list of instructors and their credentials at the end. Institutions offering both undergraduate and graduate programs may publish separate catalogues.

■ course-integrated

bibliographic instruction designed to complement the content of a specific course of study, integral to completing the library research component embedded in the course.

■ course-related

bibliographic instruction designed to support the needs and objectives of a specific course of study, but not essential to the completeness of the course.

■ courseware

a computer application designed to assist teachers and librarians in creating Web-based courses and online tutorials. Courseware requires little knowledge of HTML and may include presentation management software, the ability to include graphics and audio/video files, online chat and threaded discussions, automarked quisses, course calendaringand grading.

■ court hand

the cursive style of writing used by scribes from about 1100 AD until the end of the 16th century in copying charters, legal records and other official documents, in contrast to the book hand used for copying literary and devotional works in manuscript form.

■ court library

a large private library housed in a monumental building, similar to the libraries known to have existed in ancient Rome, financed by a wealthy nobleman, aristocratic family, or high-ranking church dignitary of the Italian Renaissance, whose love of books manifested itself in collecting. An expression of the humanist revival of interest in classical culture, court libraries were open for use by outsiders at the discretion of the owner and some even functioned as lending libraries for educated readers.

■ courtesy book

a literary genre popular during the Renaissance, devoted to the detailed description of the code of personal conduct, training and view of life expected of a gentleman, soldier and courtier by the society in which he lived.

■ **cover**

the outer protective material attached to the bound leaves of a manuscript or printed publication, consisting in books of two panels (front and back), each attached to the inlay over the spine along a flexible joint. Books bound in paper, cloth, or leather over boards are said to be published in hardcover. The cover of a machine-bound book is called a case. Books bound in flexible paper covers are called paperbacks. Periodicals are almost always issued in soft cover.

■ **cover letter**

a letter of introduction, usually no longer than one page, sent with a resume or curriculum vitae when applying for employment. A good cover letter usually indicates that the applicant meets all the qualifications listed in the job posting and expresses an interest in being considered for the position. In a more general sense, a brief letter of explanation sent with a document.

■ **cover paper**

the heavier grades of paper used for the outer cover of pamphlets, trade catalo sand paperback books, manufactured in a range of colours and finishes.

■ **cover story**

the article in a magazine or trade journal that corresponds to the headline and illustration on the cover, usually longer and more extensively illustrated than other feature articles in the same issue. Some periodical indexes and bibliographic databases are designed to indicate whether an article is a cover story.

■ **cover title**

the title printed or impressed on the cover of a publication as issued by the publisher (in books usually on the spine), which may be a shortened form of the title proper.

■ **coverage**

the extent of a library collection (or section of a collection), or of a catalogue, index, abstracting service, database, bibliography, or other finding tool, usually indicated by the number and types of publications indexed and a publication date range. The range of subjects or fields indexed determines the scope of such a resource. Also refers to the amount of attention (time, space, number of commentators, etc.) given a specific topic in the media.

■ **coverage**

in indexes, the range of years and number and type of publications included.

■ **covers bound in**

a term used in the book trade to describe a volume in which the original covers are enclosed in a later binding. This usually occurs in rebinding when the bindery decides to retain the original covers as endpapers or flyleaves.

creasing

in binding, the process of impressing a dull rule or disk on a sheet or leaf of paper to create an indentation along the line where a fold is to be made. By compressing the fibres, creasing produces a cleaner fold and increases the number of times the sheet can flex before it detaches at the fold.

creator

in archives, the individual or agency responsible for creating, receiving, accumulating, or otherwise producing records or documents for which some form of disposition must be made once their archival value has been appraised. Also refers to the person responsible for producing an original work of visual art.

credential

a letter, certificate, degree, or other document certifying that a person, organisation, or institution is qualified to fill a specific position, offer a service, or exercise authority in a given field.

credensa

originally, a sideboard from which a lord's food was tested for poison ('credence'). In libraries, a furnishing that doubles as a bookshelf and study table, having two or three tiers of shelves under a flat surface low enough to accommodate a person standing or seated on a high stool or chair.

credit

any textual statement at the beginning or end of a motion picture, video recording, or television program, identifying by name the director, producer, screenwriter, performers, narrator and other persons responsible for creating the work, usually with musical accompaniment. In filmmaking, considerable artistic attention is devoted to the style in which credits are presented, to set the tone for what is to follow (or add a final touch).

Also refers to an amount printed on a vendor's monthly statement, or on a separate credit memo, usually following a minus sign, indicating that it has been deducted from the total amount owed, for items returned or prepaid but not shipped.

credit line

a brief statement giving the name of the author, artist, agency, or publication that is the source of a picture, photograph, or quotation used in an article or book, usually printed immediately below the illustration or quotation, or at the end of the caption. Credit lines are sometimes printed together in a separate section in the front matter or back matter of a book, or in a paragraph on a separate page in a periodical.

crime in the library

because many libraries in the United States and other countries are open to the public, they are not immune to the disruption caused by unlawful behaviour, including theft of materials and equipment, verbal abuse and assault on patrons and staff, indecent exposure, drug use and sale by patrons and staff, mutilation of materials, vandalism of equipment and facilities, arson and more recently, computer crimes. Statistics indicate that crime is increasing in libraries, placing an additional burden on library budgets to provide adequate security.

■ cum privilegio

a Latin phrase meaning 'with permission,' printed in old books to notify readers that the work was published with the approval of existing secular or ecclesiastical authorities. The Roman Catholic Church still requires imprimatur and nihil obstat in books representing its official teachings. Synonymous with cum licentia.

■ cumdach

an Irish word for a rectangular box made of bronze, brass, or wood, usually ornamented in elaborate style with gold, silver and precious stones, used to store and protect medieval manuscript books. Synonymous with book shrine.

■ cumulative index

1. an index designed to save the user's time by combining in a single sequence the entries listed in two or more previously published indexes, for example, the ten-year indexes to Current Biography Yearbook. Most printed periodical indexes are issued in monthly or quarterly paperback supplements, cumulated at the end of the publication year in one or more annual volumes. In a more general sense, any index that combines in a single sequence entries for previously published volumes of a book or periodical.

2. a compilation (usually annually) of previously published indexes. The cumulation includes all the information in the prior, individual indexes, which can then be discarded.

■ cuneiform

from the Latin cuneus (wedge) and forma (shape or form), referring to the pictographic characters used in ancient Akkadian, Assyrian, Babylonian, Persian and Sumerian inscriptions from about 4,000 to 100 BC, each of which consisted of an arrangement of wedge-shaped marks incised in a wet clay tablet using a sharp, pointed implement called a stylus. If a text was long enough to be continued on more than one tablet, each tablet was numbered and incised with a catchword at its foot to link it to the next. The last tablet usually ended with a colophon.

■ curator

a person responsible for the development, care, organisation and supervision of a museum, gallery, or other exhibit space and all the objects stored or displayed in it. Also, a person in charge of a special collection, trained to assist users in locating and interpreting its holdings.

■ curiosa

books or pamphlets that are highly unusual in subject or treatment, usually somewhat indecent by conventional standards.

■ **currency**

the quality of being in progress, recent, or up-to-date. In information retrieval, the extent to which the content of a document or source reflects the existing state of knowledge about the subject. In the research process , the importance of currency varies, depending on the discipline. In medicine and the sciences, information can become outdated in less than five years, but in the arts and humanities, materials decades old may be just as useful as more recent information. Because periodicals are issued at regular intervals, they provide more current information than books, which must be updated in supplements and revised editions. Some online catalogues and bibliographic databases allow the user to limit search results by publication date to retrieve only recently published materials. The opposite of noncurrent and outdated. In archives, newly acquired records usually remain current for a designated period of time, after which their status is changed to semicurrent and they are moved to a temporary holding area to await final disposition.

■ **current awareness publications**

an index which provides information (usually the tables-of-contents) on the very latest issues of periodicals. Since it may take several months after publication for citations and abstracts to appear in standard indexes, these provide the most timely information available on a topic.

■ **current awareness service**

a service or publication designed to alert scholars, researchers, readers, customers, or employees to recently published literature in their field(s) of specialisation, usually available in special libraries serving companies, organisation sand institutions in which access to current information is essential. Such services can be tailored to fit the interest profile of a specific individual or group. Some online catalogues and bibliographic databases include a 'preferred searches' option that allows the library user to archive search statements and re-execute them as needed.

■ **current bibliography**

a bibliography that includes only references to recently published sources on a subject, or in a specific field or discipline. The opposite of retrospective bibliography.

■ **current contents**

a periodical that reproduces the tables of contents of the leading scholarly journals in an academic field or discipline, to assist researchers in keeping abreast of the most recently published literature in their areas of interest or specialisation, usually published weekly or monthly. Because currency is the raison d'etre of this type of publication, libraries may limit back files to the most recent 3-5 years.

■ **current issue**

the latest number of a serial publication, bearing the most recent issue date. In some libraries, current issues are displayed with the front cover facing forward on sloping shelves or on a periodical stand to facilitate browsing. Back files are typically stored in a different location, sometimes on microfilm or microfiche to conserve space. Synonymous with current number.

■ **current periodical**

the most recent issues of journals and magazines, not yet bound between hard covers; since current periodicals are in high demand, they are non-circulating.

■ **curriculum**

all the required and elective subjects/courses taught at a school or institution of higher learning, usually listed by department and course number in an annual course catalogue. Courses required of all students for graduation constitute the core curriculum.

■ **curriculum guide**

a written plan covering one or more facets of curriculum and instruction (goals and objectives, teaching strategies, learning activities, specific resources, evaluation and assessment techniques) for use within an instructional unit as small as a classroom or as large as a school district or state.

■ **curriculum room**

a room or designated area within an academic library containing curriculum-related materials such as kits, textbooks, workbooks, educational software and juvenile fiction and nonfiction, for the use of students enrolled in teacher education courses. Synonymous with curriculum lab.

■ **Curriculum Vitae (C.V.)**

a brief summary of a person's professional career, including basic biographical information, degrees and post-graduate education, honours and awards, employment history, publications and presentations, memberships, service, etc., for use in employment (hiring, tenure, promotion, etc.).

■ **cursive**

a right-sloping style of handwriting also known as running script, in which the letters within words are connected, having been written continuously without lifting pen or pencil from paper or other writing surface. Used in humanist manuscripts and papal documents of the Renaissance and for writing letters. In printing and word processing, any typeface that has the appearance of handwriting.

■ cursor

1. a small illuminated point, vertical bar, underline, or other symbol on a computer screen which can be positioned by the user via a keyboard, mouse, or other control device to indicate where a new character will appear when typed as input, or a new operation is to occur when initiated by the user. In Windows and other graphical user interfaces, the cursor may change shape when moved from one window or dialog box to another, turning into an I-beam for text-editing, an arrow or finger for selecting an option from a menu or toolbar, an hour-glass while an operation is in progress, or a small pen in graphics programs. In many applications, the symbol blinks steadily to make it easier to locate on the screen. Synonymous with pointer.

2. on the display screen of a computer, the small lighted rectangle, arrow, or other symbol which indicates where the next character will appear.

■ custodian

the person responsible for the care and protection of something of value. Over the past one hundred years, the model of librarianship has evolved from custodianship of materials in physical form, to one in which the librarian is seen as a mediator of access to information in a wide range of formats, including electronic resources. However, custodianship remains a high priority in archival and special collections.

■ custody

in archives, the official guardianship of books, manuscripts, papers, records and other documents, based on physical possession, with or without legal title or the right to control access or disposition. The person responsible for such care is their custodian.

■ custom binding

a book bound to the specifications of its owner or a dealer, or in accordance with special instructions from the publisher, rather than the general instructions for the edition.

■ cut

an illustration printed (captioned or uncaptioned) with the text page, as opposed to a plate printed on a separate leaf, usually of different quality paper, to be added to the publication in binding.

■ daily

issued on a daily basis, with the possible exception of Sundays. Also refers to a serial issued daily, especially a newspaper.

■ damaged

an item returned to the library in such poor condition that it cannot be placed back on the shelf for circulation, for example, a water-soaked or pet-chewed book. The borrower is normally charged the cost of repair or replacement. New items received from the shipper in damaged condition are returned by the library to the seller for credit or replacement.

■ dandy roll

the cylinder that exerts pressure in mechanised papermaking, smoothing the surface and creating designs such as the watermark, countermark and the lines characteristic of laid and wove paper.

■ dash

a short length of horizontal rule used for punctuation, to separate text and for decorative effect. In printing, dashes vary in length from the two-em (longest) to the hyphen (shortest). In typing, a dash is made by striking the hyphen key twice in succession (—). In descriptive cataloguing, the dash is given a space on either side, but when used in subject headings to indicate subdivision, no spaces are included.

■ data

the plural of the Latin word datum meaning 'what is given,' often used as a singular collective noun. Facts, figures, or instructions presented in a form that can be comprehended, interpreted and communicated by a human being, or processed by a computer.

■ data bank

1. sometimes used synonymously with database, the term applies more specifically to a collection of nonbibliographic data, usually numeric. Large data banks containing information about individuals (social security numbers, credit history, health records, etc.) have become the subject of controversy as the rapid development of high-speed information technology poses new threats to personal privacy. 2. the actual, substantive, factual information which goes into a database.

■ data compression

a method of reducing the amount of memory required to store data on a computer by encoding it and minimising redundancy. Compressed data requires less transmission time, but more computation time to restore it to its original form for processing.

■ data conversion

the process of translating data from one form to another, usually from human-readable to machine-readable format or vice versa, from one file type to another, or from one recording medium to another (example: film to videotape or videodisc).

■ data processing

the systematic performance of a single operation or sequence of operations by one or more central processing units on data converted to machine-readable format, to achieve the result for which the computer program that controls the processing was written, for example, the compilation of circulation statistics from records of circulation transactions occurring in a library over a given period of time.

■ database

1. a large, regularly updated file of digitised information (bibliographic

references, abstracts, full-text documents, directory entries, images, statistics, etc.) related to a specific subject or field, consisting of records of uniform format organised for ease and speed of search and retrieval and managed with the aid of database management system software. Content is created by the database producer which usually publishes a print version and leases the content to a database vendor that provides electronic access to the data after it has been converted to machine-readable form, usually on CD-ROM or online via the Internet using proprietary search software. Most databases used in libraries are catalogues, periodical indexes, abstracting services and full-text reference resources leased annually under licensing agreements that limit access to registered borrowers and library staff. Abbreviated db.
2. a standardised collection of information in computerised format, searchable by various parameters; in libraries often refers to electronic catalogues and indexes.

■ Database Management System (DBMS)

a computer application designed to control the storage, retrieval, security, integrity and reporting of data in the form of uniform records organised in a large searchable file called a database. The range of available DBMS software extends from simple systems intended for personal computers to highly complex systems designed to run on mainframes.

■ date due slip

a card or slip of paper inserted in an item charged from a library collection, or a small printed form attached to the inside of the front or back cover (or to one of the endpapers), on which is stamped the date the item is due back in the library. Date due slips are sometimes removed by borrowers in an attempt to avoid overdue fines, but automated circulation systems have put an end to this strategy.

■ date line

the line printed at the beginning of a story in a newspaper or article published in a magazine, indicating the date and place of origin of news that is not local.

■ date range

an interval of time marked by a beginning and ending date. Some online catalogues and bibliographic databases allow the user to limit a search to a specific range of publication dates. A year followed by a hyphen (1946-) limits retrieval to information published in the year specified or any succeeding year, a year preceded by a hyphen (-1945) limits retrieval to sources published up to and including the year specified and a year followed by a hyphen and a subsequent year (1939-1945) limits retrieval to sources published in those or any intervening years.

■ deaccession

the process of deleting from an accession record documents and other materials which are to be removed from a library collection. Also refers to any item so removed. The opposite of accession. In archives, the process of removing records or documents from official custody, undertaken after careful consideration, usually as the result of a decision to transfer the material to another custodian, or because the legal owner desires its return or the material is found upon reappraisal to be of doubtful authenticity or to be inappropriate for the collection.

■ **deacidification**

a general term for a variety of costly preservation processes that chemically reduce the acid content of paper documents to a pH of 7.0 (neutral) or higher, usually undertaken at a professional conservation center to prevent further deterioration. An alkaline buffer may be deposited in deacidification to neutralise any acids that develop in the future. Brittleness is not reversed by deacidification. Mass deacidification is the shipment of a quantity of documents to a center for processing in small batches, rather than individually.

■ **dealer**

an individual or commercial company in the business of buying and selling new books, used bookstand/or rare books for resale to libraries, collectors and other booksellers.

■ **decennial**

issued every ten years. Also refers to a serial publication issued every ten years.

■ **deckle edge**

the uneven or feathered edge of a sheet of handmade paper, created by the flow of liquified fibrous stock between the frame (deckle) and sieve of the mould used in manufacture. The same effect is achieved in machine-made paper by exposing the edge to a jet of air or water. In quality bookbinding, deckle edges are considered tasteful, but since books tend to collect dust when stored on an open shelf and rough edges are difficult to clean, this feature is not practical.

■ **declassified**

a document no longer protected against unauthorised disclosure because the security classification assigned to maintain confidentiality has been officially changed or cancelled. The opposite of classified.

■ **dedicated**

in computing and communications, a device or channel reserved for a specific use. In libraries, dedicated servers are used to run the online catalogue and provide access to the library's Web site.

■ dedicated line

a direct pathway to the Internet or some other computer network via a separate telecommunications channel not shared with multiple users as in dial-up access, but available around the clock to a specific user or group of users, for a designated purpose. When accessed through a common carrier, the channel is called a leased line.

■ dedication

a brief note in which the creator of a work addresses it to one or more persons, usually a colleague, mentor, or family member, as a sign of honour, appreciation, or affection. In books, the author's dedication appears in the front matter, usually printed on the recto of the leaf following the title page.

■ dialog box

in a graphical user interface, a box that opens for the user to supply additional information before the program continues.

■ dialog

a supplier of computer databases for online bibliographic searching.

■ dialogue

conversation, real or imagined, between two or more persons, especially the exchange of ideas and opinions between individuals who do not share the same point of view. Also refers to a written work in the form of a conversation between two or more people, or to the portions of a work of fiction (novel, short story, play, etc.) consisting of words spoken by the characters, as opposed to passages of narrative or description. In the text of a narrative work, dialogue is set apart by the use of quotation marks.

■ dial-up access

connection to a network, online service, or computer system from a terminal or workstation via a telephone line, usually in exchange for payment of a monthly fee to a service provider, as opposed to access via a dedicated line. Dial-up access requires a modem to convert the digital signals produced by a computer into the analogue signals used in voice transmission and vice versa.

■ diary

a private written record of day-to-day thoughts, feelings and experiences, kept by a person who does not expect them to be published. Also refers to the blankbook or notebook in which such experiences are recorded. Diaries are sometimes published posthumously and some have become famous literary and historical works, for example, the Diary of Samuel Pepys and more recently that of Anne Frank. Also refers to a small notebook in which the consecutive dates of the year are listed, with blank space for scheduling appointments, meetings, important deadlines, etc.

■ dictionary

a single-volume or multi-volume reference work containing brief explanatory entries for terms and topics related to a specific subject or field of inquiry, usually arranged alphabetically (example: Dictionary of Neuropsychology). The entries in a dictionary are usually shorter than those contained in an encyclopaedia on the same subject, but it is not uncommon for the word 'dictionary' to be used in the title of works that should more appropriately be called encyclopaedias (example: Dictionary of the Middle Ages). Also refers to a work listing the words of a language in alphabetical order, with orthography, syllabication, pronunciation, etymology and definition(s). Some dictionaries also include synonyms, antonyms and brief biographical and gazetteer information. An unabridged dictionary is comprehensive in the number of words and definitions included. An abridged dictionary provides a more limited selection of terms and less information in each entry. In a visual dictionary, the terms are illustrated. Dictionaries are known to have developed from Latin glossaries as early as the 13th century. Dictionaries of the English language, limited to difficult words, were first compiled in the 17th century. The most famous is the Oxford English Dictionary (1989), conceived in Britain in 1857 by the Philological Society. Some English dictionaries are limited to a specialised vocabulary (example: Dictionary of American Slang). In libraries, at least one large printed dictionary is usually displayed open on a dictionary stand. Smaller portable editions are shelved in the reference section.

■ dictionary catalogue

1. a type of catalogue, widely used in the United States before the conversion of the card catalogue to machine-readable form, in which all the entries (main, added, subject) and cross-references are interfiled in a single alphabetic sequence, as opposed to one divided into separate sections by type of entry (author, title, subject).
2. a catalogue with all entries (author, title, subject and added entries) arranged in a single alphabetical sequence.

■ dictionary stand

a free-standing piece of display furniture usually made of wood, at least waist-high with a sloping top and a book stop, used in libraries to display an open dictionary or other large reference work. A dictionary stand is narrower than an atlas case and may contain shelves for storing other volumes. Small revolving tabletop models are also available from library suppliers.

■ differential pricing

the controversial practice of charging libraries a substantially higher price for periodical subscriptions than the amount an individual subscriber is required to pay, which some journal publishers claim is justified because a library subscription makes the publication available to more readers, an effect known in the publishing trade as pass-along.

■ diffuse authorship

a work created by four or more persons or corporate bodies in which no single individual or body can be identified as the primary author. In libraries, such works are catalogued under the title, with an added entry for the first-named person or body.

■ digest

an orderly, comprehensive abridgment or condensation of a written work (legal, scientific, historical, or literary), broader in scope than a synopsis, usually prepared by a person other than the author of the original. Headings and subheadings may be added to facilitate reference. Also refers to a periodical or index containing excerpts or condensations of works from various sources, usually arranged in some kind of order.

■ digital

data recorded or transmitted as discrete, discontinuous voltage pulses represented by the binary digits 0 and 1, called bits. In digitised text, each alphanumeric character is represented by a specific eight-bit sequence called a byte. The computers used in libraries transmit data in digital format. The term is also used in a general sense to refer to the wave of information technology generated by the invention of the microcomputer in the second half of the 20th century, as in the expression 'digital divide' and 'digital library.'

■ digital archives

archival materials that have been converted to machine-readable format, usually for the sake of preservation or to make them more accessible to users.

■ digital collection

a collection of library or archival materials converted to machine-readable format for preservation, or to provide access electronically.

■ digital divide

a term coined by former Assistant Secretary of Commerce for Telecommunication and Communication, Larry Irving, Jr., to focus public awareness on the gap in access to information resources and services between those with the means to purchase the computer hardware and software necessary to connect to the Internet and low-income families and communities that cannot afford network access. Public libraries are helping to bridge the gap between information 'haves' and 'have-nots' with the assistance of substantial grants from industry leaders such as Microsoft's Bill Gates.

■ digital imaging

the field within computer science covering all aspects of the capture, storage, manipulation, transmission and display of images in digital format, including digital photography, scanning and bitmapped graphics. In libraries, images of text documents are created for electronic reserve collections and digital archives. They are also available in full-text bibliographic databases and reference resources

■ digital library

a library in which a significant proportion of the resources are available in machine-readable format, rather than in print or

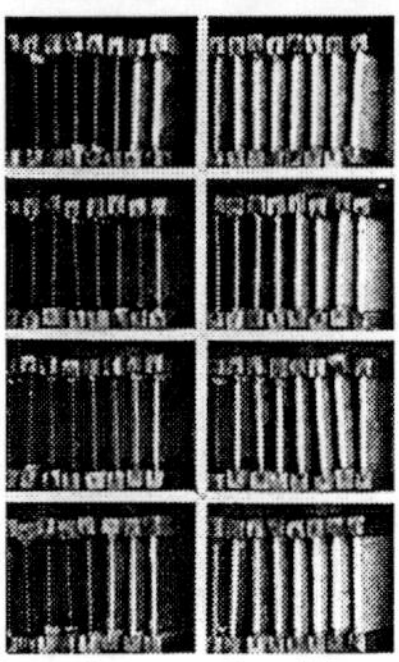

on microform. In libraries, the process of digitisation began with the catalogue, moved to periodical indexes and abstracting services, then to periodicals and large reference works and finally book publishing. Abbreviated d-lib.

■ dissertation

a lengthy, formal written treatise or thesis, especially an account of scholarly investigation or original research on a specialised topic, submitted to a university in partial fulfilment of the requirements for a Ph.D. degree. Dissertations submitted at universities in the United States, Canada, Great Britain and other European countries are indexed and abstracted in Dissertation Abstracts International (DAI) available in print, on CD-ROM and online from Bell & Howell. In most academic libraries, copies of dissertations may be requested on interlibrary loan or ordered via document delivery. Abbreviated diss.

■ Dissertation Abstracts International (DAI)

a service of Bell & Howell that provides indexing and abstracting of Ph.D. dissertations and master's theses in all academic disciplines, submitted at universities in the United States, Canada, Great Britain and other European countries since 1861 (dissertations abstracted since 1980, theses since 1988). DAI is available in print, on CD-ROM and as an online bibliographic database directly from Bell & Howell or via OCLC First Search (updated monthly). Print copies of dissertations can be obtained from Dissertation Express (Bell&

Howell) upon payment of a fixed fee.

dissertation

a treatise (thesis) written by a candidate for a Ph.D.

distance learning

a method of instruction and learning designed to overcome barriers of time and space by allowing students to study in their own homes or at local facilities, often at their own convenience, using materials available electronically or by mail. Communication with the instructor is normally by telephone or e-mail. Telecommunication networks and teleconferencing have facilitated distance learning. Libraries are working to support distance learning by providing online catalogues and databases, electronic reserves, electronic reference service, online tutorials and electronic document delivery service.

distinctive title

a title that is unique to a specific work. Distinctiveness of title is important in registering copyright and makes the entry for a document easier to retrieve from a library catalogue or other finding tool in a search by title.

distribution copy

in reprography, a microform copy from which additional copies of equal legibility can be reproduced.

distribution imprint

the statement printed on the verso of the title page of a book giving the official name(s) of the distributor(s) from which copies can be obtained, as distinct from the imprint of the publisher that issued the edition, or the printer responsible for printing the edition.

distribution list

in e-mail software, a feature that allows the user to establish a list of e-mail addresses under a common name, enabling messages to be sent simultaneously to everyone on the list when addressed to the list name. Although the term is sometimes used synonymously with mailing list, the latter generally supports a much larger group, requiring special software for automatic maintenance.

distribution rights

legal arrangements made by a publisher to transfer to another company or person the exclusive right to market a publication, usually within a designated geographic area. In books, distribution rights are usually indicated in the distribution imprint on the verso of the title page.

distributor

an agent or agency that owns the exclusive or shared rights to market a published work, usually within a designated geographic area. In domestic publishing, the distributor is usually, but not always, the publisher. Foreign publications are often distributed by a domestic publishing company under an agreement with the original publisher. Abbreviated distr.

■ docking station

a piece of computer hardware that enables a laptop to function as a desktop computer by providing a single large plug and socket that duplicates the individual cable connections to monitor, keyboard, mouse and printer. Some docking stations include built-in peripherals such as audio speakers and CD-ROM drive and a network interface card to allow the user to connect to a local area network. Because no standard exists for docking stations, compatibility with the specific type of laptop is an important consideration in making a purchase decision.

■ doctored

a book that has been altered from its original condition, usually as a consequence of mending, repairs, restoration, or the addition or removal of parts.

■ docudrama

a shortened form of the term documentary drama, a dramatisation of events that actually happened, usually produced for film or television. Although some elements may be fictionalised, a serious attempt is made to be historically accurate.

■ document

a physical entity consisting of any substance on which is recorded all or a portion of one or more works, in the words of Marshall McLuhan, the 'medium' in which a 'message' (information) is communicated. Document formats range from print (books, manuscripts, pamphlets, periodicals, reports, maps, charts, prints, etc.) to microform and nonprint media. Abbreviated doc. Also, any form printed on paper, once it has been filled in, especially one that has legal significance or is supplied by a government agency (example: an application for copyright protection). Also refers to a word processing text file (file type .doc) or any file created on a Macintosh computer.

■ document camera

a table-top device used in bibliographic instruction and other visual presentations to project text and/or images from an opaque surface or transparency onto a large screen using an LCD projector. Document cameras have superseded overhead projectors in well-equipped libraries.

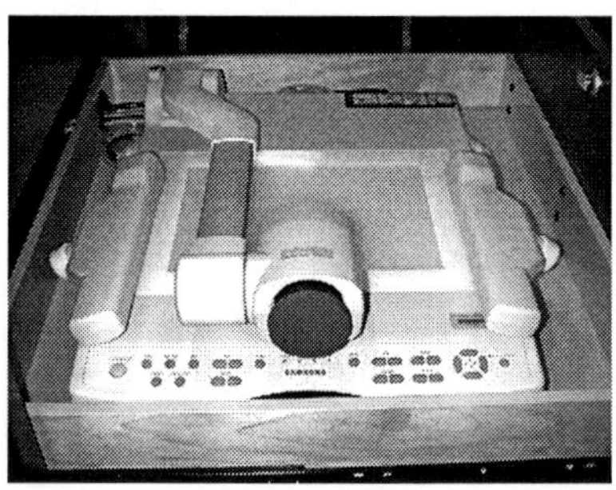

Document Delivery Service (DDS)

the provision of published or unpublished documents in hard copy, microform, or digital format, usually for a fixed fee upon request. In most libraries, document delivery service is provided by the interlibrary loan office on a cost-recovery basis. The patron is usually required to pick-up printed material at the library, but electronic full-text may be forwarded via e-mail. Also refers to the physical or electronic delivery of documents from a library collection to the residence or place of business of a library user, upon request.

document trail

all the authenticated sources of information about a topic, recorded in any medium, traced backward in time to determine conclusively the origins of an existing state of affairs, a technique used in archives to establish provenance and in news reporting to uncover the details of a story.

document

1) a physical entity of any printed work, such as a book, manuscript etc.
2) a government publication or public document.

documentary

a motion picture that records actual events or depicts social conditions without fictionalisation, often through the use of historical footage and still photographs, usually accompanied by a narration dramatically structured to highlight important individuals who participated in the action. The term was coined by the Scottish film-maker John Grierson in the late 1920's to describe the cinematic works of Robert Flaherty, the first person to produce films of social commentary depicting actual people in real-life situations.

documentation

the acquisition, organisation, storage, retrieval and distribution of specialised documents, especially of a legal, technical, or scientific nature. Also refers to a collection of documents pertaining to a specific subject, especially when used to substantiate a point of fact. In scholarly publication, the practice of citing the source of a direct quotation or excerpt, an idea that is not original, or factual information, to support a thesis or argument and/or avoid plagiarism or infringement of copyright, particularly important in the writing of history and biography. In archives, the process of writing and organising descriptions of records for reference purposes and to facilitate the development of finding aids for users. In data processing, detailed descriptive information required to develop, operate and maintain machine-readable data files and systems. In a more general sense, a systematic written description of any procedure (or set of procedures and/or policies), including the history of its application within a specific context. In France, a term used in nearly the same sense as information science.

■ documentation center

an organisation or agency that specialises in receiving, processing, preserving, abstracting and indexing publications, usually within a scholarly discipline or field of research and study. Documentation centres also issue bulletins on the progress of such work for distribution to interested parties and may also prepare bibliographies on special topics, make copies or translations and engage in bibliographic research.

■ documents

the division of the library that collects, catalogues and provides reference assistance for government publications.

■ dog-eared

the condition of a book that shows definite signs of wear, especially pages that have been folded down at a corner to mark a place.

■ domain

all the hardware and software resources controlled by a single computer system. In a local area network (LAN), all the clients, servers and devices under the control of a single security database, administered under a common set of rules and procedures. On the Internet, all the clients, servers and devices sharing a common portion of the IP address, the highest level domain being the category of host, indicated in the United States by the three-letter suffix at the end of the domain name. In database management, all the possible values of the data contained in a specific field present in every record in a file. In indexing, the range or extent within which documents or items are selected for inclusion in a bibliography, index, or catalogue. When the domain is one or more tangible

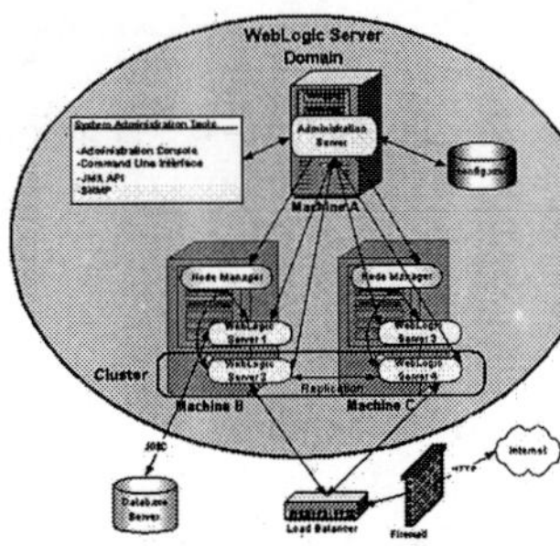

collections, the result is a catalogue. In an indexing and abstracting service, the domain is usually the published literature of an academic discipline or group of related disciplines. In a national bibliography, the domain is the published output of an entire country.

■ domain name

the address identifying a specific site on the Internet. In the United States, domain names usually consist of three parts separated by the period (full stop). In the address www.thisuniversity.edu, the first part (www) indicates the protocol or language used in accessing the address, the second part (thisuniversity) represents the name of the institution or organisation hosting the site and the last part (edu) is a high-level domain code indicating the category of entity serving as network host. Here are some of the top-level domain codes:

.com - commercial enterprise
.edu - educational institution
.gov - government agency
.mil - military installation
.net - network
.org - nonprofit organisation

■ Domain Name Server (DNS)

dns translates between a machine name and that machine's numerical IP internet address.

■ Domain Name System (DNS)

a table used to translate numerical IP addresses (example: 123.496.78.6) into the alphanumeric domain name addresses (www.thisuniversity.edu) familiar to Internet users and vice versa.

■ donation

in archives, a voluntary deposit of records by a person or organisation, in which both legal title and physical custody are formally transferred by the donor.

■ donor file

a systematic record of the names of persons and/or organisations that have donated materials to a library or archives. A well-maintained donor file should document any restrictions on the preservation, use, or disposition of donated items or files and provide current contact information. In a weeding project, it is wise to check discards against such a file to ascertain if a prior agreement was made with the donor concerning final disposition.

■ door stop

library slang for a piece of equipment so obsolete that it cannot be given away. Such items are usually consigned to a storage room in the basement until renovation or a move into a new facility makes disposal unavoidable.

■ dos

an acronym for Disk Operating System (pronounced 'dahss'), the first operating system for IBM-compatible personal computers, developed for IBM in a version called PC-DOS by Bill Gates' fledgling company Microsoft. Gates subsequently marketed the Microsoft version (MS-DOS) which became the underlying control program for early versions of Windows. Windows NT and later versions of Windows are not dependent on DOS, although they are capable of supporting DOS applications. Because it is nongraphical, line-oriented and command-driven, the DOS interface is not as user-friendly as Windows.

■ dos-a-dos

an English term for a type of binding in which two books are bound back-to-back, sharing the back cover, with the fore-edges of one aligned with the spine of the other, so that they open in opposite directions. Popular during the 17th century, this style was used to bind in a single volume the New Testament with the Prayer Book and Psalms.

■ dot

a full stop used to divide the elements of an Internet address.

■ dot.com

a commercial enterprise that does all or a substantial portion of its business over the Internet (example: Amason.com).

■ drop initial

a large decorated or undecorated initial letter in a manuscript or printed work, aligned horizontally with the tops of succeeding letters in the same line, but extending below the line into a space left by indenting the next line (or lines). Drop initials are used mainly at the beginning of a chapter or other major division of a work. Synonymous with drop cap.

■ drop shipment

publications ordered from a jobber by the acquisitions department of a library, sent by the publisher directly to the library at the request of the jobber, usually to reduce shipping costs when the jobber does not have the items in stock.

■ drop-down title

the shortened version of the title of a book, printed on the first page of the text, usually the same as the running title.

■ due date

the date of the last day of the loan period, stamped or written by a library staff member on the date due slip affixed to an item when it is checked out at the circulation desk. Fines may be charged for materials returned after the due date if they are not renewed. In the online catalogue, the due date may be displayed to indicate the circulation status of an item currently checked out. Synonymous with date due.

■ dues

titles ordered from a publisher that cannot be supplied until additional stock arrives from the printer, usually new books for which stock has not been received or backlisted titles in the process of being reprinted. Such items are usually back ordered.

■ dummy

a single prototype of a book, made up of the same number of leaves (usually blank) of the same grade of paper as the final product, trimmed and sewn but usually unbound, to give the binder an idea of bulk and page size and to assist the graphic designer in planning the layout of the dust jacket. Also refers to the complete layout of every page of a print job, including typeface, type size and the position of text block, headings, illustrations, captions, etc.

■ dummy

a block, usually of wood, used when a book has been re-located from the site where a patron would expect to find it according to the catalogue. The dummy is placed on the shelf and is labelled with the name and actual present location of the item it has replaced.

■ **dump**

a computer operation that copies raw data from one location to another in a system, usually with little or no formatting, for example, the transfer of the contents of memory to a printer or computer screen to display the status of a program at the moment it crashed, useful in diagnosing the nature of a problem.

■ **duodecimo (12mo)**

a book, approximately 8 inches in height, made by folding a full sheet of book paper to form signatures of twelve leaves (twenty-four pages).

■ **duotone**

an illustration in which the image, originally done in black-and-white, is printed in two colours, usually black and either dark blue or dark green. Duotone allows tint to be applied to an image at considerably less expense than full-colour printing.

■ **duplex**

in communications, a channel capable of transmitting signals in both directions (sending and receiving) at the same time. In computer networks, this is usually achieved by using paired wires or by dividing bandwidth into two frequencies. A half-duplex connection is capable of transmitting signals alternately but not simultaneously in either direction (example: two-way radio). Synonymous with full-duplex. Also refers to a printer attached to a computer or computer network, which has the capability to print both sides of a sheet of paper, a means of conserving paper in libraries that allow printing from public access workstations.

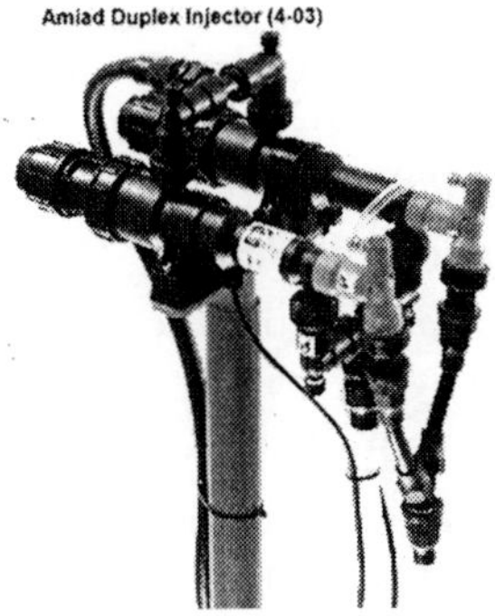

■ **duplicate**

an additional copy of an item already in a library collection, which is not needed. Public libraries often order high-demand items in multiple copies, then weed duplicates as they cease to circulate. In reprography, an exact copy of an original document (either positive or negative) which can be used in place of the original. Also refers to the process of making single or multiple copies of an original document.

■ **duplicate paging**

the numbering of pages in duplicate, usually on facing pages, used mainly in books containing parallel texts, for example, a text in translation and the same text in the original language.

■ **duplicate record**

a bibliographic record that occurs more than once on a library's catalogue. In MARC files, this usually occurs when a record is used more than once in OCLC cataloguing procedures. When a bibliographic database is created or updated, duplicate records are removed in a batch process known as deduping.

■ **duplication center**

the library's photocopy service center.

■ **durability**

the degree to which a material retains its physical integrity when subjected to stress, for example, heavy use in the case of some library materials. A durable material, such as the buckram used as a covering in some library bindings, will generally last a relatively long time under conditions of normal use. The opposite of fragile.

■ **dust jacket**

the removable paper wrapper on the outside of a hardcover book, usually printed in colour and given a glossy finish to market the work to retail customers and protect it from wear and tear. The front of the dust jacket bears the title, the author's full name and a graphic design. The title also appears on the spine of the jacket, with the author's last name and the publisher's name or symbol. In most trade titles, a promotional blurb written by the publisher appears on the inside flap. The back flap usually provides brief biographical information about the author, which may include a small portrait photograph. The ISBN is printed on the back of the dust jacket, usually in the lower right-hand corner, following brief quotes from positive reviews of the work. Textbooks, reference bookstand sci-tech books are usually published without a dust jacket.

The first protective paper jacket was provided by a publisher in England in 1833. Since then, dust jacket design has become a highly skilled form of graphic art and a significant factor in the cost of book production. In illustrated children's books, the design used on the dust jacket is usually done by the illustrator. Abbreviated dj. Synonymous with book jacket and dust cover.

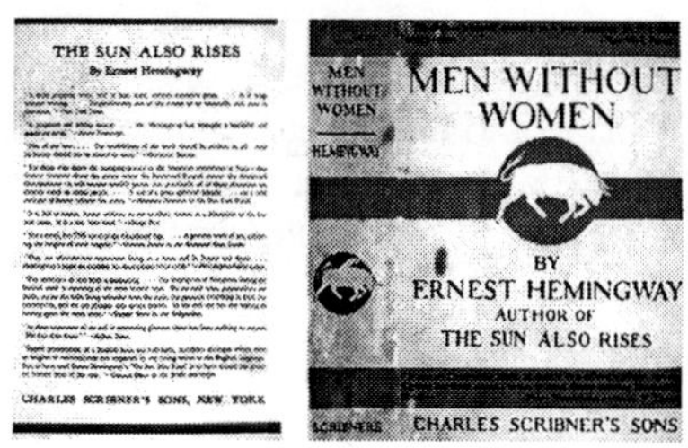

■ **dvd**

an initialism that stands for digital videodisc, a type of optical disk of the same size as a compact disc, but with significantly greater recording capacity, partly because it is double-sided. DVD

is expected to supersede video CDs, laserdiscs and videotape as the preferred medium for motion pictures for home use. DVD players can also read most CD media.

■ **dwell**

in tooling, the length of time the heated finishing tool is in contact with the leather or cloth surface being decorated.

■ **dynamic map**

a map on which flow lines and/ or arrows of varying width are used to indicate the direction and amount of movement (migration), action (military manoeuvres), or change in conditions (weather). Synonymous with flow map.

■ **e.g.**

an abbreviation of the Latin phrase exempli gratia meaning 'for the sake of example.'

■ **ear**

a small decorative design printed on either side of the title in the flag at the head of the front page of a newspaper. Also refers to a small projection found on the upper right-hand edge of the lowercase 'g' in some typefaces.

■ **early book**

books produced during the earliest periods in which human activities were recorded—on clay tablets in Mesopotamia, on papyrus scrolls in ancient Egypt, on tree bark or palm leaves in Asia, etc.—usually to record sacred prayers and rituals, traditional sagas and epics, lists of dynastic succession, laws and legal decisions, property ownership and taxation, magical incantations, astronomical observations and astrological predictions, important medical knowledge, etc. Due to the amount of labour required, early books were usually produced in single copies.

■ **easel**

a metal, wood, or plastic rack or stand on a tripod base, designed to allow an open book or periodical to be displayed face-out as part of an exhibit or presentation. Large models are used to display flip charts in presentations.

■ **easel binding**

a type of comb or spiral binding designed with rigid extended covers that can be folded back to form the base of a triangle, allowing the book or notebook to stand upright when opened, with the spine across the top. The text is printed parallel with the spine and the pages are turned up and over, instead of from side to side.

■ **easy book**

a heavily illustrated book with limited text, written to appeal to the interests and reading ability of children from preschool to third grade, usually shelved in a separate section of a school library or children's room in a public library.

■ **ebsco**

a commercial company that provides subscription management services, electronic journal access, online bibliographic and full-text databases and an online book ordering service to libraries and related institutions. EBSCO is currently one of the three leading aggregators of journals available in electronic full-text.

■ **eclogue**

a short pastoral poem, or part of a longer one, traditionally in the form of a dialogue between a pair of shepherds, for example, Spenser's The Shepheard's Calendar (1579). The term lost its pastoral connotation in the 18th century and now refers to a poem in which a serious theme is developed through a monologue or dialogue, as in Rosalind and Helen (1819) by P. B. Shelley.

■ **edited**

a single work, or two or more shorter works by the same or different authors, prepared for publication by a person other than the author, whose name usually appears as editor on the title page. In the bibliographic description, the editor's name is given in the title and statement of responsibility area following the phrase 'edited by.' For works with more than one editor, the names are listed in order of appearance on the chief source of information, followed by the word 'editors.'

■ **editing**

in publishing, the process of revising and preparing for publication material submitted by an author in manuscript or typescript form, usually performed by one or more editors. Also refers to the work of gathering together and preparing for publication in a single volume or uniform set of volumes the previously published works of one or more authors, usually done by someone else. In data processing, the revision of a document, such as a machine-readable bibliographic record, usually by selecting from an edit menu an option to cut, copy, paste, or delete portions of text, or by reformatting the text in some manner. Film editing is the process of selecting from the total amount of footage shot those portions which are to be included in a motion picture, then splicing them together in a sequence of scenes that tells a story (feature film) or conveys factual information about the subject (documentary). A similar process occurs in audiotape and videotape production.

■ **edition**

1. all the copies of a book published in a single typographical format, printed from the same typesetting and issued at one time by the same publisher, or at intervals without alteration. An edition may consist of several impressions

in which the text and other matter is not substantially changed. In older publications, the terms impression and edition are virtually synonymous since type was broken up for reuse after the first printing. In the case of nonprint items, all the copies produced from the same master copy and issued by the same entity. In a more general sense, the format (particularly the size and shape) in which a work is published. Some books, especially reference books and textbooks, are revised and republished. Unless the publisher stipulates that a work is a revised edition or expanded edition, the first revision is known as the second edition. Subsequent revisions are numbered in the order in which they are published. The latest edition is the most current, but older editions may contain useful information deleted from later ones. Also refers to a work published in a specific form for a particular market or purpose, for example, a book club edition, deluxe edition, export edition, library edition, limited edition, trade edition, or special edition. In library cataloguing, the edition is indicated by ordinal number and/or description in the edition area of the bibliographic description. Abbreviated ed. In newspaper publishing, one of two or more printings issued on the same day, for example, the 'Early Edition' or the 'Late Edition.' In radio and television, a program broadcast at a particular time of day ('Morning Edition').

2. all copies of a bibliographic item produced from the same master copy. A citation will not usually indicate a 'first edition,' but will note later editions: 'revised edition,' 'fifth edition,' etc.

3. one of the various editions of a newspaper or magazine printed at different times of the day, etc.; for example: ' daily edition,' 'evening edition' or 'special edition.'

■ editor

a person who prepares for publication the work(s) of one or more authors. An editor may be responsible for selecting material included in a collection or for preparing manuscript copy for the printer, including annotation of the text, verification of the accuracy of facts and bibliographic citations, polishing grammar and style, organising front and back matter, etc. Periodicals and large reference works often have a general editor or editor-in-chief who supervises the work of an editorial staff. In large publishing houses, the editing process may be divided into separate functions, each performed by a different person:

Acquisition editor: scouts and evaluates new works for recommendation to the publisher.

Manuscript editor: assists the author in developing and organising the work.

Copy editor: perfects details of grammar and style, checks the accuracy of facts, quotations, citations, etc.

Managing editor: coordinates resources required for publication and develops the publication schedule.

Production editor: oversees the transition from editorial process to production (printing, binding, distribution).

Also refers to the individual in charge of the content of a newspaper, magazine, or journal and in some cases its publication, whose name is given in the masthead.

■ editorial

a brief essay expressing clearly and unequivocally and sometimes with artful persuasiveness, the opinion or position of the chief editor(s) of a newspaper or magazine with respect to a current political, social, cultural, or professional issue. Editorials appear on the editorial page of a newspaper, usually at the end of the news section. The editorial page may also include columns written by syndicated columnists, letters to the editor and political cartoons. In a news magazine, editorials and columns usually appear at the beginning before the feature articles, or sometimes on the last page(s).

■ editorial board

a group of people responsible for controlling the editorial content and overseeing the publication of a periodical, whose names are usually given in the masthead. In magazine publishing, the editorial board establishes the overall editorial policy and tone to be followed by staff writers, selects columnists and decides which letters to the editor will be published. In journal publishing, the board usually controls the evaluation and selection of articles submitted by independent scholars for publication.

■ editorial content

the portions of a periodical containing content controlled by the editor(s) or editorial board (articles, columns, editorials, letters to the editor, illustrations, political cartoons, etc.), as opposed to the space devoted to advertisements, notices and announcements, etc.

■ editorialise

to put forth an opinion or position on a subject, usually with intent to persuade the listener or reader to adopt or at least consider the point of view of the speaker or writer. Also, to inject personal opinions or comments into an otherwise objective discussion or account, a technique used in essays, editorials, columns, letters to the editor and other forms of persuasive writing, but considered inappropriate in scholarly publication and in works of fiction.

■ educational videotape

a videotape designed and marketed to schools and libraries as a teaching tool, sometimes for use in conjunction with a specific curriculum unit. Educational videos tend to be priced higher than feature films and mass market nonfiction videos.

■ eggshell

a smooth, slightly pitted finish given to uncoated paper or board, which produces a soft nonglossy surface resembling the shell of a bird's egg. Most antique papers have this type of finish.

■ electronic book

a book composed or typed on a computer, or converted from print to digital (machine-readable) format by scanning or some other process, for display on a computer screen. Although the first hypertext novel was published in 1987 (Afternoon, A Story by Michael Joyce), e-books did not capture public attention until the online publication of Stephen King's novella Riding the Bullet in March, 2000. Within 24 hours, the text had been downloaded by 400,000 computer users.

■ electronic collection

library materials in digital format, including e-sines, e-journals, e-books, reference works published online and on CD-ROM, online bibliographic and full-text databases and other Web-based resources.

■ electronic database

a general term for many methods of storing information electronically. In the library this includes CD-ROMs and the library catalogue.

■ electronic document delivery

the transfer of information traditionally recorded in a physical medium (print, videotape, sound recording, etc.) to the user electronically, usually via e-mail or the World Wide Web. Libraries employ digital technology to deliver the information contained in documents and files placed on reserve and requested via interlibrary loan.

■ electronic journal

a Web site graphically modelled on an existing print journal (example: Library Journal), or which provides access to an online journal that has no print counterpart (Electronic Journal of Differential Equations). The rapidly rising cost of print journal subscriptions has led many libraries to explore electronic alternatives.

■ electronic magazine

a Web site graphically modelled on an existing print magazine.

■ electronic newsletter

a newsletter published online, usually via the Internet, with or without a print counterpart.

■ electronic publishing

the publication of books, periodicals (e-journals, e-sines, etc.), bibliographic databases and other information resources in digital format, usually on CD-ROM or online via the Internet, for in-house users, subscribers and/or retail customers, with or without a print counterpart. Synonymous in this sense with e-publishing. Also used synonymously with desktop publishing.

■ electronic records

bibliographic or archival records stored on a medium, such as magnetic tape/disk or optical disk, that requires computer equipment for retrieval and processing.

■ electronic reference

reference services requested over the Internet, usually via e-mail, instant messaging ('chat'), or Web-based submission forms, answered by the reference department of a library, independently or through a collective system. Synonymous with digital reference and online reference.

■ electronic reserves

items placed on reserve which an academic library makes available online to be read on a computer screen, downloaded to diskette, or printed as needed. Permission may be required to use works not in the public domain. Software for electronic reserves systems is available from commercial vendors.

■ electronic style

accepted format for citing (in footnotes, endnotes and bibliographies) information available in digital formats, such as computer software, abstracts and full-text articles retrieved from bibliographic databases, messages posted to newsgroups and mailing lists and documents available on the World Wide Web.

■ elegy

in classical literature, a lyric poem composed in couplets of alternating hexameter and pentameter lines, a form known as elegiac meter. In English literature through the 17th century, a song or poem of melancholy or solemn contemplation. In contemporary usage, a formal poem lamenting the death of a particular person (example: In Memory of W. B. Yeats by W. H. Auden) or the phenomenon of mortality in general (example: Elegy Written in a Country Churchyard by Thomas Gray).

■ element

in library cataloguing, a discrete unit of data constituting part of an area of description within the bibliographic record created to represent an item, for example, the publication date in the edition statement or the number of pages or plates in the physical description. Also refers to a unit of information within a field of a record in a bibliographic database, for example, the journal title or volume number in the source field of an entry representing a periodical article.

■ elephant folio

in nonspecialty publishing, a large folio usually about 14 x 23 inches in size. The term double-elephant refers to the very large paper size used to print works such as Birds of America by John James Audubon.

■ elhi book

a term used in the educational book trade in the United States to refer to a textbook published specifically for elementary and high-school students, usually revised and updated regularly by publishers anxious to retain market share. In a more general sense, any book published for elementary and/or high school age readers. Also spelled el-hi.

■ el-hi textbooks & serials in print

a reference serial published by R. R. Bowker in which elhi textbooks currently in print are indexed, by author, title and a classified list of subjects. A separate index is provided for textbooks published in series. Elhi serials are indexed by subject and title.

■ elision

from the Latin elisio meaning 'a striking out.' The omission of a vowel or silent consonant at the beginning or in the middle of a word (example: you've for you have or ne'er for never), or the omission of a vowel, consonant, or syllable in the pronunciation of a word or phrase. In orthography, the omission is indicated by an apostrophe.

■ ellipsis

the use of square brackets [ ] or three full points ... or a series of asterisks **** in handwritten or printed text to indicate the omission or suppression of a word or words (four points if the omission ends a sentence). Often used to reduce the length of a quotation without altering its meaning or significance.

■ encyclopaedia

a book or numbered set of books containing authoritative summary information about a variety of topics in the form of short essays, usually arranged alphabetically by headword or classified in some manner. An entry may be signed or unsigned, with or without illustration or a list of references for further reading. Headwords and text are usually revised periodically for publication in a new edition. In a multivolume encyclopedia, any indexes are usually located at the end of the last volume. Encyclopedias may be general or specialised, usually by subject (Encyclopedia of Bad Taste) or discipline (Encyclopedia of Social Work). In electronic publishing, encyclopedias were one of the first formats to include

multimedia and interactive elements. Also spelled encyclopaedia. Synonymous with cyclopedia.

■ encyclopedia of associations

an annual reference serial published by the Gale Group, providing detailed directory information on over 22,000 nonprofit American membership organisations of national scope. Each entry typically includes the organisation's official name, address and phone/FAX numbers; the primary official's name and title; founding date, purpose and activities; size of membership and dues; national and international conferences; and publications. Each edition includes an alphabetically arranged name index and keyword index and a separate volume containing geographic and executive indexes. Companion volumes are available from the same publisher for international organisations and regional, state and local organisations.

■ end panel

a single or double-faced flat piece of wood, steel, or other rigid material securely attached to the end of a range of library shelving, usually extending from floor to top of unit to cover the shelf ends facing an aisle or open area. End panels also help provide structural rigidity to shelving, important in regions prone to earthquake. The panels may be painted or covered with material that aesthetically enhances the library's decor. End panels in wood may be custom-made to match library furnishings.

■ end user

person with an information need.

■ epic

a lengthy narrative poem in which the language, characters and action are heroic and exalted in style. Most epics have a comparatively simple plot, a theme (or themes) reflecting the universal human condition, a hero of superhuman mental and physical capacity who is nonetheless fatally flawed, a setting imaginary or remote in time and place, with supernatural forces playing a decisive role in the action, upon which may depend the fate of an entire society or people. Epics are usually closely tied to the legends, oral traditions and history of a specific culture (Iliad and Odyssey of Homer, Beowulf, etc.). Literary epics, such as the Aeneid of Virgil and Paradise Lost by John Milton, are consciously modelled on traditional examples.

■ epigram

in the classical period, an inscription or epitaph, but in modern usage a tersely witty, often antithetical saying, ingeniously composed in prose or verse, delivered with aplomb to make a point in a manner calculated to enhance one's reputation in the company of people who value feats of intellectual and literary virtuosity. The satirical form, established in ancient Rome by Martial, was cultivated in England from the late 16th to the early 20th century.

■ epigraph

a brief quotation or motto included in the front matter of a book, usually following the dedication, or at the beginning of each chapter, expressing an idea or theme the author intends to develop more fully in the text.

epilogue

a part added as a conclusion at the close of a literary work, for example, the statement of the moral at the end of a fable. The term also refers to the final section of a speech, also called the peroration and to a brief speech delivered at the end of a dramatic performance, requesting the approval of audience and critics.

episodic

a literary work consisting of a number of more or less self-contained but loosely connected incidents (episodes) strung together by the author to form a narrative [example: Idylls of the King (1859) by Alfred, Lord Tennyson].

epistemology

from the Greek episteme (knowledge) and logos (theory), the branch of philosophy devoted to the theoretical study of the nature, methods and validity of human knowledge, including the relationship between the knower (subject), the known (object)and the process of knowing.

epistle

a composition in poetry or prose, written in the form of a letter so elegant in style that it is considered a literary work worthy of publication. Also refers to one of the letters of the New Testament of the Christian Bible.

epistolary novel

a form of novel that reached its greatest popularity during the 18th century, in which the narrative is developed by the author in a series of letters (example: Clarissa by Samuel Richardson). Sometimes a novelist begins a work in epistolary style, then switches to conventional narrative (Busman's Honeymoon by Dorothy L. Sayers).

epitaph

from the Greek epi ('upon') and taphos ('tomb'), a brief valedictory verse on the life and death of a person (or persons), composed as an inscription on a grave marker, sometimes by the deceased before death. Epitaphs are usually complimentary, but may be humorous or ironic. One of the most famous was written by Simonides of Ceos (556-468 BC) commemorating the 300 warriors who died at Thermopylae.

epithet

from the Greek word epitheton, meaning 'something added.' A descriptive name or title expressing an important quality or attribute, usually added to distinguish a person (William the Conqueror), epoch (Age of Enlightenment), or thing (John Knox cap) from others of the same name or class. In library cataloguing, the epithet follows the personal name in the heading under which the item is catalogued.

■ **epitome**

a statement of the essence of a subject, in the briefest possible form. Also refers to a very brief but accurate written statement of the main points of a work, usually prepared by a person other than the author.

■ **eponym**

a single name under which several authors are published. Also, the name of a person or character so closely associated with a quality, process, or activity that the name is used in signifying it (Herculean, pasteurisation, Platonic, Romeo). Also refers to a person who gives, or is reputed to have given, his or her name to an institution, structure, place, etc. (Guggenheim Museums), or to a distinguishing title derived from the name of a person, designating a people, place, thing, or period (Periclean Athens, Carolingian minuscule, Elisabethan drama).

■ **escape key**

a key located in the upper left-hand corner of a standard computer keyboard, usually labelled Esc, which allows the user to go backward one step in a sequence of operations, terminating the current operation.

■ **escapist literature**

fiction written as light entertainment, intended mainly to divert the mind of the reader into a world of imagination and fantasy. Popular genres include romance, science fiction, thrillers, etc.

■ **esl**

an abbreviation of 'English as a Second Language,' a branch of English language study and teaching.

■ **essay**

a short prose literary composition addressed to the general reader, usually dealing thoughtfully and in some depth with a single theme, seen from the personal point of view of the essayist who does not necessarily attempt the systematic or comprehensive analysis one would expect in a dissertation or treatise. There are no limitations on style or content—essays can be formal or informal, descriptive, narrative, persuasive, humorous, satirical, historical, biographical, autobiographical, or critical. In some cases, essays that appear on the surface to be straightforward can have a deeper, more philosophical meaning. Essays published in collections and Festschriften are indexed in Essay and General Literature Index published by H. W. Wilson.

■ **estimated price**

the price that the acquisitions department of a library anticipates will be charged when an item or subscription is ordered from a publisher, jobber, dealer, or subscription agency. The price actually paid may be higher or lower due to a discount, shipping charges, etc.

■ **estray**

in archives, the legal term for a record or document no longer in the possession of its original creator or legitimate custodian.

■ et al.

an abbreviation of the Latin phrase et alii, meaning 'and other people' used in bibliographic citations after the first of more than three collaborators, instead of listing all the names. Also, an abbreviation of et alibi ('and elsewhere') and et alia ('and other things').

■ et seq.

an abbreviation of the Latin phrase et sequens meaning 'and the following one.' Plural: et seqq. ('and those that follow').

■ etc.

an abbreviation of the Latin phrase et cetera meaning 'and the rest' or 'and so forth,' used to shorten a list.

■ etymology

the origins of a word, traced back as far as possible in time, usually by the methods of comparative linguistics. Some specialised language dictionaries are devoted specifically to etymology. The most comprehensive is the Oxford English Dictionary.

■ eulogy

a written or spoken composition in praise of someone or something, especially a person who is deceased (example: Ben Jonson's eulogy on Shakespeare).

■ ex libris

a Latin phrase meaning, 'From the books of...' printed on a bookplate followed by a blank space for the owner's name. Abbreviated ex lib.

■ exact sise

the actual size of the binding of a book, as measured in inches or centimetres, independent of the dimensions of the leaves or any other size designation. In library cataloguing, exact size is given in centimetres in the physical description area of the bibliographic record. Synonymous with absolute size.

■ excerpt

a lengthy verbatim selection taken from a speech or written work, usually longer than a quotation. Reprinting an excerpt without permission may be an infringement of copyright. Excerpts are sometimes published in the form of a digest.

■ exhibit

a physical object placed on display in a museum, gallery, or other public place, usually because of its historical, cultural, or scientific importance, or its aesthetic qualities, extraordinary characteristics, or monetary value. Libraries typically exhibit rare and valuable books, manuscripts, personal papers and memorabilia associated with authorship, publishing, book history and reading. Exhibits may be permanent or rotated periodically, depending on the availability of materials suitable for display and the policy of the library. Also refers to the event during which such objects are displayed. Also, a booth or table at which a book publisher, jobber, or dealer, or a library vendor or supplier, displays its products and services at a conference to attract prospective customers. Companies and organisations that lease exhibit space are called exhibitors.

■ exhibit catalogue

an art book in hard or soft cover, containing reproductions of the works of art displayed in an exhibition or series of exhibitions held at a museum or gallery. The illustrations are usually numbered and may be arranged in the order in which the items are exhibited, with or without prices. Accompanying text may be minimal. Exhibit catalogues are often issued by museum publishers. Synonymous with exhibition catalogue.

■ extract

one or more lengthy quotations from a book or other work, set within the main text of another work, usually indented and sometimes printed in distinguishing type. When printed in the same type size as the text and without indention, an extract is enclosed in quotation marks and preceded and followed by a blank line. In a more general sense, any piece taken from one work and used in another, sometimes to represent the whole, as in a scene from a motion picture used in a trailer.

■ extract type

in printing, notes and lengthy quotations or extracts are distinguished from the body of the text by setting them in a smaller size of the same typeface.

■ extra-illustrated

a volume into which additional illustration and sometimes printed matter has been inserted, not part of the publication as issued. Synonymous with privately illustrated.

■ extranet

a private computer network designed to serve the employees of a company or members of an organisation (as in an intranet)and also to provide various levels of accessibility to selected persons outside the organisation (business partners, customers, clients, etc.), but not the general public. When transmission occurs over public telecommunication channels (the Internet), the system is pass worded to exclude unauthorised users. Services may be fee-based or offered at no charge.

■ extranet

a collaborative network linking businesses or institutions in order to share information externally

■ extrapolation

the addition of one or more new subjects at the end of an array in a classification system, based on a shared characteristic or characteristics.

■ fable

a fictitious story which uses animal characters to express or teach a moral lesson (example: Animal Farm by George Orwell).

■ **fabliau**

in medieval literature written in old French, a humorous metrical story told in eight-syllable lines that relates incidents of ordinary life in a realistic style and at the same time conveys a moral message. Fabliaux often satirise the faults of clergymen or other prominent persons, or the foibles of ordinary people. They can be broadly humorous, as in some of Chaucer's Canterbury Tales.

■ **face**

in publishing, the outside of the front cover of a book. In printing, the raised surface of a unit of metal type, from which the impression of a single character is taken in printing. Also used as an abbreviation of typeface.
Also refers to the unbroken front of a single-sided bookcase or shelving unit, or one side of a double-sided bookcase or shelving unit, or range of double-sided units.

■ **face out**

placement of a book or periodical on end with the front cover forward, usually to attract browsers to a library display or exhibit, or to encourage sales in a retail outlet. In some libraries, current issues of periodicals are displayed on sloping shelves designed to allow the front covers to face forward.

■ **face up**

in printing, the position of a full-page illustration printed on the recto of a leaf so that it appears on the right-hand side of the opening in a book or other publication.

■ **facet**

the entire set of subclasses generated when a class representing a subject in a classification system is divided according to a single characteristic. The number of subclasses depends on the specific characteristic applied. In his Colon Classification, S. R. Ranganathan identified five categories of facet recognisable in any class: personality, matter, energy, space and time. In a more general sense, any one of several distinct aspects of a subject.

■ **flexible binding**

a cloth or leather covered book bound in a material that bends easily, rather than the rigid boards used in most hardcover editions. Synonymous with flexcover.

■ **flextime**

time worked in excess of the maximum number of hours per day, week, or month specified under the terms governing employment, for which the employee is granted time off at a later date. Synonymous with comp time.

■ **flicker book**

a type of toy book published during the 19th century, containing a sequence of closely-related cartoon-style illustrations designed to give the impression of animation when the pages are fanned from cover to cover, similar to the visual effect created by the rapid projection of frames in a motion picture.

■ **flier**

an inexpensive, widely distributed handbill or circular of small size (usually 8 1/2 x 11 inches), used flat or folded for advertising and announcements. Also spelled flyer. Synonymous in the U.K. with leaflet.

■ **flip chart**

a large-sized pad of paper designed to be mounted on an easel, to display information in graphic or tabular format during a presentation. As the session proceeds, pages can either be torn off or turned over the top. Unlike slide projection or presentation software, a flip chart allows the presenter to manipulate information content manually as it is presented, sometimes in response to feedback from the audience. Transparencies are visible to a larger audience but require overhead projection equipment. Also spelled flipchart.

■ **flush**

said of a line of type aligned along a right or left margin without indention.

■ **flush binding**

a binding in which the covers are trimmed even with the leaves after having been attached to the sections. Most paperback books have flush covers.

■ **flyleaf**

the half of an endpaper not pasted to the inside of one of the boards of the cover. The term is also used for one or more blank leaves at the beginning of a book following the front free endpaper, or at the end preceding the back free endpaper, when the text does not fill the last few pages. The purpose of the flyleaves is to protect the first and last leaves of the text block from damage. Also spelled fly leaf.

■ **fly-title**

a title printed on an otherwise blank leaf indicating the beginning of a chapter or other major division of a book, such as an essay in a collection, or a story, play, or poem published in an anthology. In England, a synonym for half title or bastard title.

■ **fog index**

a numeric formula used in publishing to gauge the degree of readability (clarity) of a piece of writing, based on average sentence length and number of words of three or more syllables per sentence. The higher the index number, the less intelligible the writing, an important consideration in judging the sales potential of a work. The measure is imprecise because it does not take into consideration the writer's style, which may break long sentences into phrases and make difficult words easier to comprehend from the context.

■ fold sewn

a binding in which the gathered sections are attached to each other by sewing through the back fold, with a kettle stitch linking adjacent sections at the end of each pass of the thread. Hand fold sewing can be all along, two on, or three on.

■ folded book

a novelty book format consisting of one long strip of paper folded accordion-style, with one or both ends attached to separate rigid covers and no back. Used for pictorial display of wide-angle panoramas, particularly in China. More complex folded books have been created by contemporary artists for whom the book is a form of visual art. Synonymous with folding book.

■ foot

the bottom edge of a book or page in a bound publication. The opposite of head. Synonymous with tail.

■ footage

a length or quantity expressed in feet, for example, the number of running feet in a segment of film joined to other segments in editing to create a motion picture.

■ footer

a line or lines at the bottom of a Web page, giving the name of the person (or persons) responsible for creating and maintaining the site and its host. The footer may also include the date of last update, a copyright notice and a contact link or Internet address. Also refers to the lines at the bottom of an e-mail message indicating the name, title and affiliation of the sender and any contact information, as distinct from the header at the beginning of the message and the body containing the text. Also used synonymously in printed documents with running foot.

■ foxing

reddish-brown or yellowish spots resembling freckles on the paper of old documents (books, prints, etc.), a condition probably caused by fungus and/or a chemical reaction under humid conditions, particularly common in paper made by machine during the late 18th and 19th centuries. Although the cause (or causes) are not fully understood, the fact that foxing often begins near the edge of a leaf or sheet and spreads inward suggests that exposure to the atmosphere may play an important role. In some types of documents, foxing can be reduced or eliminated by a technique called washing, but preservationists proceed with caution because some methods can cause further damage. Synonymous with fox marks.

fps

an abbreviation of 'frames per second.'

frame

a separately scrollable area in the window of a computer application or in a Web page that has been divided into more than one scrollable area.

In filmstrips, motion pictures and video recordings, one of the individual still images arranged in sequence to tell a story or create the illusion of movement when projected in rapid succession. Projection speed is measured in fps (frames per second). Librarians use the frame (or frames) bearing the title of the work as the chief source of information in cataloguing such an item. Also refers to a single subdivision of the grid on a sheet of microfiche, or one of the units comprising a length of microfilm. In binding, an ornamental rectangle impressed in the surface of the cover of a book some distance from the edges. Also refers to a rigid border of wood, metal, plastic, cardboard, etc., used to mount a picture, print, photograph, slide, etc.

frankfurt book fair

the largest and one of the oldest book trade fairs in the world, held annually in Frankfurt, Germany in October, providing an opportunity for publishers to exhibit their publications, negotiate international sales rights, make arrangements for co-published editions, etc.

frayed

the condition of a cloth book cover on which the threads along at least one edge have broken and pulled loose due to abrasion, exposing the board underneath.

free hand

handwriting of any period that does not follow established rules with respect to abbreviation, contraction, punctuation, uppercase and lowercase, etc.

free resource

a source of reliable information that can be obtained without charge (example: telephone directories). Prior to the emergence of the Internet, government, business and nonprofit organisations provided most of the free information available to librarians and library users. Today, information is available at no charge from a considerably wider range of sources via the World Wide Web, but the user must exercise discrimination in assessing accuracy and authority.

free speech

freedom under the First Amendment to the U.S. Constitution

to write or say whatever one wishes without fear of censorship or prosecution, within certain limitations (libel, slander, etc.).

■ **frequency**

the interval at which a periodical or other serial publication is issued (daily, semiweekly, weekly, semimonthly, monthly, bimonthly, quarterly, semiannually, annually, irregularly, etc.). Scholarly journals are usually published quarterly, magazines weekly or monthly and newspapers daily or weekly. Frequency and changes of frequency are indicated in the note area of the bibliographic description of a serial. In statistics, the number of times a unit of measurement occurs within a class or during a specified period of time. In electronics, the number of repetitions of the period of an alternating current (signal), expressed in hertz (cycles per second).

■ **full score**

a music score in which each of the parts is written on a separate stave, usually for the use of the conductor. For orchestral and choral works, this usually requires a large page size. From top to bottom, the standard arrangement of instrumental parts in a full score is: woodwinds, brass, percussion and strings, with any solo part in a concerto appearing above the violins. Voice parts, arranged in descending order of vocal register, are placed above the string section, with any solo parts given above the chorus. Only the largest music libraries collect this type of score.

■ **full stop**

the period, a punctuation mark used in text to indicate the end of a sentence and in bibliographic records to separate elements of description. When used to divide the parts of an Internet address, it is called a dot. Synonymous with full point.

■ **full text**

when the entire content of an item, such as an article, book, or encyclopaedia, is available in electronic format.

■ **full-colour printing**

a method of reproducing in print an infinite range of colours by controlling the overprinting of three colours of ink (yellow, magenta and cyan), with black added to create gradations of light and dark. The term colour separation refers to the process by which a full-colour original is photographed through coloured filters or scanned by a colour sensing machine to separate the colours and allow negatives to be produced that define the area to be printed with each colour of ink.

■ **full-motion video**

video transmission in which the image changes at the rate of 30 frames per second (fps). Motion pictures run at 24 fps. Video that has been digitised and stored on computer can be displayed at varying frame rates depending on the speed of the computer.

full-page

a term used in printing to refer to an illustration, plate, or map that fills an entire page in a book or other publication, with or without margins and caption. Also refers to an article that fills all the available space on one page of a newspaper.

full-page border

continuous ornamentation, plain or simple, extending around the perimeter of a page on all four sides. A three-quarter border extends around three of the four sides. In medieval illuminated manuscripts, a decorative band surrounding a miniature or portion of text on all four sides, usually covering the surface of the page in a dense carpet of multicoloured vines, leaves, flowers, birds and animals, except for very narrow margins.

galley

in printing, a long narrow tray open at one end, into which assembled lines of type are transferred by the compositor from a manual composing stick, or from a typesetting machine, to await make-up into pages. Galleys were originally about 10 x 6 inches in size and made of wood, but in the early 19th century, metal trays came into use and their length was extended to about 22 inches to accommodate several pages of type. Also used as a shortened form of galley proof.

galley proof

an impression taken from type composed in long columns, arranged in trays called galleys, before it has been made up into pages, to allow the author and proofreaders to inspect the text and make any corrections before the work goes to press. Although galley proofs usually do not include illustrations and indexes, reviews may be written from them. Synonymous with galleys and slip proof.

game

a set of materials designed for play according to an established set of rules, usually housed in a container to keep the pieces together. Educational games are usually stored in the curriculum room or children's room of a library.

gap

in the record representing a serial in a library catalogue or union catalogue, an indication that items issued are missing from the sequence held by the library. This happens when a subscription is cancelled and later resumed, or when issues or volumes are lost due to damage or theft. Most libraries make an effort to fill gaps in periodical subscriptions with microfilm or microfiche if online full-text is not available.

garland

a type of anthology containing a collection of prose extracts or short literary compositions, usually ballads or poems.

gate count

the number of times a counting device, attached to or located near the security gate at the entrance or exit from a library, is activated during a designated period of time (day, week, or month). Gate counts provide statistical information on traffic patterns which can be helpful in establishing library hours and anticipating staffing needs.

■ **gatefold**

an illustration, map, or other insert, larger than the volume in which it is bound, which must be unfolded horizontally to the left or right to be fully viewed. Also, a method of folding a sheet of paper into three sections in which the two ends are folded toward each other over the center, like a triptych, used in advertising, performance programs, restaurant menus, etc.

■ **gazette**

a news sheet in which current events, legal notices, public appointments, etc., are recorded on a regular basis. Formerly, a journal devoted to current news. Also, a journal officially issued by a government, particularly in Great Britain. The word is derived from the name of an Italian coin that was equivalent at one point in time to the price of a news sheet.

■ **genealogy**

the study of the descent from a common ancestor (or ancestors) of a specific individual, family, or group of persons. Genealogical research often requires the use of archival materials. Genealogical resources are increasingly available in digital form. Also refers to an enumeration of ancestors and their descendants in natural order of succession, usually in the form of a 'family tree.' In works of history and biography, genealogical tables are sometimes printed on the endpapers or at the beginning of the text.

■ **general encyclopaedia**

an encyclopaedia that provides basic information on a broad range of subjects, but treats no single subject in depth, as distinct from a subject encyclopaedia that provides greater depth of coverage within a limited scope (example: Encyclopaedia of 20th Century Humour).

■ **general interest magazine**

a magazine of interest to a wide audience (example: Reader's Digest). Most public libraries make an effort to subscribe to the most popular general interest magazines, but are more selective in subscribing to special interest magazines.

■ **GIF**

graphics Interchange Format; an algorithm for image compression developed for the commercial Internet provider CompuServe; graphics files in this format use the extension .gif.

■ **gift**

one or more books or other items donated to a library, usually by an individual, but sometimes by a group, organisation, estate, or other library. In academic libraries, desk copies and review copies are sometimes received as gifts from members of the teaching faculty. Donated items are usually evaluated in accordance with the library's collection development policy and either added to the collection or disposed of, usually in a book sale or exchange with another library.

gift book

an elaborately printed, expensively illustrated, ornately bound book of poetry or prose, usually published annually, popular as a gift item during the early part of the 19th century. Also known as a keepsake. In modern usage, a book purchased as a gift for another person (or persons). Coffee table books are often purchased for this purpose. Also spelled giftbook.

gifts

the library department responsible for handling materials received as gifts from individuals and other institutions.

gigo

in computing, an initialism that stands for 'garbage in, garbage out,' a slang expression for the axiom that the quality of output a user receives from a computer is directly proportional to the quality of the input submitted.

gilt edges

in deluxe editions, gold leaf is sometimes applied to the head, tail and/or fore-edge of each copy, then burnished to create an especially luxurious appearance. In the book trade, the abbreviation 'ge' means gilt edges, 'aeg' means all edges gilt, 'gt' means gilt top and 'teg' means top edge gilt. Left unburnished, a gilt edge is called antique.

given name

one or more names chosen for a person, usually by the parents at birth or christening, sometimes the same as that of a living relative or ancestor, but distinct from the surname identifying members of the same family. Given names can be compound.

glair

an adhesive preparation made from egg whites, used in edge gilding and tooling to permanently fix silver and gold leaf. Glair is usually purchased dry as albumen and mixed with water or vinegar prior to use. It melts with the application of heat and sets up quickly as soon as the hot finishing tool is removed, securing the leaf firmly to the surface. Also spelled glaire.

glossary

an alphabetical list of the specialised terms related to a specific subject or field of study, with brief definitions, often appearing at the end of a book or at the beginning of a long entry in a technical reference work. Long glossaries may be separately published, for example,

■ **glyphic**

in printing, a typeface derived from a carved or chiselled form, rather than from a calligraphic hand.

■ **gnawed**

a book that shows signs of having been chewed by an animal on at least one edge or corner, a condition that reduces its value considerably in the used book market and makes it a candidate for weeding in libraries.

■ **gold foil**

an inexpensive substitute for gold leaf, made by spraying a thin deposit of gold or a look-alike substitute onto an adhesive backing, used extensively to decorate edition bindings and library bindings and also in hand-binding when economy is desired. Syonymous with blocking foil.

■ **gold leaf**

gold beaten by hand or mechanical means into very thin sheets, used in bookbinding to embellish lettering, tooling and the edges of the sections. The gold leaf used in bookbinding is sold in sheets 3 1/2 inch square, made from an alloy of 23 carat gold and 1 carat silver and copper, beaten to a thinness of 1/200,000-1/250,000 of an inch. Silver is used less often for the same purpose.

■ **gothic novel**

originally, a type of novel in which a medieval castle formed the setting for a plot with chillingly sinister overtones, intended to evoke irrational fear in the heart of the reader. Horace Walpole's Castle of Otranto, A Gothic Story (1764) established this genre. In modern usage, a subgenre of romance fiction, popular during the 18th and early 19th centuries, in which the setting is dark and gloomy, the action grotesque or violent, the characters strange or malevolent, the plot mysterious and the mood often one of decadence or degeneration (example: Wuthering Heights by Emily Bronte). Synonymous with roman noir.

■ **gouge**

a nick or hole made accidentally in the cover or spine of a book. Also refers to a finishing tool used in bookbinding to make curved lines on a book cover.

■ **governance**

the arrangements by which the faculty and administration of an academic institution control and direct institutional affairs (bylaws, elective offices, committees, etc.). In some academic libraries, participation in governance may be a factor in tenure and promotion decisions affecting librarians who have faculty status.

■ **grace period**

a designated period of time following the due date during which a borrower may renew an overdue item or return it to the library without incurring a fine. To encourage the return of long overdue materials, some libraries also set aside one day (or several days) each year during which overdue items may be returned without penalty. Not all libraries provide a grace period. Synonymous with amnesty period and fine-free period.

■ graduate library

the academic library at a university that maintains separate collections (and usually facilities) for undergraduates and graduate students, containing the major research collections, staffed and equipped to meet the information needs of graduate students and faculty.

■ grain

in a sheet of machine-made paper or board, the direction in which most of the fibres lie, determined by forward movement of the papermaking machine in manufacture. Books are printed with the grain parallel to the spine because paper bends more readily with the grain than against it. One way to determine the grain in a sheet of paper is to do a tear test—paper tears more cleanly with the grain than across it. There is little or no grain in a sheet of handmade paper. Woven material used as covering material in bookbinding also has grain—as a general rule, the warp threads run parallel to the spine. Grain in leather depends on the direction in which the hairs lay before removal, indicated by tiny puncture marks on the surface.

■ grangerised

an edition into which illustrations, letters and/or other matter is inserted after publication. The practice began in 1769, when James Granger (1723-1776) published A Biographical History of England containing blank leaves for the insertion of portrait engravings after printing. Synonymous with privately illustrated.

■ grant

funds received from a private foundation or government sponsored organisation by an individual, group, or institution, in support of a worthy project or cause. In most cases, the recipient must compete for such funds by submitting a proposal. The art of obtaining grants is called grantsmanship. Guides for proposal writing are available in academic libraries and large public libraries.

■ grant-in-aid

funds received by a library or library system from a state or federal government agency in support of regular operations, or a special project or program, as opposed to funds derived from the community or district served. In most cases, the library must apply in a competitive process by submitting a proposal.

■ grantsmanship

the art of successfully obtaining and administering grants and grants-in-aid, including the ability to recognise when an idea is fundable, locate funding sources, research the information necessary to fill out the application, establish a realistic timetable, write the proposal and manage the grant process once funding is approved. When grant funding is a high priority, a college or university usually employs a trained and experienced grants administrator to help teaching faculty and librarians negotiate the process.

groupware

computer software designed to support more than one user connected to a LAN, usually colleagues working together on related tasks whose offices are not in the same location. Although groupware is an evolving concept, most products include a messaging system, document sharing and management software, a calendaring and scheduling system for coordinating meetings and tracking the progress of group projects, electronic conferencing and an electronic newsletter.

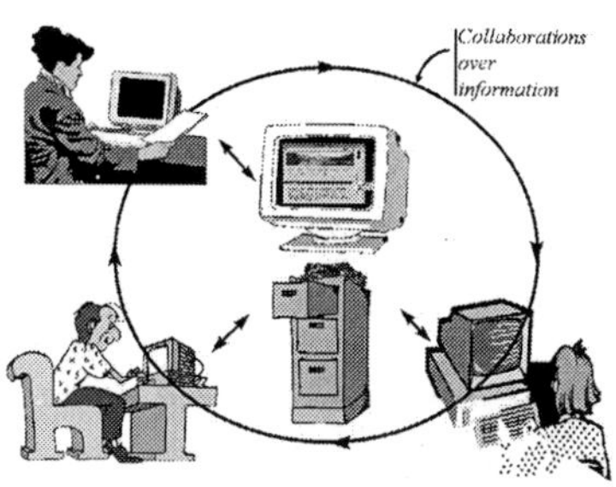

guard

a flexible strip of cloth or strong paper inserted along the inner margin between two leaves prior to sewing the sections of a book, used to mount a plate or insert too stiff to turn like a normal page. Synonymous in this sense with hinge. Also, a strip of paper or other material added to reinforce a signature in a book.

GUI

(pronounced 'gooey') graphical user interface; a program in which the user executes commands, selects files, etc. by using a mouse or other pointer device to select items (such as program icons, commands in a drop-down menu or options in a dialog box) rather than by typing in text commands.

guide

information provided by a library, usually in the form of a printed handout or leaflet, that 1) explains how to use a library service (online catalogue, interlibrary loan, etc.); 2) describes important resources on a subject (World War II), in a discipline (history), or of a specific form (periodical articles, government documents, biography, etc.); or 3) explains how to accomplish something (compile an annotated bibliography, cite sources in a particular bibliographical style, etc.). In archives, a type of finding aid that provides a summary or general description of the contents of an archival collection, or that describes archival holdings related to a specific subject, geographic area, period in history, etc., or of a certain type of material (diaries, letters, photographs, etc.).

■ **guidebook**

a handbook that provides useful current information for travellers to a city, state, region, country, or other geographic area, or for visitors to a museum, park, historical site, etc.

■ **guillemets**

french quotation marks printed << like this >>, also seen in some German texts. Synonymous with duck-foot quotes.

■ **guillotine**

a power-driven or hand-operated machine with a long, sharp-edged blade, used in binding to cut and trim large numbers of flat or folded sheets to the desired dimensions.

■ **gutenberg bible**

the earliest known book to have been produced from movable type, probably printed between 1450 and 1455 at Mains, Germany by Johann Gutenberg and his associate Peter Schoffer, with the financial assistance of a merchant named Johann Fust. Also known as the Masarin Bible because a copy was found by a French bookseller in the private library of the bibliophile Cardinal Masarin (1602-1661) one hundred years after his death. It is a Latin bible printed in black ink in gothic type set in two 42-line columns per page. Of approximately 180 copies printed, only forty-eight copies are known to have survived, which makes them very rare and valuable. Twelve are printed on vellum and thirty-six on paper.

■ **gutenberg, johann, c. 1399-1468**

a goldsmith by trade, Johann Gensfleisch sum Gutenberg is credited with the invention printing from movable type, probably at Mains in Germany. His first printed work was a 42-line Bible set in gothic type probably printed no later than 1456. Uncertainty regarding Gutenberg's accomplishment arises from the lack of recorded information about his life and the fact that no extant work bears his name, nor have any of his presses survived. The printing press spread rapidly to the Netherlands, Italy, France and England, becoming well-established in Europe by the 1480's. The Gutenberg Museum was established in Mains in 1900 as a center for the study of Gutenberg's life and work and early history of typography.

■ **gutter**

the blank space formed by the inner margins of facing pages in an open book, from the binding edge to the area that bears printed matter. The width of the gutter is an important factor in determining whether a book can be rebound.

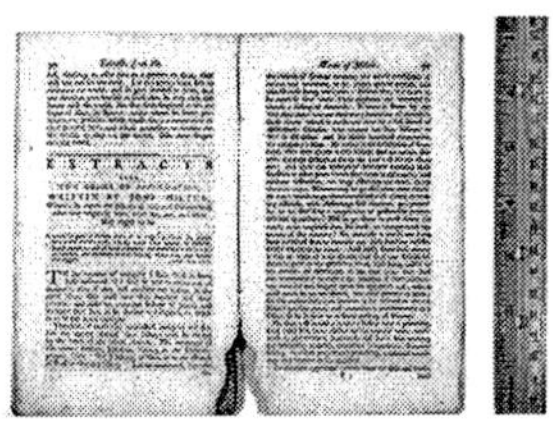

■ gutter press

tabloid newspapers and magazines that publish salacious gossip, usually of a personal nature concerning the lives of prominent people. Synonymous with yellow press.

■ gutting

the practice, abhorred by publishers, of reviewing a book, not by critically evaluating its strengths and/or weaknesses, but by revealing the main lines of its plot, ruining the experience of first-time readers. Also refers to the practice in publishing of carefully quoting out of context, in the blurb on the dust jacket and in advertising, only the most complimentary passages from reviews which, in their entirety, expressed mixed or even negative opinions of the work.

■ hachure

a series of short lines drawn or printed on a land map to indicate gradient: long thin, widely-spaced lines indicating a moderate grade and short, thick, closely-spaced lines a steep grade, with direction of slope indicated by direction of line.

■ hacker

a slang term for a person with extensive knowledge of computers and computing, who uses his skills to access supposedly secure computer systems for the intellectual challenge such activities provide. The best hackers take pride in leaving no 'tracks' to reveal their presence.

■ hagiography

a form of biography, widespread during the Middle Ages and Renaissance, in which the life described is that of a saint. Also refers to a book containing such writing, often a collective biography covering the lives of two or more saints. An author who writes about the lives (and legends) of saints is a hagiographer.

■ hard disk

a magnetic medium capable of storing a large quantity of data, which resides permanently within a computer, as opposed to a portable disk (floppy, Sip, etc.) that can be inserted in a disk drive by the user whenever a data file needs to be opened or saved and removed once the operation is completed. In microcomputers, the hard disk is usually the c. drive. In networked systems, users may also have access to a portion of the hard drive on a shared server.

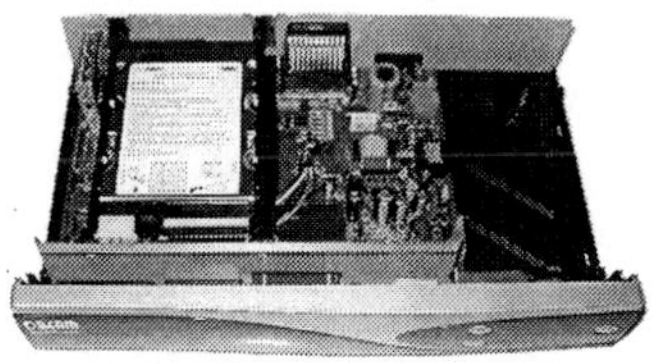

■ hardcover

a book bound in an inflexible board case or cover, usually covered in cloth, paper, plastic, leather, or some other durable material, as distinct from a book bound in a cover made of flexible material. In modern publishing, a new trade title is usually issued first in hardcover, then in a paperback edition after sales in hardcover decline. Synonymous with cloth bound, hardback and hard bound.

■ hardware

mechanical, electrical, electronic, or other physical equipment and machinery associated with a computer system, or necessary for the playback or projection of nonprint media. Basic microcomputer hardware includes a central processing unit (CPU), keyboard and monitor. The TechEncyclopedia describes the distinction between hardware and software as the difference between 'storage and transmission' and 'logic and language.'

■ head

the top edge of a book. Also refers to the margin at the top of a page, as opposed to the margin at the tail or foot of the page. Also, a word or phrase used as a brief headline in a book or periodical.

■ heuristic

from the Greek word heuriskein meaning 'to discover.' A course of action or method of problem-solving in which progress toward the best possible outcome or solution is continuously evaluated through trial and error. Both positive and negative results are incorporated as feedback into the discovery process, allowing procedure to be adjusted as the best next step is determined. Library research is usually a heuristic process.

■ historiated border

an ornamental band around a miniature or portion of text on the page of an illuminated manuscript, decorated with figures of animals and/or human beings, sometimes in a scene illustrating the accompanying text.

■ historiated initial

an initial letter in an illuminated manuscript, decorated with animal and/or human figures. Sometimes in a scene that illustrates the accompanying text.

■ historical atlas

a book of maps showing the progressive changes that have occurred over a given period of time in a geographic area or in the development of a spatial phenomenon.

■ historical bibliography

the branch of bibliography devoted to the study of the history and methods of book production, including hand-copying, illustration, publishing, printing, papermaking, binding and preservation. Historical bibliography has merged with the field of book history.

hollow

the open space between the cover and the back of a book in which the sections are not glued directly to the cover. A hollow back allows a book to open flat and stay open without damaging the spine.

hollow back

a type of binding in which the cover is not glued to the back of a book, leaving an open space that allows the binding to flex easily when the volume is opened, without cracking the spine. Most hardcover trade editions are bound with a hollow back. Synonymous with loose-back and open back.

holograph

a document written entirely in the handwriting of the person (or persons) to whom it is attributed. A holographic reprint is a reproduction of such a document, made by mechanical means. Also refers to a three-dimensional image of an object recorded on photosensitive film by the pattern of interference made by a split laser beam, in a process called holography.

home page (or homepage)

several meanings. Originally the web page that your browser is set to when it starts up. The more common meaning refers to the main web page for a business, organisation, person or simply the main page out of a collection of web pages

home page

1. the World Wide Web document displayed first when one's browser starts up.

2. the main web page for an individual or organisation.

hyponym

a word or phrase that can be replaced without exception by another, without changing the meaning of a sentence, but not vice versa, for example, asure by blue or sparrow by bird.

i.e.

an abbreviation of the Latin phrase id est meaning 'that is.'

ibid

an abbreviation of the Latin ibidem meaning 'in the same place' used with a page number (or numbers) in footnotes, endnotes and bibliographies to indicate a source that has been cited fully in a preceding note or entry.

ibid.

abbreviation for Latin ibidem, 'in the same place'. Used in references and citations to refer to the last work cited, saving re-typing thc author and title.

icl

inter Campus Loan - the process of having an item brought in from another campus.

icon

1. a small graphic element or symbol displayed on a computer screen, which the user can select with a pointing device such as a mouse to summon a menu of options, access a data file, or initiate a process or operation in an application program that uses a graphical user interface, for ex-

ample, a small image of a trash can or recycle bin to which unwanted documents can be moved for disposal. Also refers to a picture, image, figure, or representation. In Eastern Orthodox religious imagery, a picture of Jesus, Mary, or an apostle or saint. Also spelled ikon or eikon.

2. a pictorial image used in a graphical user interface to represent a program, a command, a link to a Web page, etc. ;

■ iconic document

a publication or other document in which the content is presented in predominantly graphic or pictorial form. Examples include atlases, children's picture books, exhibit catalogues, visual dictionaries, posters, postcards, etc.

■ iconography

the art of illustration or representation by means of pictures, figures, or images, developed to a high degree in the artistic tradition of the Eastern Orthodox faith. Also refers to the study of the pictorial representation of objects or people, in portraits, paintings, photographs, sculpture, coins, etc.and to the result of such study, especially when it takes the form of detailed lists of representations.

■ ideal copy

in analytical bibliography, a detailed description of the most perfect copy of the first impression of an edition, based on close inspection of as many copies as possible, to which all other copies of the same impression and any subsequent impressions, are compared in determining issue and state.

■ imprint

information about the publication of a book; usually, the publisher's name, place and date of publication is provided on the title pageant the printer's name and place is given on the verso of the title page.

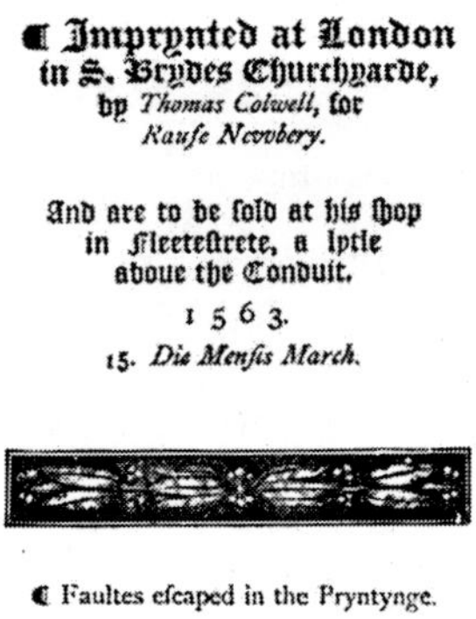

¶ Imprynted at London
in S. Brydes Churchyarde,
by *Thomas Colwell*, for
Raufe Newbery.

And are to be ſold at his ſhop
in Fleeteſtrete, a lytle
aboue the Conduit.

1 5 6 3.

15. *Die Menſis March.*

¶ Faultes eſcaped in the Pryntynge.

■ in press/to be published

in the process of being printed, but not yet available.

in print

a book currently available from the publisher, either as a front list or backlist title, as opposed to a title no longer available.

in process

newly ordered library materials shipped by the vendor and received by the library, but not yet ready for circulation because technical processing has not been completed. In some online catalogues, the phrase 'in process' is added in the temporary catalogue record to indicate the circulation status of a new item that has arrived but is not ready to be checked out. Most libraries will expedite processing at the request of a registered borrower.

isbn

international Standard Book Number

An internationally agreed on standard number that identifies a book uniquely.

issue

to produce books or other printed materials for public sale or distribution.

Also, all the copies of an edition of a book printed from the same setting of type as the first impression, which may include minor variations or revisions such as a new title page, an additional appendix, an updated bibliography, or a slightly different format. Also used synonymously with state to refer to the priority of copies within a first edition. Also refers to all the copies of a periodical published on the same date, bearing the same issue number. Purchase of a subscription entitles the subscriber to receive one copy of each successive issue for a prescribed period of time. In libraries, all the issues for the same publication year may be bound in one or more physical volumes, with the bibliographic volume number stamped on the spine(s), to create a back file.

issue date

the specific date or period (spring, summer, fall, winter) by which a particular issue of a serial publication is identified, usually printed on the front cover and on each page as a running foot.

issue number

the number assigned by the publisher to a separately issued part of a serial publication to distinguish it from other parts published at different times. Issue numbers are assigned consecutively, starting with the first issue of each publication period. When a serial is published in volumes, issue numbers recommence with each volume.

italic

a cursive form of type, first used in an Italian edition of Virgil, which slants heavily to the right, used in combination with roman type for emphasis and to indicate foreign words or phrases in a text. In the preceding sentence, the word 'emphasis' is in italic and in the following sentence, the book title appears in boldface italic. Warren Chappell states in A Short History of the Printed Word (1970) that italic is rooted in a variety of humanistic script known as cancellaresca or 'chancery' that reached its highest state of development in 16th century Italy when rounded letterforms were elongated to become elliptical.

■ jargon

the specialised vocabulary and idioms of a group of people engaged in the same activity or line of work, for example, the MARCese used by library cataloguers in reference to the bibliographic record and its component fields. In a more general sense, speech that is unintelligible or incoherent.

■ jestbook

a collection of jokes, witty anecdotes, epigrams, exempla and ribald tales, usually with didactic endings. Introduced into Europe from the Muslim world during the 8th century, jestbooks enjoyed greatest popularity during the 16th and 17th centuries. Because of their ephemeral nature, few early examples survive. Also spelled jest book. Synonymous with facetiae.

■ jewelled binding

a binding in which the boards are covered in designs done in gold or silver inset with ivory and precious or semi-precious stones, usually with a similarly decorated clasp to keep the vellum leaves of the body pressed firmly together. During the medieval period, this style was used for devotional books commissioned by the Catholic Church and members of the nobility from the 6th century onwards. The lavish use of costly materials was considered an act of religious piety, rather than ostentation and the colours of the gems often had symbolic meaning. Extremely valuable, the rare survivals are sold by the world's most prestigious auction houses.

■ job description

a detailed description of the duties and responsibilities associated with a specific position in an organisation, used in training, performance evaluation and the allocation of workload.

■ job lot

copies of a book or other publication offered by the publisher at lower than list price to a wholesale bookseller known as a jobber, usually to reduce or close out stock of a particular title.

■ jobber

in the United States, a wholesaler that stocks large quantities of new books and nonprint materials (audiobooks, videotapes, music CDs, etc.) issued by various publishers and supplies them to bookstores and libraries on order, usually at a substantial discount (10-40%). Titles out of print from the publisher may still be available in limited quantity from a book jobber. Large jobbers also offer customised services such as continuation orders, approval plans, cataloguing, technical processing, etc. Using a jobber allows a library to operate more efficiently by consolidating book ordering.

joint

in bookbinding, the narrow portion of covering material affixed directly to the endpaper along the groove separating the board from the inlay over the spine, forming the hinge that allows the cover to open and close like a door. A book has a front joint connecting the front board to the spine and a back joint connecting the back board to the spine. On the inside, the hinge is formed by the fold in the endpaper, reinforced in some editions with a cloth strip.

joint author

a person who collaborates with one or more others to produce a work in which all who contribute perform the same function. The contributions of the individual collaborators may not be indicated and are usually not separable. In cataloguing, the main entry is made under the name of the author listed first on the chief source of information (the primary author), with added entries for the other authors, unless the primary responsibility clearly rests with one author. Bibliographic style manuals differ in the maximum number of joint authors named in a citation. Synonymous with co-author.

kelmscott press

a private press founded in 1891 by the architect, designer, writer, calligrapher and typographer William Morris (1834-1896) who sought to revive, in modern book production, the aesthetic of the medieval period and early printing. Although the press survived only until 1894, the 53 books it issued set a very high standard of beauty and craftsmanship.

kerf

a shallow groove cut into the binding edge of the sections of a book, perpendicular to the spine near the head and tail of the text block, to allow the kettle stitching to be recessed. Also spelled cerf.

kermit

an asynchronous communication protocol developed and maintained by the Kermit Project at Columbia University, which enables files to be transferred from one computer system to another. Accurate, flexible and customisable, Kermit includes terminal emulation and can be installed on almost any operating system. Although it is not in the public domain, Columbia University allows Kermit to be used as shareware, but encourages users to purchase the product in support of the Project.

kettle stitch

in hand-binding, a special end stitch taken near the head and foot of each section to lock the sewing thread after it passes down the fold, linking adjacent sections through their folds and producing two rows of kettle stitches perpendicular to the binding edge, one near the top and the other at the bottom of the spine. In some editions, a shallow groove called a kerf is cut into the binding edge at each end of the spine to recess the kettle stitching. Synonymous with catch stitch.

■ kiosk

a small circular pavilion, usually located near the entrance to a library, used for displaying announcements, dust jackets removed from new books, reading lists, comments and suggestions from library users (sometimes with responses from library administration)and other information concerning library operations and programs. Also refers to a free-standing furnishing equipped with a multimedia computer to allow users to retrieve information 'on the run' via a touch screen, used in airports and other public locations to provide directions, scheduling information, etc.

■ kit

a set of related instructional materials in more than one medium, designed to be used as a unit with no single medium predominating, usually in the classroom or in a school library. Kits are often stored in a container to keep the parts together. In academic libraries, they are usually shelved in the curriculum room. Synonymous with multimedia item. This category also includes items consisting of a single-medium package of textual material, such as a set of activity cards.

■ knowledge

information that has been comprehended and evaluated in the light of experience and incorporated into the knawel's intellectual understanding of its subject.

■ known-item search

a search in a library for a specific work, as opposed to a search for any work by a known author or for works on a particular subject. If the title of the work is known, the easiest way to locate a copy is to search a library catalogue or bibliographic database by title. When the user is uncertain of the precise wording of the title, the best strategy may be to search by author's name. If at least 2-3 significant words in the title are known with certainty, a keywords search may retrieve an entry for the work.

■ kraft paper

a heavy, unbleached grade of coarse paper, usually mocha brown in colour, used for paper bags and wrapping paper. In publishing, kraft paper is used for the outer wrapper on magazines to protect the glossy cover from damage in mailing. In binding, a narrow strip of kraft paper may be used as a second lining to reinforce the layer of thin fabric called crash (or super) affixed to the binding edge of the sewn sections as the first lining to hold them firmly together.

kunstlerroman

from the German word Kunstler ('artist') and the French word roman ('novel'), a novel that traces the growth of a writer's creative genius from childhood to maturity, with particular attention to major trials and obstacles and their influence on the development of the artist's character and work (example: A Portrait of the Artist as a Young Man by James Joyce).

kwac

an acronym for Keyword and Context (also known as Keyword alongside Context), an algorithmically generated index in which keywords from the title (and sometimes the text) of a document are printed as headings along the left-hand margin of the page, with the portion of the title or text following each keyword indented under the heading, followed by the portion of the title or text preceding the word.

label

a small paper form on which information can be written, typed, or printed, designed to be affixed to the surface of an item such as a book, usually for purposes of identification or classification. Libraries use labels extensively in technical processing. They are available precut from library suppliers in various colours, shapes and sizes, either blank or preprinted, with or without adhesive backing. Labelling tape is also available for making customised labels mechanically. When labels are used in preservation, they should be acid-free.

labelling

the controversial practice of affixing a warning mark or label to library materials considered unsuitable for young children or that contain language or images which some readers or viewers might find offensive or distressing. The practice is followed by some public television stations in the United States when programs containing adult language or graphic images of sex and/or violence are broadcast at times when children are likely to be watching.

lacuna

a gap in a library collection, usually in the holdings on a specific subject or by a particular author, which the library seeks to fill in order to meet the needs of its users. Also refers to a missing portion of a page, or missing pages, in a manuscript or text, especially when caused by damage or normal wear and tear. Plural: lacunae.

lampoon

a biting satire written in prose or verse, usually directed against an individual in public life or an institution that has become the object of public scrutiny. Lampoons written in verse were popular in England during the 18th century. The form was given new life in 20th century by publications such as the Harvard Lampoon and its close relative, the National Lampoon. Because this form of humour exposes its subject(s) to public ridicule, libel laws impose restraint.

■ language

the system of conventional sounds and symbols developed over time by a specific human population as a means of expressing and exchanging thoughts, feelings, information and knowledge. A language consists of a vocabulary and rules of grammar, syntax and orthography. A national language is the official language of a specific country, used in its government publications and educational institutions. Some countries have more than one national language, for example, Canada where both English and French are officially recognised. In library cataloguing, the language in which a work is written or spoken. A note is made in the bibliographic record only when the language of the text is not apparent from the rest of the bibliographic description, as in the case of a film subtitled in a language different from that of the dialogue or narration. In some online catalogues and bibliographic databases, it is possible to limit search results by language.

■ language dictionary

a dictionary that lists the words of one language, in alphabetical order, with definitions in another. Some language dictionaries are divided into two parts, first listing the words of a language with definations in another and then vice versa.

■ lapsit services

library services and programs designed for very young children (12-24 months old) in conjunction with their adult caregivers, including nursery rhymes, songs, finger plays and storytelling, often with the aid of a flannel board or puppets.

■ laptop

a small portable battery-operated personal computer, usually equipped with a built-in keyboard and mouse and a flat panel monitor that folds over the keyboard to form a cover. Modern research libraries are retrofitting study areas to provide network connectivity for patrons who use laptops and some academic libraries are installing them in classrooms used for bibliographic instruction. Synonymous with notebook.

large paper edition

an edition in which the leaves are larger in size than the trade edition (and usually printed on better quality paper) making the margins wider than normal. Limited and deluxe editions are often printed in this way.

legible

writing or printing that can be easily read or deciphered by the human eye, the opposite of illegible. Legibility is an important consideration in the design of printed material.

legislative history

a chronological account of the steps involved in the passage of a bill into law, including events leading up to the first draft, committee hearings, lobbying efforts, floor debates, compromises, final vote, enactment and any subsequent history, such as a presidential veto or court test.

legislative reference service

an agency or unit of government that provides research assistance to legislatures and other government agencies on issues related to proposed legislation. This function may include assistance in drafting and indexing bills. At the federal level, legislative reference service is provided by Congressional Research Services, a division of the Library of Congress.

lending library

a library or other institution that sends materials on request to another library, usually via interlibrary loan.

letter

in writing and printing, a character or symbol used to represent a speech sound. All the letters of a written language constitute its alphabet. The Latin alphabet used to write the English language contains 26 letters, each with an uppercase and lowercase form. Also refers to a handwritten, typewritten, or printed personal or business message of one or more persons, usually enclosed in an envelope and delivered to the addressee by post or courier.

letter to the editor

a letter, usually printed at the discretion of the publisher on the editorial page of a newspaper or magazine, in which a reader expresses his or her views on the subject of a previously published article or editorial, or on the editorial policy of the publication in general, sometimes followed by a brief response from the editor(s).

letter-by-letter

a method of alphabetisation in which any punctuation marks and divisions are ignored in a heading consisting of two or more words and the heading treated as a single word ('newt' appearing before 'New Testament'). The Chicago Manual of Style recommends a modification in which the method is followed only to the first comma or parenthesis, to keep identically spelled surnames together. Most dictionaries are alphabetised in this fashion. Synonymous with all through and follow through.

■ libel

a written or printed statement or representation intended to expose a person, group of persons, or corporate entity to public ridicule or contempt, or to damage in some other way the reputation of its subject. Also refers to the act of publishing such a statement. Burden of proof is on the plaintiff to show that actual damage occurred.

■ librarian

a professionally trained person responsible for the care of a library and its contents, including the selection, processing and organisation of materials and the delivery of information, instruction and loan services to meet the needs of its users. In an online environment, the role of the librarian is to manage and mediate access to information which may exist only in electronic form.

■ librariana

a catch-all term for the body of information, works and memorabilia that has accumulated on the subject of libraries, librarians and related topics, particularly items of historical interest.

■ librarianship

the profession devoted to applying theory and technology to the creation, selection, organisation, management, preservation, dissemination and utilisation of collections of information in all formats. In the United States, often used synonymously with library science. A person formally trained or certified to perform such services is a librarian.

■ library

from the Latin liber meaning 'book' (in Greek and the Romance languages the corresponding term is bibliotheca). A collection or group of collections of books and/or other materials organised and maintained for use (reading, consultation, study, research, etc.). Institutional libraries, organised to facilitate access by a specific clientele, are staffed by librarians and other personnel trained to provide services to meet user needs. By extension, the room, building, or facility that houses such a collection, usually but not necessarily built for that purpose.

■ library administration

the control and supervision of a library or library system, including planning, budgeting, policy-making, personnel management, public relations and program assessment, with responsibility for results. Also refers collectively to the persons responsible for managing a library, usually a board of trustees or dean, library director and his or her immediate staff.

■ library advocate

a person who appreciates libraries and their role in society, to the extent of speaking and acting publicly in their support, especially when funding and the freedom to read are at stake.

■ library binder

a commercial binder that specialises in serving the needs of libraries. Most libraries regularly send their periodical back files to a library binder to be bound into annual volumes. Special binding may also be needed for heavily used items and trade paperbacks. Library binders are organised in the Library Binding Institute.

■ library binding

an especially strong, durable binding used for periodical back files and for rebinding worn volumes and new paperbound publications for which circulation is expected to remain high over a comparatively long period of time. Includes pre-library binding.

■ library bond

an interest-bearing or discounted security issued by a library district, or by the government entity of which a library or library system is a part, usually to finance the construction and/or renovation of facilities, or some other major capital project. A bond places the library district under a general obligation to pay the bondholder (investor) a specified amount of interest, usually at regular intervals and to repay the principal amount of the loan within a designated period of time. The bond is backed by a majority of voters in the district, who consent to be taxed at a slightly higher rate to raise sufficient revenue to pay the interest and principal on the loan. Bond measures pass more easily in times of prosperity than in economic recession.

■ library card

a small paper or plastic card issued by a library to a registered borrower, which must be presented at the circulation desk in order to check out materials from its collections. Identification is usually required of new applicants. In most libraries in the United States, library cards are barcoded for electronic circulation. Periodic renewal may be required to verify current street address and telephone number. Synonymous with borrower card.

■ library classes

a variety of courses and one-shot classes and workshops offered by the library, numerous 'short courses' on databases, indexes, programs and many subject-specific sessions on request by faculty or students.

■ library closure

the closing of a library or branch in a library system, temporarily or permanently, usually due to budgetary constraints or demographic changes in the area served. Library closings are announced in the news section of American Libraries, the monthly magazine of the American Library Association.

■ **library collection**

the total accumulation of books and other materials owned by a library, catalogued and arranged for ease of access, which often consists of several smaller collections (reference, circulating books, serials, government documents, rare books, special collections, etc.). The process of building a library collection over time is called collection development. Synonymous with holdings.

■ **library conference**

a formal gathering of librarians, library directors and others associated with libraries, for the purpose of meeting colleagues, discussing issues and events and learning about new products, services, technologies and recent developments in the library science and information science profession. Most library associations sponsor regular conferences at which officers are elected, committees and task forces formed, policies formulated, awards announced, etc. Conferees are generally charged a registration fee based on the sections of the conference they plan to attend.

■ **library cooperation**

methods by which libraries and library systems work together for the mutual benefit of their users, including centralised processing, cooperative cataloguing, international exchange of bibliographic information, union catalogues, resource sharing, etc.

■ **library director**

the person who has overall responsibility for supervising the operations of a library or library system, including planning, budgeting, policy-making, personnel management and program assessment. In public libraries, the library director is usually subject to the oversight of a board of trustees; in academic libraries, by a dean of academic affairs or provost.

■ **library discount**

a discount off the list price of a book or other publication, given by most publishers and jobbers on purchases made by an institutional library. Most publishers offer a flat rate, usually 5-10%. Jobbers may link the discount rate to size of order or volume of purchasing. As a general rule, specialised titles are given a shorter discount than trade books, or not discounted at all because of their limited sales potential.

■ **library district**

an officially delineated geographic area in which the residents decide by popular vote whether to provide tax support for a public library or library system, or one of the geographical areas into which a state is divided for the purpose of administering libraries in accordance with a comprehensive state-wide tax plan.

library edition

an edition of a book published in a binding stronger and more durable than the usual publisher's binding, for marketing specifically to libraries, usually more expensive than the trade edition of the same title.

library education

educational programs designed to prepare students for the post-baccalaureate degree, taught by the faculty of a university department known as a library school (or school of librarianship). Modern library education began in 1887 when Melvil Dewey founded the first school for training professional librarians at Columbia University.

library equipment

mechanical and electronic devices purchased by a library for staff use, or to facilitate patron use of its services and collections, including photocopy machines, microform reader-printers, video and CD players, projection equipment, computers and computer peripherals, security devices, etc.

library extension

programs and activities that enable a library or library system to deliver traditional services outside the physical walls of its facilities, including bookmobiles, books-by-mail and direct delivery of library materials to patrons.

library faculty

the professionally trained librarians employed at an academic institution that grants faculty status to librarians. One of the advantages of faculty status is the right to participate in governance. At some institutions, library faculty are members of the same collective bargaining unit as the teaching faculty. Whether they are eligible for tenure and promotion to the same ranks as the teaching faculty depends on the contract governing employment.

library hand

a highly legible, uniform style of handwriting traditionally used by librarians for making entries in manuscript catalogues before the typewriter came into widespread use. With the conversion of card catalogues into files of machine-readable records, catalogues cards have fallen into disuse and handwritten catalogues entries are rarely seen.

library historian

a researcher who writes about the history of libraries and librarianship, from ancient to modern times.

Library History Round Table (LHRT)

a round table of the American Library Association dedicated to facilitating communication among scholars and students of library history, supporting research in library history and addressing current issues of concern to library historians, such as conservation and preservation. LHRT publishes the semi-annual LHRT Newsletter.

library hours

the hours during which a library is open to its users and any days when it is not open, usually posted near the entrance or at the circulation desk. Libraries also make their hours available by telephone and via their Web pages. Because staffing is required to keep a library facility open, hours often reflect budgetary constraints. Most libraries are equipped with a book drop for returning items when the facility is closed.

library humour

jokes, cartoons, anecdotes, unusual reference questions, witticisms, satire, occupational folklore, etc., having to do with libraries and librarianship.

Library Instruction Round Table (LIRT)

a round table of the American Library Association dedicated to promoting formal and informal library instruction in all types of libraries, as a means of helping library users acquire the information literacy skills essential for lifelong learning.

library journal

a professional journal devoted to the publication of articles about library and information science, librarianship and related topics. Most library journals also publish reviews of new publications, including books of professional interest to librarians.

library legislation

laws passed by a federal or state legislative body, pertaining to or affecting the interests of libraries and related institutions. Through their professional associations, librarians and library advocates seek to influence legislative decision-making in ways that will benefit libraries and their users.

library market

the portion of the market for books and other publications generated by sales to libraries, library systems and related organisations such as museums, archives and research institutions. The library market is segmented by type of library (public, academic, school, special, etc.). Publishers and jobbers market their products to libraries by exhibiting at library conferences, advertising in library trade journals and review publications, offering special library discounts and prepublication prices and direct mail advertising (trade catalogues and brochures).

library materials

all the items purchased by a library or library system to satisfy the information needs of its users, including books, periodicals, reference materials, music scores, maps, microforms and nonprint media, as distinct from equipment and supplies. Some libraries include subscriptions to electronic resources in the materials budget, others fund them separately. Except for gifts and special endowments, the acquisition of library materials is normally funded through the operating budget. The rapid escalation of journal subscription prices over the past decade has forced many academic libraries to cancel periodical subscriptions to maintain balance between expenditures for books and serials.

■ library science

the professional knowledge and skill with which recorded information is selected, acquired, organised, stored, maintained, retrieved and disseminated to meet the needs of a specific clientele, usually taught at a professional library school qualified to grant the post-baccalaureate degree.

■ library staff

the entire group of paid employees responsible for the operation and management of a library or library system, including its director, librarians, paraprofessionals, technical assistants, clerical personnel and pages or student assistants. In academic libraries at institutions that grant librarians faculty status, a distinction is usually made between faculty members and nonfaculty staff. In other types of libraries, a distinction may be made between professionally trained librarians and support staff. Volunteers are not considered part of the staff because they are unpaid.

■ library statistics

numerical data assembled, classified and tabulated to present useful facts and information about the operation of a library or library system, or about the activities of libraries at the local, state, provincial, or national level, usually in the form of a periodic report.

■ library supplies

expendable materials such as labels, book cards and pockets, date due slips, rubber stamps, mending tape, magnetic strips, plastic sleeves, laminate, paper for printing and photocopying, etc., which a library must order from a library supplier in order to prepare new items for circulation, maintain collections and provide services.

■ library survey

a written or oral question-and-answer instrument designed to elicit feedback from library users. Library surveys are administered by staff, or by an outside agency, to determine how well the library's services, programs and collections meet user needs and any objectives established by the library administration and/or governing institution. They are also used to generate data in library research. Also refers to the report produced as the result of such a study.

■ library system

a group of libraries administered in common, for example, a central library and its branches or auxiliary outlets. Also, a group of independently administered libraries joined by formal or informal agreement to achieve a common purpose. Under such an arrangement, each library is considered an affiliate.

■ library tour

a guided walk through a library facility, usually conducted by a librarian or library assistant, to orient new users to the location of services and resources. Some libraries have installed online library tours on their Web sites, which include clickable floor plans linked to photographs and descriptive text. Not to be confused with bibliographic instruction.

■ library trustee

a member of an appointed or elected board responsible for overseeing the growth and development of a library or library system, including long-range planning and policy-making, public relations and fund-raising. Trustees are usually library advocates but may sometimes be political appointees.

■ library use only

a circulation status code written on or affixed to a physical item in a library collection and entered in the item record in the catalogue, indicating that it is available for use within the walls of the library, but may not be checked out and removed from the premises except by special arrangement. The use of reference books, periodical indexes and in some cases bound and/or unbound periodicals is generally restricted to the library. Use of items in special collections, such as rare books and manuscripts, may even be restricted to a designated room or area of the library.

■ libretto

the words or text to which a cantata, oratorio, opera, operetta, or other work for the musical stage is set, often published in the form of a small booklet for enthusiasts who wish to follow along while attending a performance or listening to a sound recording. The person who writes a libretto is the librettist. To find librettos online, try a keywords search on the term 'librettos' in Yahoo!

■ limiting

a feature of a well-designed online catalogue or bibliographic database that allows the user to employ various parameters to restrict the retrieval of entries containing the terms included in the search statement. Limits may be set before a search is executed, after results are displayed, or both, depending on the design of the system. Limiters are not standardised but typically include: publication date, material type, language, full-text, peer-reviewed (journal articles)and locally held.

■ limp binding

a book bound without boards in flexible leather, vellum, or cloth covers, lined or unlined, a style used mainly for diaries, devotional works and light verse. The squares in limp binding often extend further beyond the edges of the sections than in a normal binding.

■ line art

in printing, an illustration of reproduction quality done in black-and-white, as opposed to a half-tone in which the range of tonal values in the original is rendered by converting the image into a field of minutely graded dots.

■ line drawing

a drawing executed entirely in lines without the use of shading, hatching, or some other graphic technique to add depth or volume to the image. Cartoons, caricatures and diagrams are often done in this style.

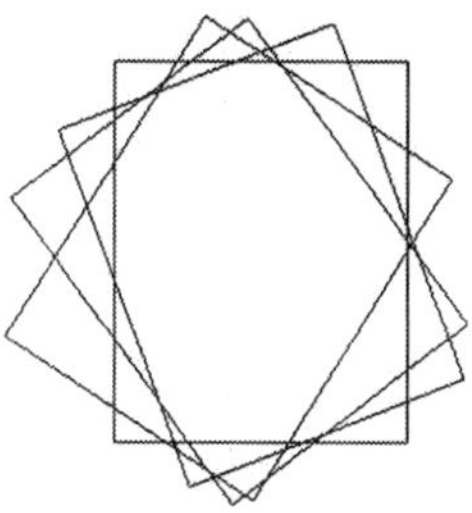

■ line-item budget

a method of budgeting used in some libraries and library systems in which anticipated expenditures are divided into discrete functional categories called 'lines' (salaries and wages, materials, equipment, etc.) for the purpose of systematically allocating resources and tracking operating expenditures.

■ lining

materials applied to the binding edge of a book with adhesive, following rounding and backing, to hold the sewn sections together securely, usually a piece of thin, loosely woven fabric called crash (gauze, mull, super), followed by a strip of kraft paper as a second layer in better quality bindings. Synonymous in this sense with back-lining. The term is also used synonymously with endpapers.

■ link

a direct connection in a hypertext document to the Internet address (URL) of another document, embedded as a word or phrase in the text, or appearing as a symbol, icon, or other graphic element which can be activated by the click of a mouse or some other pointing device. Text links usually appear underlined and in blue on the computer screen. A link is broken if it does not take the user to the desired destination when clicked. Link rot is a colloquial expression for the tendency of links to become broken due to address changes and the removal of HTML files from public access. The remedy is regular link checking. Synonymous with hyperlink.

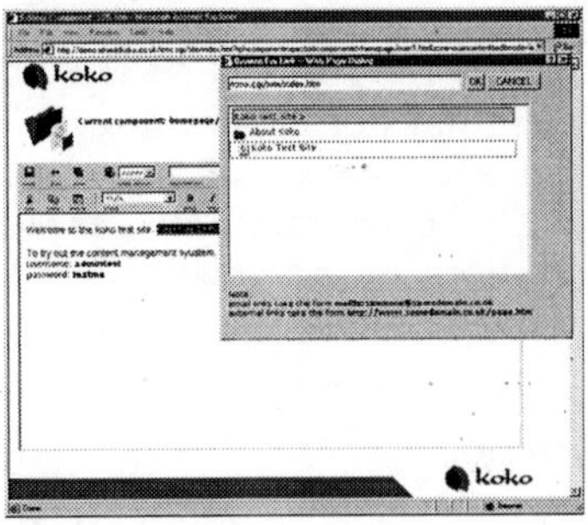

■ link checking

the process of testing the links in an HTML document to determine if they are functioning properly. Software has been developed to check links automatically. Without regular checking and updating, URL changes and dead links may accumulate in a Web page.

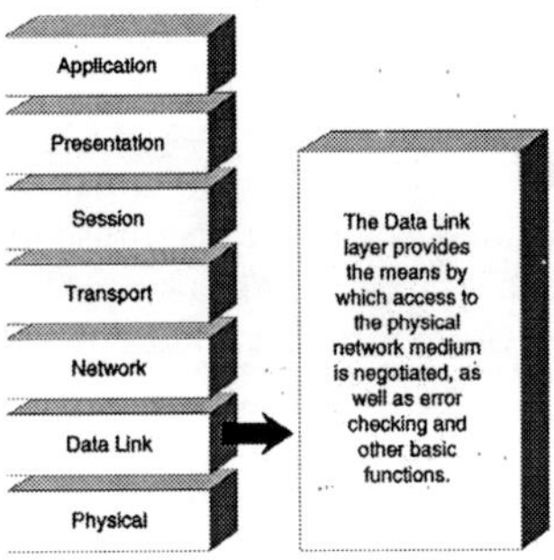

■ literary agent

an organisation or person in the business of offering professional advice to writers on the suitability of manuscripts for publication. An agent may also provide guidance and/or assistance in locating and selecting a publisher, negotiating a book contract, arranging the sale of subsidiary rights and handling the business of authorship in general, usually in exchange for a commission paid by the author, or a portion of the proceeds derived from the work. A literary agent may also act on behalf of a publisher to find works to fill a specific need. Not all authors use an agent—some prefer to deal directly with the publisher. Directory information for literary agents is available in the reference serials Literary Market Place and Writer's Market.

■ literary award

a special honour and/or reward given to an author or illustrator for creating a specific work, or in recognition of a distinguished career, usually based on the decision of a qualified panel of judges. Most literary awards and prizes given annually are funded by private individuals or foundations. Rewards may include a medal, grant and/or cash prise. Recognition usually boosts the sale of the recipient's works and can mean larger advances on royalties from publishers.

■ literary warrant

the quantity of works that have been written on a specific subject or topic. In library cataloguing, the development of portions of a classification system in response to the content of materials requiring classification. In indexing, the addition of a subject heading or content descriptor to an indexing language, based on the frequency of occurrence of the concept it represents in the title or text of documents indexed.

■ literary work

a nonsacred work written in literary form (poem, play, essay, novel, story), recognised and appreciated by educated readers and lovers of literature for the superior quality of its style and treatment of an enduring theme.

■ literati

men of letters. Scholarly, learned and/or well-educated people.

■ literature

enduring works of poetry or prose that express ideas and emotions of universal human interest in a form and style embodying excellence. Also refers to the body of works written and/or produced on a subject, in a given field of inquiry, or in a specific language, country, period, etc.

■ literature guide

a reference work that describes special features of the scholarly literature in a given discipline, including important standard reference materials and serials.

■ literature review

1. a literature review is an essay or is part of the introduction to an essay, research report, or thesis. It provides an overview and critical analysis of relevant published scholarly articles, research reports, books, theses etc on the topic or issue to be investigated. 2. a comprehensive survey of the works published in a field of study, or related to a particular line of research, usually in the form of a bibliographic essay or annotated list of references in which attention is drawn to the most significant works. An annual review is a form of serial devoted entirely to the publication of literature reviews. Synonymous with review of the literature. 3. Also, in scholarly journals that publish original research in the physical and social sciences, the first section of each article is usually devoted to a review of the previously published literature on the subject, with references in the text to a list of works cited at the end.

■ literature search

1. a systematic and exhaustive search for published material on a specific topic.

2. an exhaustive search for published information on a subject, conducted systematically using all available bibliographic finding tools, aimed at locating as much existing material on the topic as possible, an important initial step in any serious research project.

■ lithography

the process of creating illustrations or prints by drawing on a zinc plate or the surface of fine-grained limestone with a water-repellent substance to which ink adheres, a technique developed in Germany in the early part of the 19th century. When the stone is wetted, ink is repelled by the moist areas and attracted only by the design. An impression is made by applying dampened paper to the stone under pressure. In chromolithography, separate stones are used to produce multiple colours.

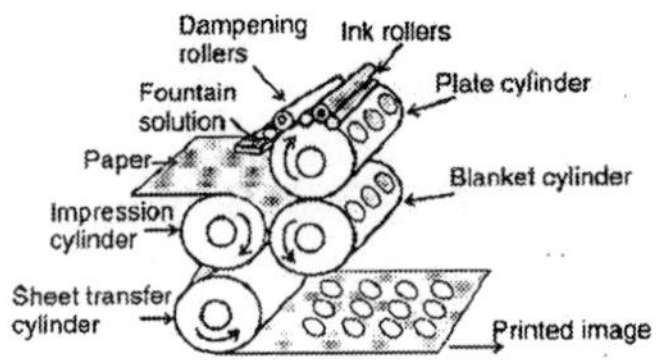

■ litterateur

a man of letters, especially one who devotes himself to the study and writing of literature in the capacity of an amateur or dilettante.

■ little magazine

a periodical of limited circulation, devoted to experimental or avant-garde poetry, fiction, essays, humour, photography and art. Little magazines flourished in the United States, Britain and France during the 1920s, but most disappeared before the beginning of World War II. Desktop publishing has given new life to this form of publication. According to Magazines for Libraries, over 5,000 little magazines are currently published in the United States, with some available online. For libraries, indexing is a problem because they fall outside the mainstream press. Synonymous with literary magazine.

■ liturgical work

a book used in the worship services of an organised religion. Liturgical works are entered under the name of the body with which they are associated (example: Catholic Church). If a well-established title exists in English, it is used as the uniform title (example: Breviary). If there is no well-known title in English, or the name of the body is given in another language, a brief title is entered in the language of the liturgy, followed by a word or phrase in parentheses indicating the variant or special text (if applicable), for example, Book of hours (Ms. Rohan).

■ local bibliography

a bibliography of books and other materials about a specific geographic area smaller than a country, usually including material about the history, geography, architecture and environment of the area, as well as works about the people born or residing in it. Useful in genealogical research.

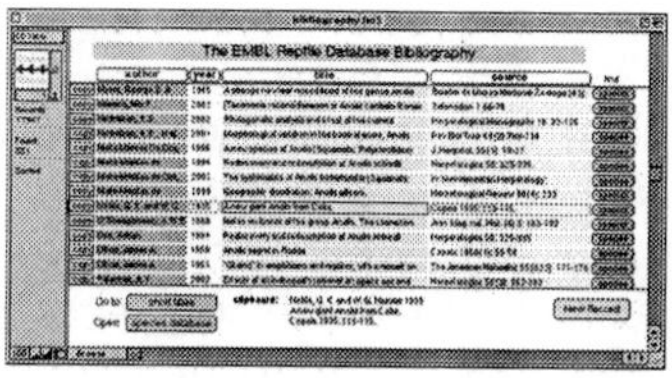

■ local collection

a library collection of books, prints, maps, photographs and other materials related to a specific geographic area and its inhabitants, usually the community in which the library is located, useful in historical and genealogical research.

■ location symbol

a code consisting of a few letters or a word displayed in a catalogue record or added to an entry in a bibliography, indicating the specific location or collection in which the item is shelved (example: Ref for items in the reference stacks). In a union catalogue, location symbols are used to indicate the libraries in the system or consortium owning at least one copy of the item. Synonymous with location code.

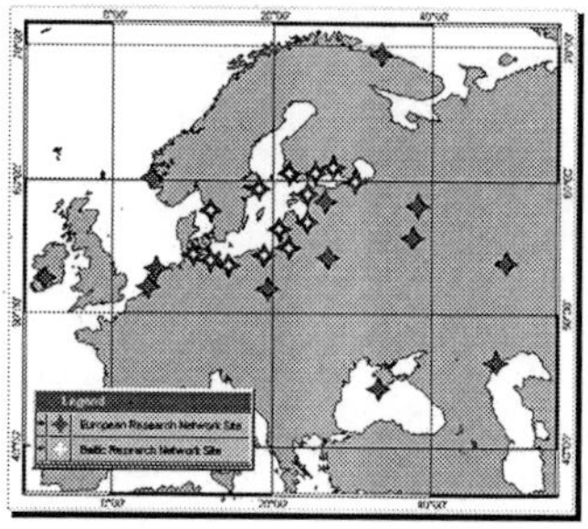

■ lyric

in classical Greece, a song or poem performed to the accompaniment of a harp-like stringed instrument called a lyre. In contemporary usage, a relatively short poem in which a single speaker expresses a personal emotion or state of mind, as opposed to narrating a sequence of events. The form includes sonnets, elegies, odes and hymns.

Aerosmith - I Don't Want To Miss A Thing

I could stay awake just to hear you breathing
Watch you smile while you are sleeping
While you're far away and dreaming
I could spend my life in this sweet surrender
I could stay lost in this moment, forever
Every moment spent with you is a moment I treasure

Don't wanna close my eyes
I don't wanna fall asleep
'Cause I'd miss you baby
And I don't wanna miss a thing
'Cause even when I dream of you
The sweetest dream would never do
I'd still miss you baby
And I don't wanna miss a thing

Lying close to you
Feeling your heart beating
And I'm wondering what your dreaming
Wondering if it's me you're seeing
Then I kiss your eyes
And thank God we're together
I just wanna stay with you in this moment forever, forever and ever

I don't wanna close my eyes
I don't wanna fall asleep
'Cause I'd miss you baby
And I don't wanna miss a thing
'Cause even when I dream of you
The sweetest dream would never do
I'd still miss you baby
And I don't wanna miss a thing

I don't wanna miss one smile
I don't wanna miss one kiss
I just wanna be with you right here with you
Just like this
I just wanna hold you close
A feel your heart so close to mine
And just stay here in this moment, for all the rest of time

Don't wanna close my eyes
Don't wanna fall asleep
'Cause I'd miss you baby
And I don't wanna miss a thing
'Cause even when I dream of you
The sweetest dream would never do
I'd still miss you baby
And I don't wanna miss a thing

■ lyrics

the words of a song or musical drama, as opposed to its music.

In libraries, songs and musicals are catalogued under the name of the composer, with an added entry under the name of the lyricist when the words are written by a person other than the composer.

■ M.L.I.S.

in the United States, the post-baccalaureate degree of Master of Library and Information Science, granted by a library school upon completion of a required course of study. To be considered for a professional position in most public and academic libraries in the United States, a candidate must have earned either an M.L.I.S. or M.L.S. degree.

■ M.L.S.

in the United States, the post-baccalaureate degree of Master of Library Science, granted by a library school upon completion of a required course of study. To be considered for a professional position in most public and academic libraries in the United States, a candidate must have earned either an M.L.S. or M.L.I.S. degree.

■ magazine

1. a popular interest periodical usually containing articles on a variety of topics, written by various authors in a nonscholarly style. Most magazines are heavily illustrated, contain advertising and are printed on glossy paper. Articles are usually short (less than five pages long), frequently unsigned and do not include a bibliography or list of references for further reading. Most magazines are issued monthly or weekly for sale at newsstands, in bookstores and by subscription. English-language magazines are listed by subject in Magazines for Libraries published by R. R. Bowker. Abbreviated mag. Also refers to a rectangular slotted container designed to hold a sequence of slides, queued for use in a slide projector.

2. a periodical, generally with a more 'popular' style and presentation than a research journal. Usually, magazine articles are authored by staff writers for an audience of the general public or interested amateurs in a given field (rather than by researchers for their peers) and edited by a magazine employee rather than an independent board of scholars. Style tends to be engaging and eye-catching and magazines often include substantial advertising. Pagination usually starts over at '1' with each issue.

■ magazine pagination

numbering the pages of a periodical, starting with one at the beginning of each issue. Magazines and trade journals are usually paginated in this way, making it more difficult to locate a specific article in a bound volume by page numbers, compared with a publication that uses journal pagination.

■ Management Information System (MIS)

a computer-based information system developed and maintained by a commercial enterprise to integrate data from all its departments (product development, production and inventory, marketing and sales, personnel administration, etc.) to support managerial and supervisory decision-making with real time analysis. MIS systems are designed to track progress towards achievement of the company's goals and objectives, including the identification of problems or obstacles that must be resolved by upper-level management. In the plural, the term refers to the study and teaching of such systems. Courses on MIS are offered as a major at some business schools in the United States.

■ mint

in the antiquarian book trade, a copy in the same immaculate, unaltered condition as when it was first published, new and virtually unused—the highest possible grade in any assessment of condition. Used books in mint condition command a higher price than copies showing signs of wear. Synonymous with as new and pristine.

■ multimedia

a document or program that integrates text, graphics, audio and video.

■ multipart volume

a work published in two or more physically separate parts that together constitute a single bibliographic volume. Reference works too large to be bound as a single volume are published in this manner.

■ multiple access

more than one point of access to a file of data (example: a library catalogue or bibliographic database searchable by author, title, subject, keywords, etc.), as opposed to a resource that has

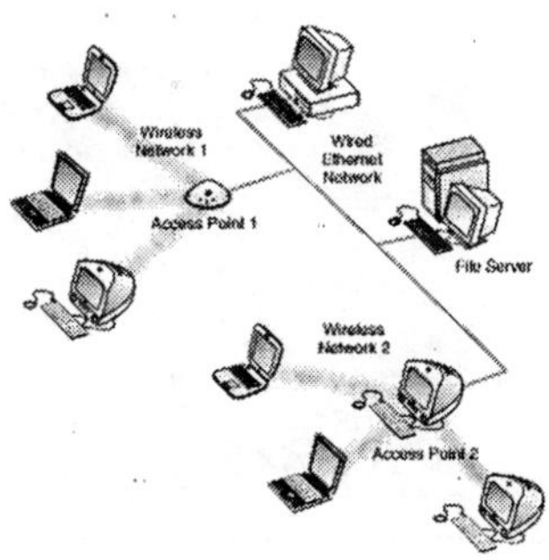

only one point of access (example: the headwords in a printed dictionary of the words of a language).

■ multiple user access

a file of data that can be used independently by more than one person at the same time, for example, a multi-volume print encyclopaedia as opposed to a single-volume dictionary. Access to online catalogues, bibliographic databases and full-text electronic resources by more than one simultaneous user may be governed by licensing agreement.

■ music library

a library containing a collection of materials on music and musicians, including printed and manuscript music scores, music periodicals, recorded music (CDs, audiocassettes, phonograph records, etc.), books about music and musicians, program notes, discographies and music reference materials.
Music collections in public libraries are selected and maintained for lifelong learning and leisure pursuits. Academic and conservatory libraries provide resources for music study and

research, including original source materials. National libraries offer unique and often rare musical heritage collections.

■ mystery

a popular novel, story, or drama about an unusual event or occurrence, such as a murder or disappearance, that remains so secret or unexplained as to excite popular curiosity and interest. The plot in mystery fiction often hinges on an attempt by a sleuth to uncover the truth. The Sherlock Holmes stories of Sir Arthur Conan Doyle are classic examples. Subgenres include detective fiction and suspense.

■ mystery play

a form of medieval religious drama, popular from the 14th to the 16th century, usually performed on a mobile wagon from a script based on a story from the Scriptures or a sequence of episodes from biblical history. In England, the performance of mystery plays was often financed by the local trade guilds in connection with important feast days, such as Corpus Christi.

■ myth

from the classical Greek word mythos meaning 'story.' A narrative rooted in the traditions of a specific culture, capable of being understood and appreciated in its own right, but at the same time part of a system of stories (mythology) transmitted orally from one generation to the next to illustrate man's relationship to the cosmos. In traditional societies, myths often serve as the basis for social customs and observances. Many of the archetypes of classical Greek mythology recur in the literature of Western culture and some have been appropriated by disciplines outside the arts and humanities. Some scholars have argued that mythic thinking is integral to human consciousness and that myths are simply a manifestation of the way culture is created by the human mind. Dictionaries of mythology are available in the reference section of public and academic libraries.

name authority file

an authorised list giving the preferred form of entry for names (personal, corporate and geographic) used as headings in a library catalogued any cross-references from variant forms.

name index

a list of the personal names appearing of a work, arranged alphabetically by surname, with reference to the page number(s) on which each name can be found in the text. Not all books have a separate name index—personal names may be included in a general index or in the subject index. When present in a single-volume work, the name index is part of the back matter. In a multi-volume work, it is usually found at the end of the last volume.

netiquette

1. a neologism formed by shortening the phrase network etiquette. The rules of civility and good manners that apply to communication via the Internet, an environment in which the visual cues available in face-to-face communication and the auditory cues perceptible in voice communication are lacking.
2. internet etiquette; unwritten rules of conduct governing communication over the Internet.

netspeak

the argot of Internet enthusiasts.

novice

a person who uses an unfamiliar computer system for the first time, as opposed to an experienced user. In the design of Web sites and graphical user interfaces, libraries and computer software companies may conduct usability tests to judge the user-friendliness of the new system. In a more general sense, any patron for whom the procedures of a library are new and often confusing. Special consideration must be shown at the reference desk.

■ number book

a form of book, common in the 18th and 19th centuries, published in numbered parts or instalments, usually at regular intervals.

■ number building

in Dewey Decimal Classification, the cataloguer must construct a class number when no existing class in the schedules precisely represents the subject of the work. This is done by adding to a base number, notation found in the table of standard subdivisions (or in one of the other tables), or from another part of the main schedules, according to established rules, for example, the addition of the decimal fraction .5 to the base number 020 to create the class 020.5 for periodicals in the library and information sciences.

■ numbered copy

a copy of a book published in a consecutively numbered limited edition, bearing a copy number assigned by hand by the publisher and an indication of the total number of copies printed, usually in the colophon or in a certificate of issue on the verso of the leaf preceding title page.

■ numeral

in writing and printing, a character or set of characters used to represent a number (example: the Arabic numeral 9 or roman numeral IX).

■ numeric and/or alphabetic, chronological, or other designation

in library cataloguing, the material specific details area of the bibliographic description in which the publication history of a serial is given, usually in the form of an open or closed entry, as distinct from the holdings note indicating the issues owned by a specific library or library system.

■ ode

a relatively long lyric poem of elaborate structure derived from songs performed by the chorus in ancient Greek dramatic performances, written to eulogise a hero (or heroes). In English literature, the object of praise may be a person or category of person, an abstraction or an inner state expressed symbolically (example:

Ode on a Grecian Urn by John Keats).

off the record

a statement or comment that the speaker does not wish recorded or made publicly known. At meetings, such remarks are not included in the minutes and may not be expressed if the proceedings are tape-recorded.

off-duty

time when an employee is 1) scheduled but not working (usually on a break or lunch hour), 2) not scheduled on a shift, or 3) not working if employed part-time. Off-duty public services librarians are sometimes recognised as staff when passing through a public area of the library and approached by patrons in need of assistance. The opposite of on-duty.

on-duty

time when an employee is expected to be at work, particularly the hours of a scheduled shift at a public service point, such as the circulation desk or reference desk. The opposite of off-duty.

one-act play

a form of modern drama in which all the action occurs in a single act . Established as a literary form by the experimental theatre movement that began in the late 19th century, the one-act play is usually short (20-50 minutes performed), with a limited number of characters, no breaks in the action and little if any change of scene, analogous to the short story in narrative fiction.

one-of-a-kind book

a book created in a single copy, as opposed to a production book issued in multiple copies. Art books created for display are usually of this type.

one-on-one

services provided by a librarian or other library staff member working alone with a single patron, usually involving a high degree of interaction, as in most transactions at the reference desk. Synonymous with one-to-one.

optical spacing

in typesetting, the technique of adjusting the distance between the individual letters in a line of capitals to create the optical illusion of even spacing, which requires placing some letter combinations closer together than others.

option

the privilege of purchasing the rights in a book or manuscript from the copyright holder for a specific purpose (example: the right to adapt a novel or short story for performance on stage or screen), usually granted for a fixed period of time designated in a legally binding agreement, in exchange for some form of compensation. In computing, a choice available to the user in the form of a menu item, button, or icon appearing in the toolbar or window of a graphical user interface, or as a text link embedded in a Web page.

■ orchestral score

the full score of a musical work composed for orchestra, giving the parts for all the instruments.

■ order cancelled (oc)

a term used on an invoice to indicate that the order for a book or other item has been cancelled by the seller, usually because copies are no longer available.

■ order record

in acquisitions, a record created and attached to the bibliographic record for an item at the time it is ordered, containing information needed to process the order (name of selector, budgetary fund, vendor, order date, estimated price, purchase order number, date received, special handling notes, date catalogedand pertinent characteristics of the item). After the item is received and processed, the order record is eventually purged.

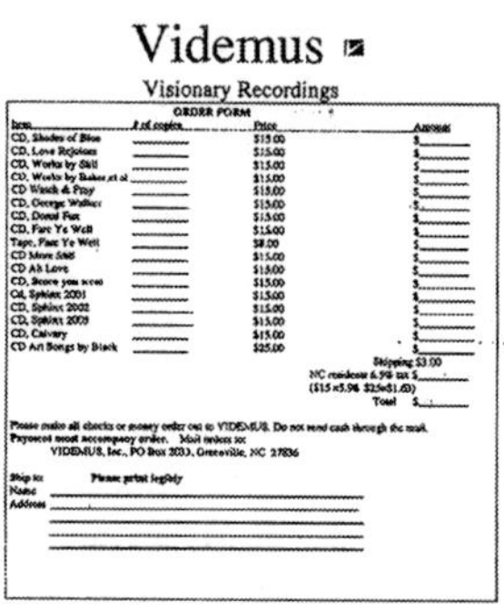

■ organisational culture

the prevailing values, expectations and conventions within an organisation or institution, often unspoken and persistent. Advancement may depend on sensitivity to such norms.

■ original

in literature, a work as written by the author or in the author's own words. In art, a finished work as completed by the artist and ready for reproduction. In science, a study that produces results never before reported, in some cases through the use of a new methodology or research design. In reprography, the source document from which the first copy is made or in some cases the first copy itself. In a more general sense, something new and fresh, not copied or based on a pre-existing model. Abbreviated orig.

■ original binding

a term used in the antiquarian book trade to indicate that a book retains the binding in which it was first issued, which may show definite signs of wear if the volume is an old one.

■ original cataloguing

1. preparation of the bibliographic record for an item without the aid of a pre-existing catalogue record for the same edition, more time-consuming for the cataloguer than copy cataloguing.
2. preparing catalogue information directly from the item in hand, rather than obtaining the

data from another source. Original cataloguing is labour-intensive and generally used only when the information is not otherwise available.

■ outreach

library programs and services designed to meet the information needs of users who are unserved or underserved, for example, those who are visually impaired, institutionalised, not fluent in the national language, illiterate, or marginalised in some other way. Large public libraries often have an outreach librarian responsible for providing such services.

■ outsourcing

the contracting of library services formerly performed in-house to an outside service provider, usually a for-profit enterprise. Part of a recent trend in the United States in the direction of privatising government services, outsourcing has affected technical services to a greater extent than public services in libraries. Cost-effectiveness is the justification most often heard for this controversial management practice. One disadvantage is that in decisions requiring judgment, an outside contractor may lack familiarity with local conditions and practices. Outsourcing has generated the least amount of controversy in conservation and preservation (particularly binding and reformatting), purchasing catalogue records in machine-readable form, acquisitions plans (approval plans, blanket order plans, subscription agents, etc.), physical processing, retrospective conversion and library automation systems. However, proposals to outsource cataloguing and selection and to privatise federal and public libraries have met greater resistance.

■ padded envelope

a flexible wrapper made of heavy-duty kraft paper and lined with soft fiber or air bubbles to protect items in shipment. Used extensively in interlibrary loan, padded envelopes are available from library suppliers in various sizes and are reusable if opened carefully. Synonymous with padded mailer.

■ page

one side of a leaf in a manuscript, book, periodical, or other printed publication, numbered or unnumbered. The right-hand page in an opening is the recto, the left-hand page the verso. Abbreviated p. and pp. (plural). Also refers to a library staff member responsible for delivering materials from closed stacks and assigned the routine task of general stack maintenance (reshelving, shelf reading, etc.). Also, to call a person by name over a public address system in a large facility, a practice avoided in libraries to minimise distraction.

■ page break

the point in a text at which one page ends and the next page begins, indicated in most word processing software by a horizontal broken line across the screen.

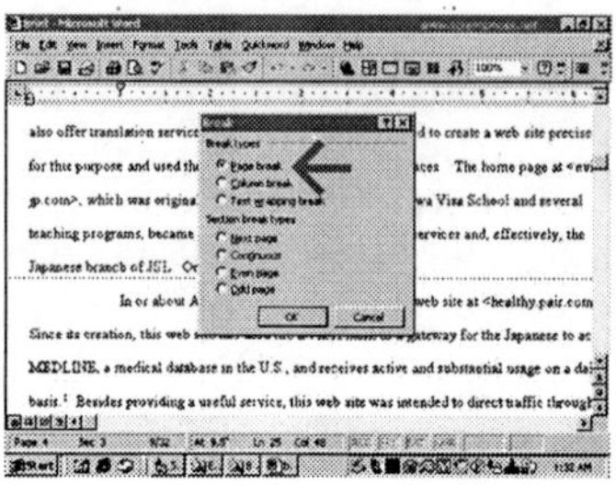

■ palimpsest

a manuscript written on parchment or vellum on which earlier writings, only partially or imperfectly erased, are still faintly visible. It was common practice, prior to the invention of paper, to reuse parchment and vellum because good quality writing material was comparatively expensive and often in short supply. A double palimpsest is one that has been erased twice. The study of palimpsests has enabled researchers to recover portions of texts and in some cases entire works, otherwise lost to history.

■ peer review

1. a formal process whereby articles submitted to a journal or conference are sent to several established scholars in that field of study. These reviewers may suggest improvements before deciding if the article should be published or included in the conference.
2. the process in which the author of a book, article, software program, etc., submits his or her work to experts in the field for critical evaluation, usually prior to publication, a standard procedure in scholarly publishing. In computer programming, source code may be certified by its owner or licenser as open source to encourage development through peer review.
3. said of a scholarly journal that requires an article to be submitted to a process of critical evaluation by one or more experts on the subject, known as referees, responsible for determining if the subject of the article falls within the scope of the publication and for evaluating originality, quality of research, clarity of presentation, etc. Changes may be suggested to the author(s) before an article is finally accepted for publication. In evaluation for tenure and promotion, academic librarians may be given publishing credit only for articles accepted by peer-reviewed journals. Some bibliographic databases allow search results to be limited to peer-reviewed journals. Synonymous with juried and refereed.

■ pen name

a name used by an author other than his or her real name, usually adopted to conceal identity. A pen name can be an allonym (name of an actual person other than the author), a fictitious pseudonym, a pseudonym based on the author's real name, or a word or phrase that is not a personal name (Spy for Sir Leslie Ward). Pen names were used more commonly during the 19th century when writing was not as respectable as it is today and therefore considered an unsuitable occupation for women. Some authors write under more than one pen name, adopting a different name when writing in a new genre or introducing a new lead character (or set of characters) in a series.

■ pendant

an additional narrative, statement, or composition that completes or complements another work, but is independent of it, for example, an essay illuminating the historical basis of a satirical work.

■ pin

an acronym for Personal Identification Number, a code used in automated systems to identify authorised users. Whether the PIN is created by or issued to the user depends on the policy governing access to the system. The practice originated in the banking industry and is used in some libraries and library systems to verify that a patron is registered to use electronic resources restricted by licensing agreement.

■ plagiarism

1. taking, using and passing off as your own, the ideas or words of another. This is the case even when you cite the source in the body of your text or in your references, or both.
2. from the Latin plagiarius meaning 'kidnapper.' Copying or closely imitating the work of another writer or composer with the intention of passing the results off as original work. In most colleges and universities, instructors impose serious penalties on students who plagiarise the works of others. To avoid plagiarism, it is best to express an idea in one's own words. When it is necessary to paraphrase closely or quote, the source should be cited in a footnote or endnote. Submission of a term paper purchased ready-made from an online term paper mill is considered plagiarism at most colleges and universities and astute professors keep abreast of the latest techniques for detecting this form of cheating.

■ plagiary

work offered as original which has, in fact, been copied (plagiarised) from another source, usually without permission.

■ pocket dictionary

a dictionary of the words of a language, published in inexpensive paperback edition. Mostly it contains no more than 30,000 to 55,000 words and are small enough to be carried conveniently in a pocket. Some include a thesaurus (example: The Pocket Oxford Dictionary and Thesaurus). Foreign language dictionaries are often published in small format for the convenience of students and travellers.

■ **pocket edition**

a small, inexpensive portable octavo edition, usually no larger than 6 3/4 x 4 1/4 inches in size, called a paperback when bound in paper covers.

■ **pouncing**

smoothing a new piece of parchment with a pumice stone to prepare the surface for writing, or using the same abrasive technique to remove writing from a previously used piece of parchment, so that another text can be written on it. The result of the erasure is called a palimpsest.

■ **precis**

a concise abridgment or summary that captures the essential thought(s) or idea(s) expressed in a longer work and retains something of the original tone and spirit.

■ **precision**

in information retrieval, a measure of search effectiveness, expressed as the ratio of relevant records or documents retrieved from a database to the total number retrieved in response to the query, for example, in a database containing 100 records relevant to the topic 'book history,' a search retrieving 50 records, 25 of which are relevant to the topic, would have 50% precision (25/50). Synonymous with relevance ratio.

■ **preconference**

a mini-conference scheduled in advance of a longer conference, usually on the preceding day (or days) for attendees who wish to spend additional time meeting with colleagues. Most preconferences are organised around a central theme which may or may not be related to that of the main conference. The theme is usually addressed by a panel, rather than a keynote speaker, with break-out sessions on related topics. Preconferees are normally charged an additional fee at registration.

■ **printout**

text, images, or other data from a computer file, printed as output on paper or some other printing surface, using a peripheral device called a printer.

■ prior publication

a work submitted to a publisher after it has already been published, usually in a different form, for example, an article initially published in a journal, later submitted by the author as a chapter in a book. Whether electronic theses and dissertations constitute, prior publication is an issue currently in debate. The policy of a publishing company with regard to prior publication is usually stated in its guidelines for contributors.

■ quadrennial

issued every four years. Also refers to a serial publication issued every four years.

■ quads

nickname for USGS topographical maps, or 'quadrangle' maps, so named because of the grid pattern they are based on.

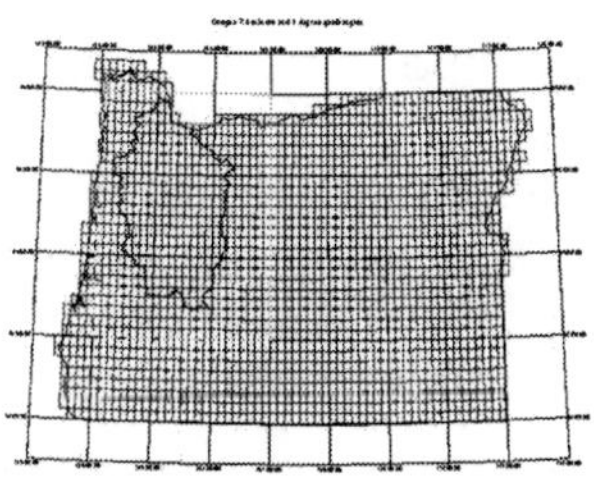

■ qualification

evidence that a person applying for employment has passed the requisite examinations, or acquired the education, experience and skills necessary to meet the requirements stated in the position description. Usually used in the plural: qualifications.

■ quarto

a book, approximately 13 inches in height, made by folding a full sheet of book paper in two right-angle folds, producing signatures of four leaves (eight pages). The precise size of each leaf in a quarto edition depends on the size of the original sheet. Some early editions are known by the number of leaves in their sections, for example, the Quarto Edition of Shakespeare's plays.

■ quasi-synonym

a word or phrase not precisely the same in meaning as another term, which is nevertheless treated as synonymous in a given indexing language, for example, the term 'Library science' used for 'Librarianship' in the Library of Congress Subject Headings list. Synonymous with near-synonym.

■ quatern book

in hand-binding, the binder traditionally bound the thirteenth book at no charge, presumably as an incentive to place larger binding orders, but by the early 19th century, this custom was restricted in England to all the copies of a single title delivered to the bindery at the same time and was not carried over into machine-binding.

■ quaternion

in bookbinding, a gathering consisting of four sheets of paper, parchment, or vellum folded once to create eight leaves, used in assembling some manuscript books and early printed books.

■ **quinquennial**

issued very five years. Also refers to a serial publication issued every five years (example: Biography and Genealogy Master Index).

■ **quinternion**

in bookbinding, a gathering consisting of five sheets of paper, parchment, or vellum folded once to create ten leaves, used in assembling some manuscript books and early printed books.

■ **quire**

originally referred to a gathering of four sheets of printing paper, forming eight leaves or sixteen pages, convenient for hand-sewn books in which the leaves were made of parchment. When paper came into widespread use after the invention of movable type, the fact that it was thinner meant more sheets could be included in a gathering. In modern usage, the word quire is synonymous with gathering, section and signature, particularly when unfolded. Also refers to one-twentieth of a ream, equal to 24 sheets of handmade paper or 25 sheets of machine-made paper.

■ **quorum**

the minimum number of members who must be present for business to be conducted at a meeting governed by the rules of parliamentary procedure. When a quorum is not present, a meeting may proceed without formally transacting business.

■ **quotation**

the copying of words of text originally published elsewhere. Direct quotations generally appear in quotation marks and end with a citation.

■ **rag paper**

paper made from cotton and/or linen rags, stronger and more permanent than paper made from wood or most other fibres, but also more expensive. Rag

content is usually indicated as a percentage. Paper made from 100% rag fiber is called all-rag.

■ ragged

refers to a page of type with lines of variable length, usually ragged right, set flush (aligned) with the left-hand margin but unjustified on the right, as in the lines of a poem.

■ raised bands

narrow, slightly elevated ridges visible across the width of the spine of a hand-bound book, produced by cords binding the sections together underneath the material applied as a covering. When faked on a decorative binding, such ridges are called false bands. The opposite of sunk bands.

■ raised capital

in printing, an initial letter, usually at the beginning of the first paragraph of a chapter, projecting above the line of type on which it appears. Synonymous with cocked-up initial.

■ ramie

fiber of the Asiatic plant species Baehmeria nivea, in the nettle family, one of the most durable materials for weaving and paper-making, used in printing bank notes.

■ Random Access Memory (RAM)

a group of high-speed memory chips that perform most of the processing in a computer, allowing users to access bytes of data in any order, rather than sequentially. At start-up, the operating system and any application programs are routinely loaded from the hard disk into RAM to allow processing to begin. Any data in current use is also stored in RAM. To retain their content, RAM chips must have electric power, which is why users must save data to a slower storage medium (hard disk, floppy disk, Sip disk, etc.) before powering down.

■ rustic capital

one of the lighter and less formal capital letters used as a book hand by scribes from the 1st to the 6th century A.D., in contrast to the heavy square capitals used in formal documents, derived from Roman inscriptions. Vertical strokes were thinned by holding the pen at an acute angle, condensing previously rounded letterforms to allow more text to be copied on a page, a distinct advantage when writing material (parchment or vellum) was costly and in limited supply. Latin: capitalis rustica. Also refers to a capital letter with a design engraved on its face, especially in the form of vines and leaves, or the textured bark of a tree.

■ sabbatical

a paid leave of absence granted to an academic professional for the purpose of research or scholarly endeavour, usually for one semester or a full academic year, following six or seven years of full-time service, sometimes involving travel. At many colleges and universities, applications are evaluated on a competitive basis by a faculty committee, or in some other manner determined by institutional governance. Librarians employed in academic libraries may be eligible for sabbatic leave depending on the provisions of the contract governing terms of employment.

■ sacred text

a written work revered by people who believe in one of the world's organised religions. In library cataloguing, such works are entered under a uniform title (Bible, Talmud, Koran, Vedas, etc.). Most libraries in the United States keep at least one English translation of the Bible in the reference collection, usually with commentaries, concordances, etc. The sacred books of the other major world religions may be available in the circulating collection of academic libraries, especially at universities offering a major or graduate degree in comparative religion.

■ saddle-stitching

a technique used to bind magazines and pamphlets in which the leaves are secured by round wire staples driven completely through the back fold at two or more places, usually by machine. Unlike side-stitching, this method allows the leaves to open flat, but its strength is not sufficient to bind publications of more than 100 pages. Synonymous with stapling and saddle-wire stitching.

■ saga

from the Old Norse word for 'thing said', a lengthy narrative in prose or verse, telling of adventure and heroic events, usually involving the history of a legendary Norse lineage. In modern usage, any long, complicated tale in which the plot has many unexpected twists and turns, particularly one recounting the fortunes of an extended family (example: The Forsyte Saga by John Galsworthy).

■ salary

a sum of money paid to an employee on a regular basis (weekly, biweekly, monthly) for performing a specific job. Most full-time librarians and technical support staff are salaried.

■ **salvage**

measures taken to recover materials, equipment and furnishings damaged outside of normal use, for example, by water as a result of a major leak or flood. Salvaged materials may require special conservation procedures such as vacuum freeze drying or fumigation. Items not salvageable are usually discarded. Also refers collectively to the materials recovered.

■ **serials**

any publication issued in successive parts, usually (though not always) at regular intervals and intended to be continued indefinitely. Serials include: periodicals, newspapers, magazines, annuals, yearbooks, journals, memoirs, proceedings, transactions and numbered monographic series.

■ **smart board**

a general term for several types of electronic whiteboard, the most sophisticated of which can be synchronised with a computer to function like an oversize touch screen, allowing users to interact directly with the display, instead of using a keyboard, mouse, or other input device. Smart boards are used for bibliographic instruction in very well-equipped academic libraries. Also spelled smart board.

■ **society**

a corporate entity consisting of a group of people who meet periodically to share a common interest, especially one that is academic or professional.

■ **special library**

a library established and funded by a commercial firm, private association, government agency, nonprofit organisation, or special interest group to meet the information needs of its employees, members, or staff in accordance with the organisation's mission and goals. The scope of the collection is usually limited to the interests of its host organisation.

■ **special offer**

an offer by a supplier or vendor to sell goods and/or services at a lower price, usually for a limited period of time, or to provide a trial period, premium, or other inducement to purchase or subscribe. Other restrictions, such as minimum purchase amount, may apply.

■ **squares**

in bookbinding, the edges of the boards of a cover, extending beyond the text block at the head, fore-edge and tail to protect the bound sections from damage. Cased books have equal margins of cover around the edges, usually 1/8 to 3/16 of an inch. The term is also used for the part of the cover that is turned in on the inside, but not covered by the endpapers after they have been pasted down.

■ standard list

a list of titles recommended for any library collection of a particular type and size, usually published under the auspices of a library association. Standard lists are difficult to keep current. Synonymous with selection guide.

■ subject encyclopaedia

an encyclopaedia in one or more volumes devoted to a specific subject, field of study, or academic discipline, as opposed to a general encyclopaedia containing information on a broad range of subjects. Entries in a subject encyclopaedia are usually written and signed by an expert on the topic and may include a brief bibliography. Examples: Encyclopaedia of the Holocaust, Encyclopaedia of Indian Foreign Relations, Encyclopaedia of Psychology

■ subject gateways

organised lists of webpages, divided into subject areas by human

■ subject heading

1. word or group of words expressing a subject under which all items on that subject are filed.
2. the most specific word or phrase that describes the subject, or one of the subjects, of a work, selected from a list of preferred terms (controlled vocabulary and assigned as an added entry in the bibliographic record to serve as an access point in the library catalogue. A subject heading may be subdivided by the addition of subheadings and sub-subheadings (example: Libraries—History—20th century). The use of cross-references to indicate semantic relations between subject headings is called syndetic structure. The process of examining the content of new publications and assigning appropriate subject headings is subject analysis. In the United States, most libraries use Library of Congress subject headings (LCSH), but small libraries may use Sears subject headings.

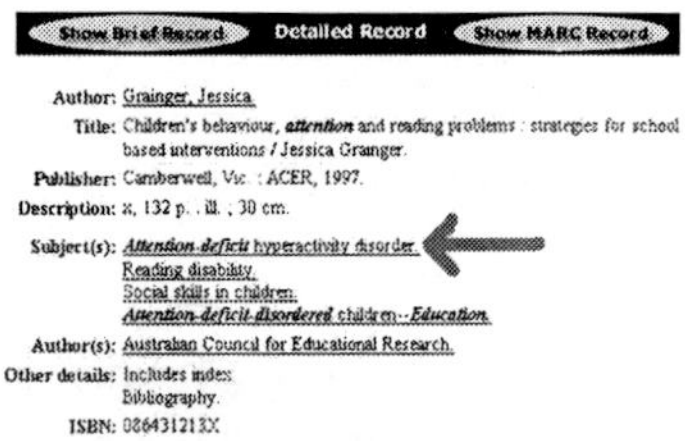

■ subpage

a Web page designed as part of a Web site, linked to the site's homepage directly, or through one or more layers of pages linked to the main page. In the Internet address (URL) www.myuniversity.edu/library/hours.html, the subdirectory /library is added to the address of the main page (www.myuniversity.edu) to direct users to the subpage of the university library and the filename /hours.html takes the user to the sub-subpage displaying library hours. For convenience, a well-designed subpage should include a direct link back to the main page.

■ **subplot**

in literature, a second complete story with the main action of a narrative work, sometimes involving the same or a related set of characters (example: the Laertes subplot in Shakespeare's Hamlet). More common in comedy than in tragedy, a subplot may be used to reinforce the main plot or as a counterpoint to it. Complex literary works may have more than one subplot, intertwined for dramatic effect.

■ **subscriber**

a person entitled to receive successive issues of a periodical for a prescribed period of time in exchange for payment of a subscription fee, payable in advance. Also refers to a paying member of a book club or rental library and to a person who receives Internet access from an Internet service provider (ISP). Libraries that pay for access to licensed bibliographic databases and individuals who sign on to receive e-mail messages from an electronic mailing list are also subscribers.

■ **subscriber's edition**

an edition of uncertain sales potential, issued only after a sufficient number of customers agree to purchase a copy, usually in response to an announcement by the publisher. The work may be printed on a better grade of paper and bound more attractively than the trade edition, with a list of subscribers included. Synonymous with subscription work.

■ **target audience**

the group or category of person for which a literary or artistic work is written or produced, or for which a library collection is developed (students, professionals, recreational readers, a particular age or interest group, etc.).

■ **task force**

a group of individuals drawn from various units within an organisation, charged with accomplishing a specific objective or set of objectives. Once the task is completed, the group is disbanded and its members return to their former units.

■ taskbar

a row of tabs in a graphical user interface, usually located across the bottom of the screen, with text labels indicating the applications and files currently open. In multitasking, a tab can be clicked by the user to bring the corresponding window to the foreground or to restore it to its original size after it has been minimised. In the Windows operating system, the Start button is also located in the taskbar,

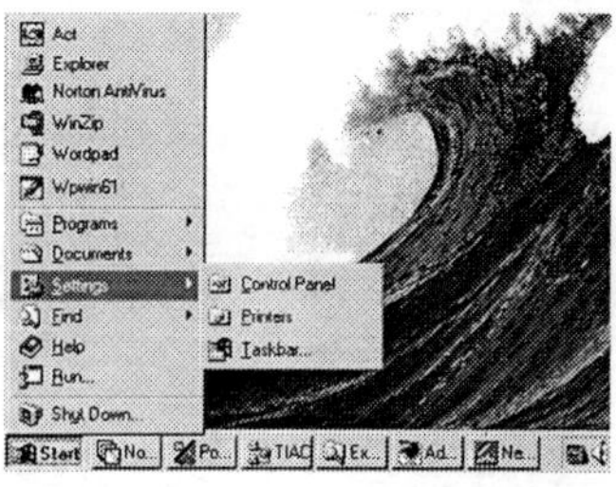

which may contain other information such as date and time.

■ taxonomy

the science of classification, including the general principles by which objects and phenomena are divided into classes which are subdivided into subclasses, then into sub-subclassesand so on.

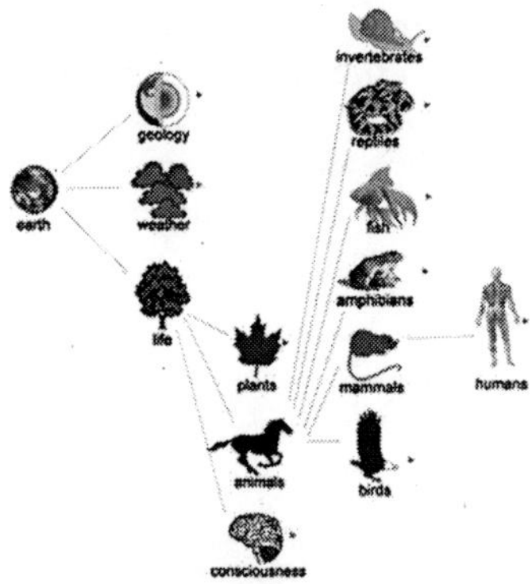

■ TCP/IP

1. protocol that allows dissimilar computers to connect to a network.
2. an initialism for Transmission Control Protocol/Internet Protocol, a set of communications protocols developed by the U.S. Department of Defense and implemented in 1982 to allow the users of host computers of different types and sizes to communicate with each other and exchange data via the Internet and other networks (intranets and extranets). Supported on most platforms, TCP/IP has become the protocol of the Internet. TCP ensures that the total amount of data (bytes) sent is received correctly and IP provides the mechanism for routing the packets of data comprising a message to the destination address as efficiently as possible.

■ teacher's manual

a booklet or soft cover book issued in conjunction with a textbook, to assist instructors in using the text to teach their classes. In library cataloguing, the presence of a teacher's manual is recorded as accompanying material in the physical description area of the bibliographic record representing the textbook.

■ tear sheet

a page of editorial content or advertising torn from a periodical or other printed publication for use as a press clipping or file copy.

■ teaser

advertising copy supplied by the marketing department of a publishing company, usually printed on the dust jacket of a new book to entice the reader to open the cover and sample the text.

■ technical journal

a journal devoted to a particular branch of engineering or technology, providing information for technicians in the field (example: Computing in Science and Engineering). Articles published in technical journals are indexed in Applied Science and Technology Index.

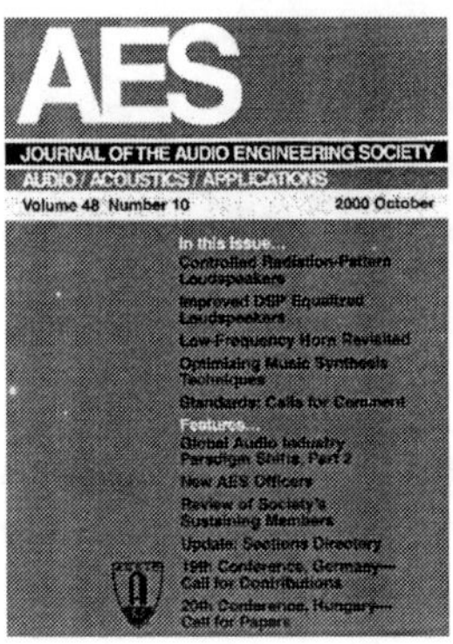

■ thematic map

a map showing one or more features or aspects of a given area of the surface of the earth or of another celestial body. Thematic maps can be quantitative, illustrating statistical data, such as average annual precipitation, or qualitative, indicating the distribution of characteristics such as predominant language, ethnic group, religious affiliation, etc.

■ thesaurus

1. guide to use of terms, showing relationships between them, for the purpose of providing standardised, controlled vocabulary for information storage and retrieval.

2. a book of synonyms and near-synonyms in a written language, usually arranged conceptually, although dictionary arrangement is not uncommon. The first thesaurus of the English language, published in 1852, was compiled by Peter Mark Roget. Also refers to an alphabetically arranged lexicon of terms comprising the specialised vocabulary of an academic discipline or field of study, showing the logical and semantic relations among terms, particularly a list of subject headings or descriptors used as preferred terms in indexing the literature of the field. In information retrieval, a thesaurus can be used to locate broader terms and related terms if the user wishes to expand retrieval, or narrower terms to make a search statement more specific. A well-de-

signed thesaurus also enables the indexer to maintain consistency in the assignment of indexing terms to documents. Plural: thesauri.

■ **thesis**

a proposition advanced and defended in a formal disputation, especially by a candidate in partial fulfilment of university requirements for a master's degree. Master's thesis are indexed annually by discipline, subject and author in Master's Theses Directories and in Dissertation Abstracts International.

■ **thesis play**

a dramatic work in which the playwright consciously attempts to illustrate a social problem and suggest to the reader or audience a possible solution (example: Mrs. Warren's Profession by George Bernard Shaw).

■ **timeout**

in computing, a routine that automatically terminates a period of waiting when a screen requiring user input receives no response within a designated time, for example, an interface that logs off whenever a predetermined period of inactivity occurs during an online session. The term is also used in communications to refer to the automatic termination of a waiting period when no response is received. Also spelled time out.

■ **Times Literary Supplement (TLS)**

first published in 1902, TLS is one of the most influential book review publications in the UK. Published weekly in newspaper format, it provides in-depth reviews of current fiction and nonfiction on a wide range of subjects, as well as reviews of contemporary theatre, opera and film. Like its American counterparts, the New York Review of Books and the New York Times Book Review, TLS is noted for its coverage of literary works. It also carries announcements of new books published by scholarly and university presses.

■ **tintype**

a positive photographic image made with a wet collodion emulsion on a thin iron plate darkened with black lacquer. As in a daguerrotype, the image is reversed laterally. Inexpensive and fast, the process was widely used for portraiture from the 1850s to the end of the 19th century, bringing photographic images within reach of the masses. In the 1880s, the wet emulsion was replaced by a dry gelatine. Synonymous with ferrotype.

■ **title**

a word, phrase, sentence, character, or characters appearing on an item, naming the work (or works) for identification and reference. Choice of title usually reflects the content of the work, distinguishing it from others of similar subject. A subtitle may be included following a colon or semicolon. Translations may have a parallel title in the original language. The full title is usually printed on the title page of a book or at the beginning of an article or essay published in a book or periodical. The title given on the title page may differ from the one printed or impressed on the spine or cover. In a film or video recording, the title is usually given in the first few frames.

In library cataloguing, the title proper is entered in the title and statement of responsibility area of the bibliographic description as it appears on the chief source of information. A work published under more than one title is catalogued under a uniform title (example: Bible). Also used in a less precise way to refer to any bibliographic item that has a title, as in the phrase 'list of titles ordered.' Also refers to a formal name or appellation given to an individual or family in recognition of privilege, distinction, office, or profession, for example: baron, saint, president, doctor, etc.

■ trade catalogue

a list of all the books (currently in print), published in a specific country or in other countries for which domestic publishers act as agents. Also, any publication that lists and describes the products manufactured and sold by a commercial company, with prices, illustrations and information on how to order, for use in sales. The publisher's catalogues sent by post to booksellers and libraries are a prime example. Some booksellers also publish their own trade catalogues for distribution to potential retail customers, or make catalogue information available on the Web (example: Amazon.com).

■ trade directory

a serial publication, usually issued annually, listing the companies and organisations engaged in buying, selling, or exchanging a specific category of goods and services. Entries include the official name, mailing address, phone/FAX numbers, key personnel and other important information.

■ trade edition

an edition produced by a trade publisher in hardcover and/or paperback publisher's binding for sale to quality booksellers and libraries. Trade editions are published for the general reader, rather than a specific segment of the market.

■ trade name

the name used to designate a specific business enterprise and the reputation it has acquired in the market place (example: Microsoft), as distinct from any trademark associated with the firm's products (Windows).

■ trade paperback

a softcover edition published by a university press or trade publisher, in larger format and better quality binding than a mass-market paperback, for retail sale in college and trade bookstores. Most trade editions are published first in hardcover, then reprinted in paperback from the same plates after sales potential in hardcover has been realised. In some instances, paperback rights are sold by the original publisher to a trade paperback publisher. Synonymous with quality paperback.

■ trade publisher

a publishing house that issues books of interest to the educated reader, for sale in college and quality retail bookstores. Few large trade publishers remain independent.

■ trademark

a letter, numeral, word, phrase, logo, device, design, sound, or symbol (or combination of these) used in connection with a product or service to signify, directly or by association, the identity of the owner, usually a commercial enterprise that has reserved to itself the use of the distinctive mark by registering it with the U.S. Patent and Trademark Office. Trademarks of successful products and services are jealously guarded by their owners to prevent competitors from imitating them. Registration, indicated by an 'R' enclosed in a small circle following the name ('TM' if registration is pending), gives the owner the right to legal redress in case of infringement. Also spelled trade mark.

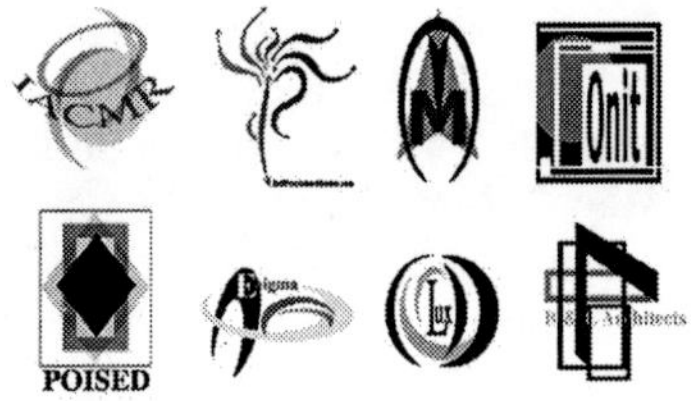

■ tragedy

a literary work in prose or verse in which a catastrophe or sudden reversal of fortune befalls the protagonist, usually due to uncontrollable circumstances (example: Arthur Miller's Death of a Salesman) or as a result of an error of judgment or serious flaw in character (Macbeth). In classical Greek drama, the weakness that brings about the downfall of the tragic hero (or heroine) is typically hubris (pride).

■ tragicomedy

a form of drama that originated in Elisabethan and Jacobean England, combining the forms and conventions of tragedy and comedy, usually by including characters of both high and low social position and by unfolding unfortunate events that unexpectedly result in a happy ending (example: Shakespeare's Merchant of Venice).

■ trailer

a very short film used primarily for advertising purposes, consisting of carefully selected extracts from a longer motion picture to be shown at a later date. In library cataloguing, the term is added inside square brackets [trailer] following the title proper in the bibliographic description to indicate material type. Also refers to the short strip of film without images at the end of a filmstrip, motion picture, or unexposed roll of film, added to allow the item to be handled without damage.

■ **type facsimile**

a reprint of a work made from a new setting of type in which every detail of the appearance of printed matter in the original edition is copied as precisely as possible. Synonymous with facsimile reprint.

■ **type family**

in printing, all the variants of the same basic type design, including uppercase, lowercaseand small capitals in both roman and italic in all sizes and weights (lightface, medium, semi-bold, boldface, condensed, expanded).

■ **type page**

the area or part of a printed page that is printed upon, excluding the margins, headlines, footlines and page numbers.

■ **type size**

the dimensions (height and width) of the body size of a type font, usually given in points. Most books are printed in type sizes ranging from 5-point to 22-point. Larger types sizes are used mainly for display matter. On the old-fashioned typewriter, pica was the most common type size.

The "Serb" Typeface Family

AHG ahg
AHG ahg
AHG ahg
AHG ahg

■ **typeface**

the upper surface of a unit of type, bearing in relief the character to be printed. Also refers to the general design or style of the characters of a font of type, including all the sizes and weights in which the font is made. Designing a new typeface is a major undertaking, even for an experienced typographer. It is therefore not unusual for a typeface to be named after the person who designed it. There does not appear to be universal agreement on the classification of typefaces. Also spelled type face. Sometimes abbreviated face.

Times New Roman
Zurich Eras
Baskerville
Avant Gard
CHARLESWORTH
FELIX TITLING
COPPERPLATE GOTHIC 67890
Georgia 12345
Goudy Handtooled
Tiranti Solid

■ **typescript**

an author's original typewritten copy of a work, in the form in which it is submitted for publication, or a typewritten copy of the original commissioned by the author or publisher, as opposed to a manuscript written by hand. Abbreviated ts. and tss. (plural).

■ ultrafiche

a card-shaped transparent microform with a reduction ratio considerably greater than that of standard microfiche or superfiche (up to 3,000 frames per 4 x 6-inch sheet). A special ultrafiche reader-printer machine is required to view and make hard copies of documents stored in this medium.

■ ultraviolet (UV)

electromagnetic radiation beyond the spectrum visible to humans as light, shorter in wavelength than violet light but longer than X-rays. The sun is the chief source of natural ultraviolet radiation. Because UV radiation can damage photographs and accelerate the deterioration of certain grades of paper, prolonged exposure of library materials to direct sunlight should be avoided and incandescent lighting installed when possible in storage areas where preservation is a high priority. UV filters can be used to reduce exposure.

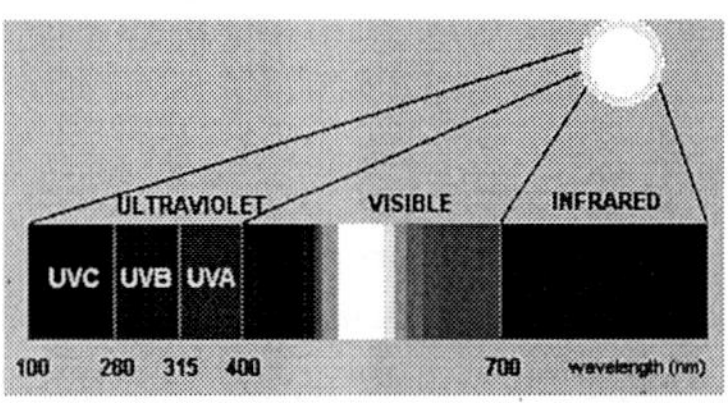

■ umbilicus

in antiquity, a knobbed wooden rod attached to one end of a papyrus scroll around which a manuscript was rolled when not in use. A vellum tag was usually attached to one end, bearing a note indicating the title or contents.

■ unabridged

a version of a written work that has not been shortened and is therefore considered to be complete. The fact that an edition is unabridged is sometimes indicated on the title page of long works issued in paperback, but unless otherwise stated, a published work is assumed to be unabridged. An unabridged dictionary is the version containing the most words.

■ unauthorised biography

a biographical work written without the consent of its subject or the subject's family if the biography is deceased, sometimes more objective in its analysis than an authorised biography because the biographer does not have to make concessions to gain access to confidential sources. However, an unauthorised biography may be less detailed or complete if the author was denied important information.

unauthorised edition

an edition printed without the consent of the author, the author's legal representative, or the original publisher, but not in violation of existing copyright law.

unbacked

printed on only one side of a blank sheet of paper, as in a poster.

unbound

1. a printed publication issued without a binding or cover, or with its cover removed. Prior to the 19th century, books were sold in the form of printed sections, to be bound to the purchaser's specifications. Also refers to an issue of a periodical or part of a serial that will eventually be bound, usually with others, to form a volume.
2. refers to the current, single issues of a periodical, before they have been bound together between hard covers to form physical volumes.

uncial

from Latin uncialis meaning 'of an inch' or 'inch-high.' A large, full majuscule script used in the earliest Biblical codices and as a book hand in manuscripts written and copied from about 300-700 A.D., in which capital letters were rounded and modified in ways suggestive of later lowercase letters, probably to increase writing speed. Half uncial gradually replaced uncial as a book hand after the 6th century. Also refers to manuscripts written in this script.

uncompression

expanding files that have been compressed.

uncut

a volume in which the bolts are not trimmed to uniform size in binding, leaving the leaves to be separated by hand by the owner of the book, with a paper knife or other thin-edged instrument. Synonymous with unopened and untrimmed.

underfunded

an organisation, institution, or project allocated insufficient monies to accomplish its goals and objectives. Chronic underfunding can lead to a decline in quality of service and is demoralising for staff and management.

undergraduate library

a separate library established, supported and maintained by a university to serve the information and research needs of its undergraduate students and the instructional requirements of the undergraduate curriculum. Sometimes administered as a branch library.

underground press

a publisher that issues printed publications unofficially or clandestinely, usually to members of a group or organisation that opposes the policies of an established government or other authority, more common during periods of civil unrest than in times of peace and prosperity. Eventually, most underground presses either disband or become 'above ground' publishing houses.

underlining

words, phrases, or passages of text underscored in pencil or ink by a previous reader, usually for future reference. As a general rule, libraries do not add heavily underlined gift books to the collection. Also refers to a formatting option available in word processing software that can be used to place a line beneath a single character, word, phrase, line, or entire passage of text.

underrun

a press run that produces fewer copies than the number ordered, sometimes causing a shortage of publisher's inventory. The opposite of overrun.

underserved

persons within the geographic area or clientele served by a library or library system who use its services infrequently for a variety of reasons, including limited awareness of available resources and services, lack of familiarity with the national language, illiteracy, poor health, lack of transportation, etc. Outreach programs help bridge these gaps.

understaffed

having an insufficient number of employees to do the work required. Signs of overwork (fatigue, absenteeism, arrears, etc.) can be the result of understaffing. Synonymous with short-staffed and short-handed. The opposite of overstaffed.

underutilised

a library service, resource, or item used less often than it ought to be, usually because its usefulness is not widely appreciated, or because it is not as accessible as other alternatives, for example, collections of theses and dissertations in some academic libraries.

undocumented

lacking official papers or other tangible evidence in support of existence, identity, validity, authenticity, provenance, etc.

unexpurgated

a text or edition that includes passages omitted from other versions or editions, usually because they were considered offensive to some readers.

unfinished

a work left incomplete at the death of the author, composer, or creator. Unfinished literary works are sometimes published posthumously.

uniform edition

two or more books printed, bound and jacketed in the same style to show that they constitute a single entity, such as a multivolume encyclopedia, or that they are related to each other in some other way, for example, the individual titles in a monographic series or the collected works of an author.

■ uniform style

the appearance of publications printed in the same typographical style on the same grade of paper, issued in a binding of the same size and design. Volumes published as a set or series are usually produced in this fashion. Also refers to the appearance of any element of a printed work that is repeated in the same style throughout the text, such as the chapter headings, running titles, headpieces or tailpieces, etc.

■ upload

to transmit a copy of one or more files from a local computer to the hard disk of another (usually more remote) computer, such as a mainframe or network server, a process that may require terminal emulation software. The opposite of download.

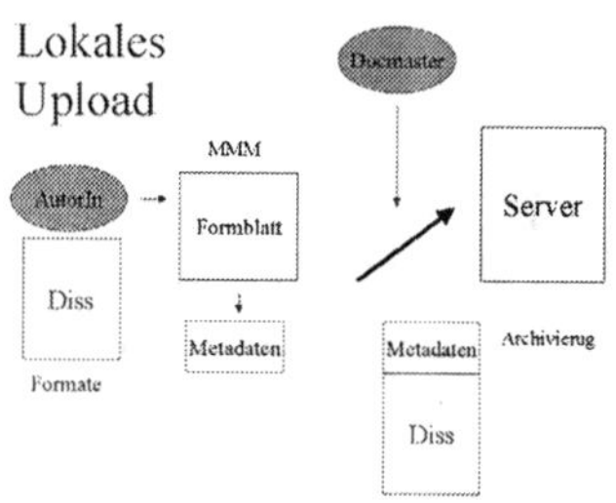

■ uppercase

capital letters, as opposed to the small or lowercase letters of a type font. The terms uppercase and lowercase are derived from the relative positions of the compartments in the wood or metal case containing elements of type bearing capital letters and small letters at a typesetter's bench in the days when type was set by hand (letterpress). Also spelled upper case.

■ use

an instruction used in an entry in a subject headings list or thesaurus of controlled vocabulary to direct the user from a synonym or quasi-synonym to the preferred term under which items on the topic are cataloged or indexed.

■ use life

the length of time or number of times an item can be used before it becomes so worn that it is no longer fit for use and has to be discarded. For books, use life depends on quality of paper, strength of binding and actions taken to protect the cover, such as enclosing the dust jacket in a washable plastic sleeve.

■ used book

a book that has had at least one previous owner. The condition of the cover and leaves is an indication of the amount of use a volume has received. Sometimes used books are found upon appraisal to be rare and valuable, especially copies of a first edition. Synonymous with second-hand book.

■ **used bookstore**

a bookstore that specialises in books that have had at least one previous owner, sometimes limited to a particular genre, such as mystery or science fiction. Unless a used book is rare or out of print, it is usually priced on the basis of condition, lower than the list price of a new copy. Some bookstores sell both new and used books. Synonymous with second-hand bookstore.

■ **utility**

a small program that expands the capability of a computer's operating system by enabling it to perform an additional task, usually something as routine as managing a disk drive, printer, scanner, or other peripheral device. Unlike the basic operating system, utilities can be added and removed as needed. A utility differs from an application program in being less complex, usually limited to a single function.

■ **utopia**

a term coined by Thomas More from the Greek ou ('no' or 'not') and topos ('place'). A literary or artistic work in which the setting is an ideal society, usually one existing in a future time or imaginary place. Utopias are created by authors who feel nostelgic about idealised past, or who wish to call attention to the need to reform existing social, political, or economic institutions. The opposite of dystopia.

■ **vancouver style**

a style of citing that uses the footnote or endnote system

■ **vandalism**

damage to library collections, furnishings, or facilities which is intentional rather than accidental, usually motivated by anger or malice on the part of the perpetrator. Vandalism detracts from the physical appearance of a library and its resources. The cost of repair or replacement puts an unwelcome burden on the budget. To avoid detection, most acts of vandalism are committed in unstaffed locations or after hours. Some libraries employ a security guard to keep an eye on areas not visible from at least one public service point when the library is open.

■ **vanilla text**

text written on a computer, usually with the aid of a text editor or word processing software, in a standard font with no formatting (boldface, italics, etc.), usually with a filename ending in .txt. Synonymous with plaintext.

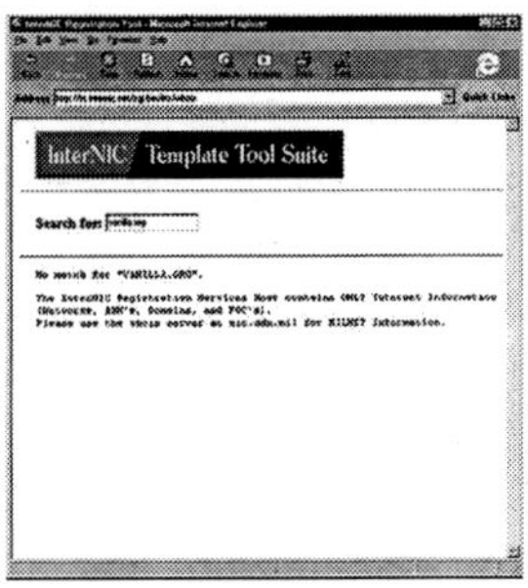

vanity publisher

a type of publisher, more common in the United States than in other countries, that specialises in producing books at the author's expense, used mainly by writers whose works have been rejected by commercial publishers and by individuals of private means who are convinced they have an important message to impart to the world. In England, vanity publishing is used primarily for poetry. Books published by vanity publishers are avoided by reviewers and rarely purchased by retail booksellers and libraries. Synonymous with vanity press.

variant

a copy of a book that differs slightly in one or more points from others of the same impression, or from a previous printing of the same edition. The differences may occur in the sections, binding, or both. Once priority of publication has been conclusively established, such variations are referred to as issues and states. Also refers to one of two or more slightly different early texts of a literary work, for example, the plays of Shakespeare that survive in multiple versions. Abbreviated var. Also, one of several forms of a word retrieved when the truncated stem of a word is used as a search term in a keywords search, for example, the terms videocassette, videodisc, video recording and videotape retrieved by truncating the root 'video' (video*).

variant edition

an edition that includes changes made in the work by the author, sometimes ranging from first composition all the way to publication in a definitive edition, allowing the reader to see the evolution of the text.

variorum edition

from the Latin phrase cum notes various meaning 'with notes from various persons.' An edition based on scholarly comparison and interpretation of several previously published versions of the text, which also includes commentary written by various editors.

Various Dates (V.D.)

a phrase used to indicate that a set or series of volumes contains works that have different publication dates.

varnish

the glossy coating applied to the printed surface of the paper cover or dust jacket on a new book, for protection and to enhance its visual appeal. Varnish can be expensive when applied in a separate press run. A second pass is not required when varnish is added to gloss ink.

vatican library

although the Catholic popes always had private libraries, in the 15th century Pope Nicholas V created a library specifically for the clerics and scholars who lived and worked in and around the papal palace. A suite of rooms was set aside and he began collecting the most beautiful manuscript books of the time. Pope Sixtus IV continued the work and the library's holdings grew rapidly from about 1,200 books in 1455 to 3,500 in 1481 when the first handwritten catalogue was made by the librarian Platina. From the beginning, the library included not only Bibles and works on theology and canon law, but also secular works, particularly the Greek and Latin classics which the popes collected in texts as close to the original as they could find. During the Renaissance, the Vatican Library became a center of classical culture in Europe and its librarians were often distinguished scholars. It continues to be one of the great libraries of the Western world, attracting scholars of all nationalities to its collections of important historical documents and rare and fine books.

■ v-chip

a microchip installed in a television set, designed to allow parents to block access to programs containing content considered unsuitable for children (violence, explicit sex, adult language, etc.). In 1996, Congress passed legislation requiring manufacturers of television receivers to install the V-chip in sets sold in the United States (13-inch or larger). However, according to the Christian Science Monitor, a survey released in July, 2001 found that only 7% of parents with children 2-17 years old use the V-chip in their television set, either because they own an older set, do not know if their set has a V-chip, or find it difficult to use. 56% said they use the rating displayed on the screen before a program begins to make decisions about their children's viewing.

■ vcr

an initialism for video cassette recorder, an electronic device designed to record onto videotape (in VHS format) signals received by a standard television receiver, for playback on a television monitor. VCRs are also used to play prerecorded videocassettes (feature films, documentaries, etc.). Although VCRs are analogue machines, adapters are available that enable digital data to be stored on videotape as computer backup.

■ vellum

a thin, fine parchment made from the polished skin of a newly born lamb, kid, or calf, dressed and polished with alum for use as a writing surface before paper came into widespread use in Europe and also in bookbinding. Also refers to a manuscript written on fine parchment and to a fine-quality off-white paper made to resemble the animal membrane.

■ **verso**

the left-hand page of a book, usually with even-numbered pages. Opposite of recto (and much more commonly-used term). The copyright date of a book is found on the verso (back) of the title page.

■ **vertical file**

a collection of loose clippings, pictures, illustrations, pamphlets, or other materials of an ephemeral nature which, because of size and format, are filed on edge in drawers or in a box, usually organised in folders by subject or some other classification system to facilitate retrieval. Also refers to the filing cabinet in which such materials are stored.

■ **vga**

an initialism for Video Graphics Array, a standard video adapter in an IBM PC, capable of producing resolutions of 640 x 480 pixels in up to 256 colours.

■ **vhs**

an initialism for Video Home System, a video recording and playback format consisting of hard plastic cassettes containing half-inch videotape. Introduced by JVC in 1976 to compete with Sony's Beta format, VHS has since become the industry standard for both home and commercial use. SVHS (Super VHS) was developed to improve resolution.

■ **vide**

the imperative form of the Latin verb videre, 'to see.' Used in the sense of 'refer to' in footnotes to direct the reader's attention to a specific passage, page, chapter, or work. Abbreviated v. or vid.

■ **video clip**

a short section of a longer work produced on videotape, used in a broadcast or incorporated into another work such as a Web page, usually for promotional purposes or to give the viewer a brief impression of the whole.

■ **videocassette**

a recorded videotape permanently enclosed in a hard plastic case containing two take-up reels to which the ends of the tape are permanently attached for playback and rewinding. In the United States, the standard format for videotapes is VHS. Most libraries shelve videocassettes in a separate section, but in some libraries they are integrated into the circulating collection by call number. To satisfy demand and encourage prompt return, the loan period for videocassettes may be shorter and the overdue fine higher than for books.

■ **virtual**

an adjective referring to activities, objects, beings and places that have no actual physical reality because they exist only in digital form (in cyberspace), for example, an e-mail 'box' or an electronic 'shopping cart.'

■ **virtual library**

1. access to electronic information in a variety of remote locations through a local online catalogue or other gateway, such as the internet. 2. a 'library without walls' in which the collections do not exist on paper, microform, or in any tangible form, but are electronically accessible in digital format. Such libraries exist only on a very limited scale, but in most traditional print-based libraries in the United States, catalogues and periodical indexes are available online and the full-text of some periodicals and reference works may also be available electronically. Some libraries and library systems call themselves 'virtual' because they offer online services. The term digital library is more appropriate because the term virtual (borrowed from 'virtual reality') suggests that the experience of using such a library is not the same as the 'real' thing, when in fact, the experience of reading or viewing a document on a computer screen may be qualitatively different from reading the same publication in print, but the information content is the same regardless of format.

■ **visually impaired**

a person whose sight makes using library materials in conventional formats difficult, if not impossible. Library services designed to meet the needs of visually-impaired persons include Braille, large print, books-on-tape and other recorded media and radio reading service. In the United States, these services are available through the federally-funded National Library Service for the Blind and Physically Handicapped.

■ **vital records**

records essential to an agency in the ongoing conduct of its business or affairs, without which it would cease to function effectively (example: the file of patron records used by a library in circulation transactions). For archivists, identifying and protecting vital records under every conceivable circumstance is a primary concern in records management and disaster planning.

■ **viz.**

an abbreviation of the Latin videlicet meaning 'namely,' 'that is to say,' or 'to wit,' used in text and footnotes to introduce a word or phrase added to explain more completely or precisely a previous word, phrase, or statement.

■ **vocabulary**

all the words used in a language. Also, all the words and phrases used by a particular person, group, or profession. Also refers to a list of words in a textbook for students learning a foreign language, usually printed at the end of the text containing them, or at the end of each chapter.

■ **vocabulary control**

in indexing, the process of creating and maintaining a list of preferred terms to indicate:

1. which of two or more equivalent terms will represent a concept as the authorised subject heading or descriptor in the classification system, and
2. the relations of hierarchy (broader and narrower terms) and association (related terms) among headings once they have been selected. Controlled vocabulary is recorded in a subject headings list or thesaurus updated as new concepts emerge and older terminology becomes obsolete.

■ **vocabulary mapping**

a function built into the search software of some bibliographic databases that allows the user to relate a specific search term to the appropriate subject heading(s) or descriptor(s), read a scope note explaining how each heading is used, view the hierarchical tree of headings to which it belongs and select broader headings or narrower terms or subheadings to include in the search. Vocabulary mapping is available in large databases, such as MEDLINE and PsycINFO, which have a well-developed controlled vocabulary.

■ **vocal score**

the score of a musical work composed for voice (opera, oratorio, cantata, etc.) in which all the parts are shown in normal size on separate staves, with any accompaniment (ordinarily written for orchestra) reduced to two staves for performance on a keyboard instrument.

■ **voice mail**

a messaging system that allows a person to send, receive and store audio messages using a standard telephone receiver. Also spelled voicemail.

■ **voice recognition**

technology capable of recognising the sounds of human speech and converting them into digital signals for processing as input by a computer, used mainly in communications. In computing, command systems capable of recognising a few hundred words eliminate the need for a mouse or keyboard in repetitive operations. Discrete systems, used in dictation, require the speaker to pause between words. Continuous recognition handles natural language at normal speed, but requires considerably more processing capability. Systems capable of understanding large vocabularies spoken at any speed are anticipated in the foreseeable future.

■ **voice-over**

in motion pictures, video and television, a narration, commentary, or prepared text spoken by a person who is not seen on the screen, a technique widely used in advertising. In documentaries, the name of the narrator is usually given in the credits.

■ **volume**

in the bibliographic sense, a major division of a work, distinguished from other major divisions of the same work by having its own chief source of information and, in most cases, independent pagination, foliation, or signatures, even when not bound in a separate cover. In a set, the individual volumes are usually numbered, with any indexes at the end of the last volume. For a periodical, all the issues published during a given publishing period (usually a calendar year), bound or unbound. The volume number is usually printed on the front cover of each issue and on the same page as the table of contents. In bound periodicals, it is impressed on the spine. In the physical sense, all the written or printed matter contained in a single binding. Volume as material entity does not necessarily correspond with volume as bibliographic entity. Abbreviated v. or vol. Also refers to the loudness of the sound(s) produced by a receiver (radio or television) or an electronic playback machine (phonograph, audiocassette or CD player, VCR, etc.), usually regulated by a volume control device that can be manipulated by the listener.

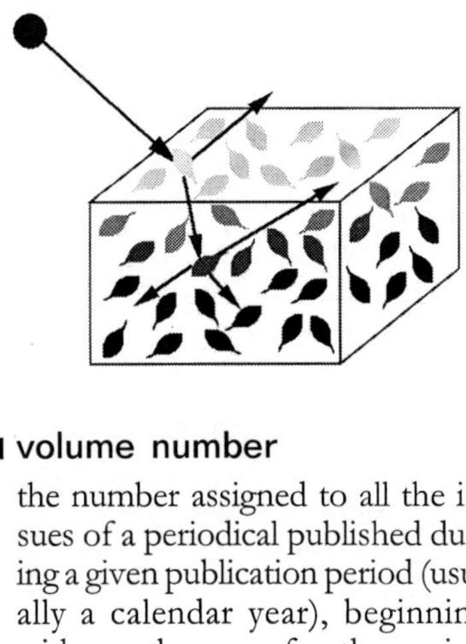

■ **volume number**

the number assigned to all the issues of a periodical published during a given publication period (usually a calendar year), beginning with number one for the period (year) in which the title was first issued. If the issues are bound in one or more physical volumes, the number is printed or impressed on the spine(s). In a multivolume reference work, such as an encyclopaedia, the volume number appears on the spine and on the title page.

volume rights

the rights, usually negotiated with a publisher by the author or author's agent, to publish a work in volume form, including hardcover, paperback, book club and textbook editions. Volume rights also include publication of the work in its entirety in a single issue of a periodical and reprinting, in full or in part, in an anthology.

volume

1. a unit in a set or series.
2. a single bibliographic unit, i.e. a book.
3. a bound periodical containing several issues.

volumen

latin for 'a thing rolled up.' A writing surface used in antiquity, consisting of papyrus or vellum sheets attached end-to-end, with text handwritten in columns on one side only, the lines running parallel with the edges of the roll. The last sheet was attached to a straight stick with knobbed ends called an umbilicus around which the manuscript was rolled. The rolls were stored in a box called a capsa or on deep shelves with a vellum label or ticket attached to one end for identification by title or contents. Synonymous with scroll.

volunteer

a person who works for a library or other organisation without material recompense. Library volunteers are often retirees who wish to make a contribution by remaining actively engaged in their community. They perform a variety of tasks, depending on their skills and talents, including reshelving, physical processing, mending, storytelling, landscape maintenance, etc.

wall shelving

single-sided shelving placed against a wall and sometimes attached to it, as opposed to free-standing shelving (usually double-sided) designed to stand on its own away from a wall or other support. Shelving of both types is manufactured in sections to allow libraries to assemble ranges of varying length.

wallpaper

the decorative background pattern or image against which windows, menus, icons and other visual elements are displayed and manipulated in a graphical user interface (GUI), usually created in JPEG or GIF file format. Some systems allow the user to select a wallpaper from a variety of different designs. Files of wallpaper designs are also available online from third-parties. Wallpapers can be custom-designed to display a distinctive element, such as a logo, trademark, or other symbol of institutional identity.

■ wan

wide Area Network; any computer network over an area larger than a single building or campus.

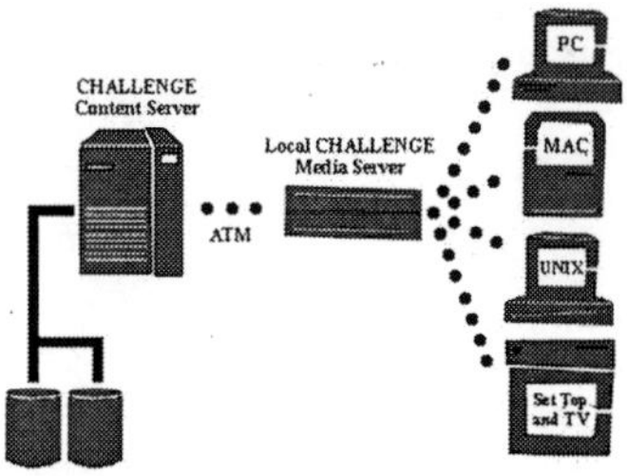

■ warping

a twist or bend in a book cover that occurs after binding or casing, severe enough to prevent the volume from lying flat, usually caused by dampness. In newly bound books, the condition may be caused by differences in the expansion and/or contraction of the materials used in the case or cover. Warping can be minimised in binding by using well-dried boards, endpapers with the grain running from head to foot and adhesives of low water content and by proper pressing. In libraries, it is controlled by storing books in a dry, well-ventilated place.

■ warranty

a fixed period of time, specified in the sales agreement, during which the seller is required to repair or replace a piece of equipment that does not function properly. Once the warranty period has expired, the purchaser must pay for repairs unless a maintenance contract has been signed. As a general rule, length of warranty is an indication of the manufacturer's confidence in the product.

■ web index

a search engine that organises Web sites by subject content in a hierarchy of subject categories, from the most general to the most specific. For example, links to Web sites for 'library and information science organisations' are listed in Yahoo! under:

Reference
Libraries
Library and Information Science
Organisations

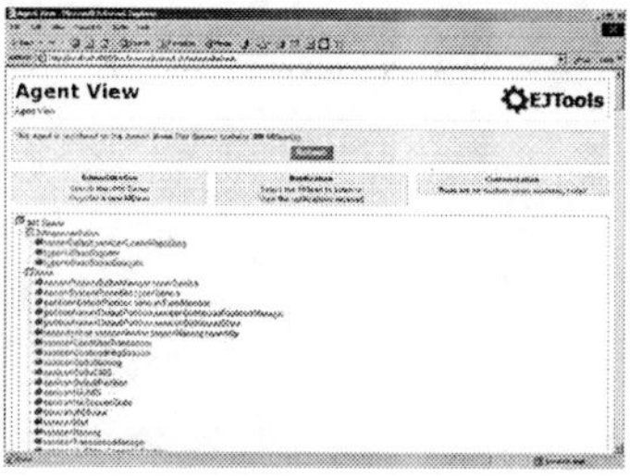

■ web page

1. an electronic document written in HTML script, stored on a Web server and accessible using Web browser software at a unique Internet address called a URL, usually one of a group of related, interlinked files that together comprise a Web site. A Web page may include formatted text, graphic material, audio and/or video elements and links to other files on the Internet.
2. a single HTML document (file), a web 'page' may be many screens long when viewed, or many pages long if actually printed out.

■ web search

to use one of the hierarchical subject guides or search engines available from a Web browser to identify and retrieve information housed on the World Wide Web. A variety of search engines are available by clicking the browser's 'Search' button, note that the search syntax used, the set of data being searched and the retrieval parameters are different for each search engine.

■ web server

a computer capable of providing Internet access to Web-based resources and services in response to requests from client computers on which Web browser software is installed. A Web server includes the necessary hardware and also the operating system, TCP/IP protocols, server software and information content of the Web sites installed on it. Web server

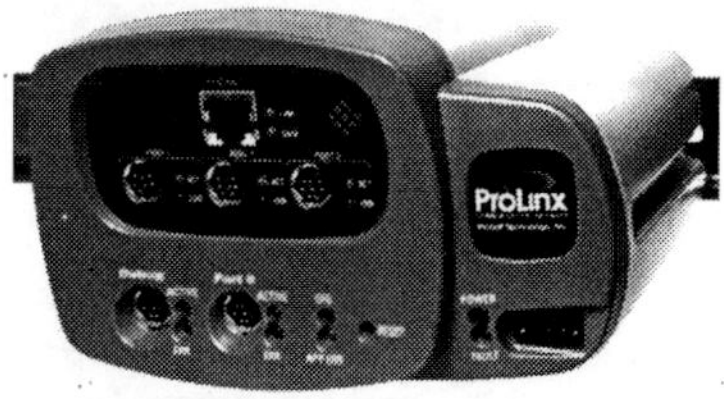

software is designed to accept requests from users to download HTML text, image and audio files.

■ web site

1. a file of related web pages of text and graphics linked through hypertext.
2. a group of related, interlinked Web pages installed on a Web server and accessible 24 hours a day to Internet users equipped with browser software. Most Web sites are created to represent the online presence of a company, organisation, or institution, or are the work of a group or individual. The main page or welcome screen, called the homepage, usually displays the title of the site, the name of the person (or persons) responsible for creating and maintaining it and date of last update. Also spelled Website.

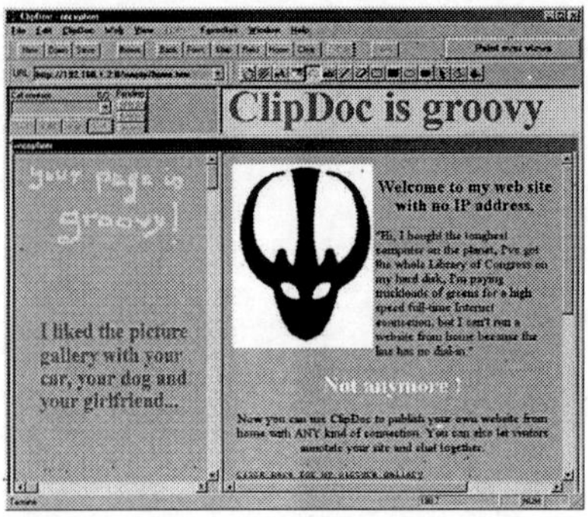

■ window

1. a rectangular, scrollable viewing area in the graphical user interface of a microcomputer application that can be opened by the user, overwriting the entire screen or a portion of it. Windows can be resized, minimised to an icon when not needed, selected for editing and reference, or closed by the user at any time to facilitate multitasking (the use of two or more programs at the same time). Also refers to the opening cut out of the center of a mat, through which a mounted print is viewed, or out of the center of a card through which a mounted slide or frame of microfilm is viewed.

2. a user-friendly operating system developed in 1985 by Microsoft for PCs running on DOS, progressively upgraded to its current version. Windows got its start by emulating the graphical user interface (GUI) developed by Apple and has since become the industry standard for desktop microcomputers.

■ wire coil

a continuous length of metal wire threaded through holes punched along the binding edge of the leaves of a book or notebook in

spiral binding. Flexible hard plastic is also used for this purpose.

■ wireless

a method of connecting to the Internet via electromagnetic airwaves, rather than wire or cable. Telecommunication charges are eliminated, but an Internet service provider is still required to gain access to the Internet. Wireless technology enables the ISP to offer greater bandwidth without the expense of adding cable to its own connection. However, in most wireless systems 'line of sight' is required, which means that the radio antenna installed at a library must have an unobstructured path to the antenna maintained by the ISP. Each client antenna can serve 50-100 workstations at T1 speed. Wireless technology is also be used internally by libraries with a direct connection to the Internet, for example, to network an instruction lab equipped with PCs or laptops.

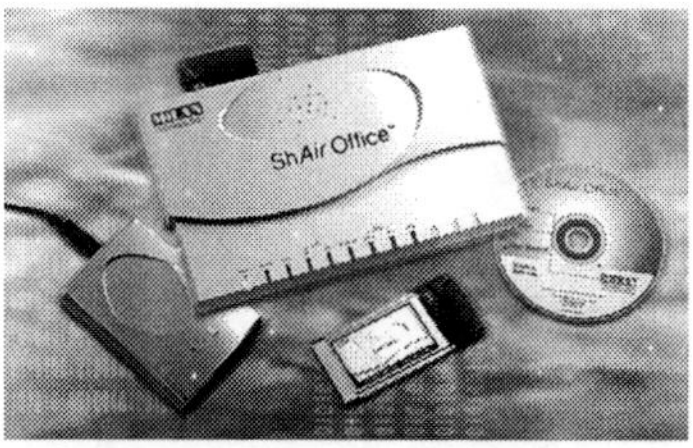

■ With All Faults (W.A.F.)

a term used by booksellers, book dealers and auctioneers to inform prospective buyers that an item is offered for sale as is and may not be returned if found to be defective.

■ word-by-word

a method of alphabetisation in which headings that begin with the same word are arranged in alphabetical order by the next word and so on, with punctuation marks treated as spaces ('New Testament' filed before 'New, William' before 'newt'). Also known as nothing before something.

■ word-by-word alphabetising

words, not letters, are used as filing units. Spaces between words are treated as filing elements.

■ wordless

a book or other publication without words, in which the story is told in a sequence of illustrations, a format used mainly in children's picture books. Without text, the 'reader' must interpret the meaning of the story from the visual images. Each reader may perceive a slightly different meaning in the pictures.

■ work

an expression of human thought or emotion in language, signs, symbols, numerals, images, or other medium for purposes of communication and record. When such an expression is issued to the public, it is a published work. If the original author or creator is unknown, the work is anonymous.

As defined in FRBR (Functional Requirements for Bibliographic Records), a distinct intellectual or artistic creation, independent of any concrete realisation or expression of its content (example: Beowulf as opposed to a specific text of the epic). The concept is abstract in specifying only the content which the various expressions of a work have in common. Under this definition, the boundaries of a work may be culturally determined. When modification of a work entails considerable independent intellectual or artistic endeavour, the result is treated as a new work (example: an adaptation of

Beowulf intended for juvenile readers).

■ work form

in technical processing, a card or paper form that accompanies a newly acquired item from the beginning of cataloguing to the point at which it is ready to be placed on the shelf, with space for library staff to note any special instructions and data necessary to prepare catalogue records, add cross-references and physically prepare the item for use. Synonymous with worksheet.

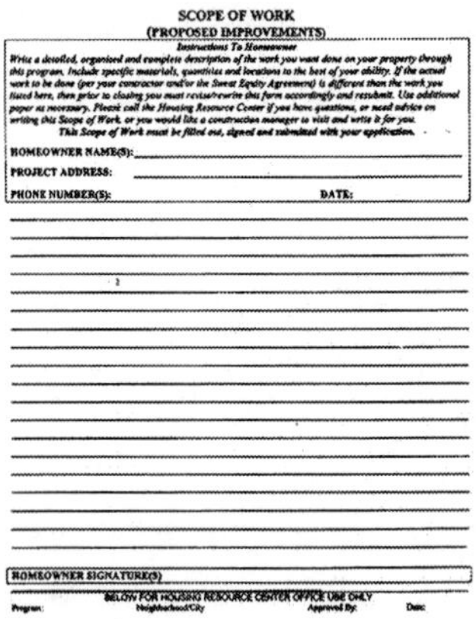

SCOPE OF WORK
(PROPOSED IMPROVEMENTS)

Instructions To Homeowner

Write a detailed, organized and complete description of the work you want done on your property through this program. Include specific materials, quantities and locations to the best of your ability. If the actual work to be done (per your contractor and/or the Sweat Equity Agreement) is different than the work you listed here, then prior to closing you must revise/rewrite this form accordingly and resubmit. Use additional paper as necessary. Please call the Housing Resource Center if you have questions, or need advice on writing this Scope of Work, or you would like a construction manager to visit and write it for you.

This Scope of Work must be filled out, signed and submitted with your application.

HOMEOWNER NAME(S): ______

PROJECT ADDRESS: ______

PHONE NUMBER(S): DATE:

HOMEOWNER SIGNATURE(S)

BELOW FOR HOUSING RESOURCE CENTER OFFICE USE ONLY

Program: Neighborhood/City Approved By: Date:

■ work in progress

a written or artistic work published or exhibited in incomplete form, sometimes in parts, to be continued or completed by the author or creator at a later date. Large reference works requiring many years of painstaking research are sometimes published as the work progresses (example: Dictionary of American Regional English).

■ work mark

one or two letters added by the cataloguer to the author mark at the end of a call number, consisting of the first letter or two of the first word of the title (initial articles excluded), to distinguish works by the same author which have the same classification (example: the d in the book number D548d to identify David Copperfield by Charles Dickens), or to subarrange editions of the same work. Synonymous with work number.

■ www

world Wide Web

■ xerography

from the Greek xeros and graphos, meaning 'dry writing.' A method of reproducing text and/or images in which dry resinous toner transferred from an electrostatically charged plate is thermally adhered to a sheet of paper or some other copying surface inside a photocopier (originally called a xerox machine). The result is a photocopy or xerox copy. Xerography is a form of reprography.

■ **x-height**

the mean height of the lowercase letters of a typeface that have neither ascenders nor descenders, sometimes used instead of point size as an indication of type size. The x-height letters of the roman alphabet are: a, c, e, m, n, o, r, s, u, v, w, xand s. The tops and bottoms of some letters such as the 'c' and 'o' may extend slightly above the mean line and below the base line. Also spelled ex-height.

■ **x-rated**

a motion picture or videorecording containing material considered suitable for adults only, usually because it contains material considered pornographic. The term is also applied to print publications containing adult material (magazines, photographs, etc.).

■ **xylography**

printing done from blocks of wood, especially by the early process of wood engraving. The results are known as xylographica.

■ **ya**

an abbreviation of young adult, an adolescent aged 12-18, usually in the ninth to twelfth grade.

■ **yahoo**

1. yet another hierarchically officious oracle, a worldwide directory of Web sites developed in 1994 by two Stanford University engineering students to organise Web content in a hierarchical system of subject categories. Yahoo Web Page also provides other Web-based services (news, weather, travel service, e-mail, shopping, games, etc.). It uses a smaller database than most other Web search engines, but searches in Yahoo! usually have higher precision because the Web sites it lists are selected by human beings, rather than robot software. Originally coined by Jonathan Swift in Gulliver's Travels (1726) to refer to an imaginary race of coarse, brutish creatures in human form, the term was later applied by Mark Twain to any boorish person.

2. one of a number of Web search engines, allows both direct searching and a hierarchical directory organised by subject classification.

■ yapp binding

a form of limp leather binding with rounded corners and squares that overlap the edges of the sections, sometimes by as much as half the thickness of the text block, named after William Yapp who used it on pocket Bibles sold in England in the mid-19th century.

■ yearbook

an annual documentary, historical, or memorial compendium of facts, photographs, statistics, etc., about the events of the preceding year, often limited to a specific country, institution, discipline, or subject. Optional yearbooks are offered by some publishers of general encyclopaedias. Most libraries place yearbooks on continuation order and shelve them in the reference collection. Yearbooks of historical significance may be stored in archives or special collections. Also spelled year book. Also refers to an annual high school or college publication commemorating a particular school year or graduating class in photographs, usually sold in hardcover to seniors by advance special order at the end of the school year.

■ yellow pages

the portion of a telephone directory or trade directory following the white pages in which the names, phone numbers and mailing addresses of commercial enterprises are listed, usually alphabetically by subject or in a classified arrangement, so named because the section is printed on yellow paper. Yellow pages are also available online and for specific professions.

■ **yellow press**

a popular name for newspapers and periodicals of the early 20th century that published news stories of a vulgarly sensational nature, comparable to the modern tabloid. Synonymous with gutter press.

■ **yellow back**

an inexpensive popular novel bound in a shiny yellow paper or board cover with a picture printed on the front, usually a woodcut in three colors, a type of publication that originated in England in the 1850's and was used until the end of the century for inexpensive reprint editions.

■ **young adult book**

a book intended to be read and enjoyed by adolescents of 12 to 18 years of age. Also refers to a book intended for adults, but considered suitable by reviewers and librarians for mature ninth to twelfth grade readers. Public libraries usually maintain a separate section of young adult literature managed by a librarian who specialises in YA services, including collection development.

■ **Young Adu95 lt Library Services Association (YALSA)**

a division of the American Library Association founded in 1930, YALSA has a membership of librarians responsible for evaluating and selecting books and nonprint materials for young adults (age 12 to 18) and for promoting and strengthening library services for young adult readers. YALSA publishes the semiannual journal Young Adult Library Services.

■ **young adult services**

library services intended specifically for adolescent patrons (ninth through twelfth graders), including collection development, programming and readers' advisory. Public libraries usually have a room or section devoted specifically to young adult materials, managed by a librarian who specialises in providing services for this age group.

■ **zero-Base Budget (ZBB)**

a financial plan that starts from zero at the beginning of each new budget cycle, with no assumptions carried over from previous experience. Under this budgeting method, every expense must be justified.

■ **zig-zag book**

a book made by folding a continuous strip of paper backward and forward accordion-style. When the pages are sewn at the back fold, the strip is printed on one side only. When both sides are printed, the folds are left unsewn to allow the volume vo be opened to its full length. This form of book is called an orihon when made from a manuscript or printed document originally produced as a roll.

■ zine

derived from 'fansine' (a contraction of 'fan magazine'), pronounced 'seen.' The term came into use during the 1980s to refer to a small, low-circulation magazine or newspaper, self-published out of passion for the subject rather than for personal gain, usually produced with the aid of desktop publishing software and high-quality photocopy machines. Zines represent the convergence of amateur publishing hobbyists, high

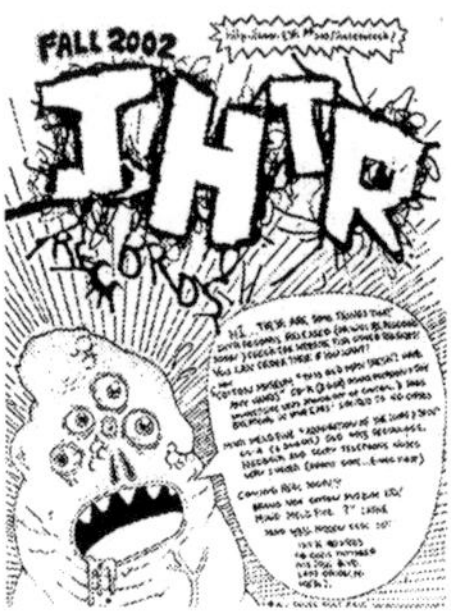

school underground newspapers, the literary small press, political radicalism and do-it-yourself popular culture. They are usually not available by subscription, often appear irregularly or infrequently and may have a lifetime of only one or two issues.

■ zip

to compress a data file using PKSIP software or some other utility capable of compressing data into PKSIP format. When such a file is restored to an uncompressed format, it is said to have been unsipped.

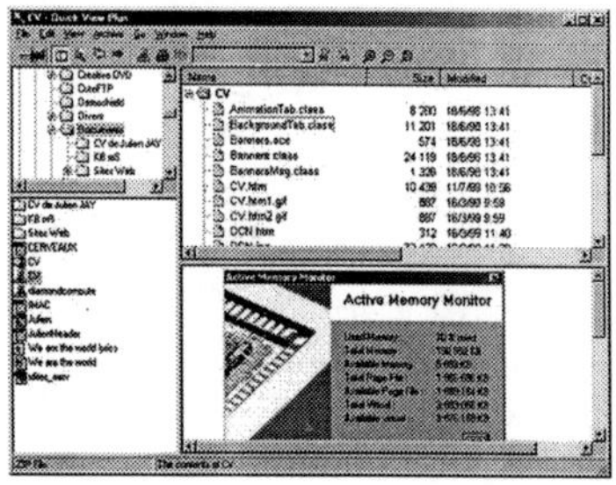

■ zip disk

a 3.5-inch removable disk cartridge developed by Iomega, capable of storing 100MB or more of data (much more than a standard floppy disk) at relatively low cost. A special Sip drive must be

installed on a microcomputer to allow a Sip disk to be used.

■ zip drive

a disk drive developed by Iomega that uses a 3.5-inch removable Sip disk capable of storing 100MB or more of data at relatively low cost, used for storing very large files and collections of files. The drive usually comes with software that catalogues the contents of the disk and provides file security.

■ zip

a method of compressing large files for transfer and storage, which can be expanded back for use with UNSIP.

■ zoom

in photography, to alter the size of an image from a stationary camera position without changing perspective by using a zoom lens to increase or decrease the focal length. In cinematography, this type of lens appears to make the camera advance toward the subject when zooming in, or retreat from it when zooming out. In word processing software, a feature that allows the user to enlarge or reduce the size of a page displayed on the screen, usually by a fixed percentage, or in small increments. Also, a feature on some photocopy machines that allows the user to specify the extent to which an original will be enlarged or reduced in size.